Soviet and Post-Soviet Politics and Society (SPPS)
ISSN 1614-3515

37

Soviet and Post-Soviet Politics and Society (SPPS)
ISSN 1614-3515

Founded in 2004 and refereed since 2007, SPPS makes available affordable English-, German-, and Russian-language studies on the history of the countries of the former Soviet bloc from the late Tsarist period to today. It publishes between 5 and 20 volumes per year and focuses on issues in transitions to and from democracy such as economic crisis, identity formation, civil society development, and constitutional reform in CEE and the NIS. SPPS also aims to highlight so far understudied themes in East European studies such as right-wing radicalism, religious life, higher education, or human rights protection. The authors and titles of all previously published volumes are listed at the end of this book. For a full description of the series and reviews of its books, see www.ibidem-verlag.de/red/spps.

Editorial correspondence & manuscripts should be sent to: Dr. Andreas Umland, Department of Political Science, Kyiv-Mohyla Academy, vul. Voloska 8/5, UA-04070 Kyiv, UKRAINE; andreas.umland@cantab.net

Business correspondence & review copy requests should be sent to: *ibidem* Press, Leuschnerstr. 40, 30457 Hannover, Germany; tel.: +49 511 2622200; fax: +49 511 2622201; spps@ibidem.eu.

Authors, reviewers, referees, and editors for (as well as all other persons sympathetic to) SPPS are invited to join its networks at www.facebook.com/group.php?gid=52638198614 www.linkedin.com/groups?about=&gid=103012 www.xing.com/net/spps-ibidem-verlag/

Recent Volumes

228   *Tima T. Moldogaziev, Gene A. Brewer, J. Edward Kellough. (Eds.)*
Public Policy and Politics in Georgia
Lessons from Post-Soviet Transition
ISBN 978-3-8382-1535-8

229   *Oxana Schmies (Ed.)*
NATO's Enlargement and Russia
A Strategic Challenge in the Past and Future
With a foreword by Vladimir Kara-Murza
ISBN 978-3-8382-1478-8

230   *Christopher Ford*
UKAPISME–Une Gauche Perude
Le marxisme anti-colonial dans la révolution ukrainienne 1917 - 1925
Avec une preface de Vincent Présumey
ISBN 978-3-8382-0899-2

231   *Anna Kutkina*
Between Lenin and Bandera
Decommunization and Multivocality in Post-Euromaidan Ukraine
With a foreword by Juri Mykkänen
ISBN 978-3-8382-1506-8

232   *Lincoln E. Flake*
Defending the Faith
The Russian Orthodox Church and the Demise of Religious Pluralism
With a foreword by Peter Martland
ISBN 978-3-8382-1378-1

233   *Nikoloz Samkharadze*
Russia's Recognition of the Independence of Abkhazia and South Ossetia
Analysis of a Deviant Case in Moscow's Foreign Policy Behavior
With a foreword by Neil MacFarlane
ISBN 978-3-8382-1414-6

234   *Arve Hansen*
Urban Protest
A Spatial Perspective on Kyiv, Minsk, and Moscow
With a foreword by Julie Wilhelmsen
ISBN 978-3-8382-1495-5

235   *Eleonora Narvselius, Julie Fedor (Eds.)*
Diversity in the East-Central European Borderlands
Memories, Cityscapes, People
ISBN 978-3-8382-1523-5

236   *Regina Elsner*
The Russian Orthodox Church and Modernity
A Historical and Theological Investigation into Eastern Christianity between Unity and Plurality
With a foreword by Mikhail Suslov
ISBN 978-3-8382-1568-6

Bo Petersson

THE PUTIN PREDICAMENT

Problems of Legitimacy and Succession in Russia

With a foreword by J. Paul Goode

ibidem
Verlag

Bibliografische Information der Deutschen Nationalbibliothek

Die Deutsche Nationalbibliothek verzeichnet diese Publikation in der Deutschen Nationalbibliografie; detaillierte bibliografische Daten sind im Internet über http://dnb.d-nb.de abrufbar.

Bibliographic information published by the Deutsche Nationalbibliothek

Die Deutsche Nationalbibliothek lists this publication in the Deutsche Nationalbibliografie; detailed bibliographic data are available in the Internet at http://dnb.d-nb.de.

Cover image: ID 114842407 © Elena281 | Dreamstime.com

ISBN-13: 978-3-8382-1050-6
© *ibidem*-Verlag, Stuttgart 2021
Alle Rechte vorbehalten

Printed in the EU

Contents

Foreword

Authoritarian legitimacy is notoriously difficult to observe. While autocrats always insist upon their legitimacy, the ever-present threat of coercion and sanction makes it difficult to know whether their claims are broadly supported in society. Scholars thus tend to distinguish between *legitimacy* as a diffuse property claimed by rulers and their supporters and *legitimation* as an ongoing process of legitimacy-seeking (usually in the form of claim-making).

Researching legitimacy — that is, societal acceptance of a ruler's right to rule — is complicated by a variety of factors and biases, not least of which being the well-known problem of "preference falsification" — or when citizens conceal their private views on a regime while presenting a public appearance of loyalty (Kuran 1995). Even in semi-autocracies and hybrid regimes, privately-held preferences may be concealed even from neutral observers (including pollsters) on the assumption that they might be allied with the regime.

Arguably, the difficulty of closing the gap between public and private preferences is one of the core reasons that regime change in authoritarian regimes appears surprising. Hence, preference falsification is not just a problem for social scientists but also for autocrats who deliberately cultivate ignorance about the inner workings of their regimes — in other words, autocracies are "engines of agnatology" (Ahram and Goode 2016). A consequence of this "structural opacity" (Schedler 2013) is autocrats' uncertainty about the information provided by subordinates as well as citizens. Today's Russia exemplifies the difficulties created by the structural opacity of autocratic rule. Throughout the 2000s, the Kremlin relentlessly surveyed society to watch for potential sources of grievance that could turn into protest movements. Some observers even mocked the regime's obsession with public opinion, calling it a "ratingocracy." Yet this approach to "managed democracy" (*upravliaemaia demokratiia*) failed to anticipate the popular resonance of the protests "For Fair Elections" that followed the combination of fraudulent

2011 parliamentary elections along with Putin's announced intention to return to the presidency for a third term in 2012.

The start of Putin's third term after the 2011-2012 protests signaled an important change in the nature of the regime. Rather than seeking better information about Russians' true sentiments, it embraced structural opacity and escalated its information warfare against domestic and international audiences, flooding the airwaves, press, and social media with a mixture of pro-government propaganda, anti-Westernism, disinformation, and conspiracy theories. Consistent with broader trends among authoritarian states worldwide, Russia's leaders became "informational autocrats" (Guriev and Treisman 2019), preferring to manipulate and divide while mimicking democracy. The new approach did not necessarily improve the Kremlin's knowledge of societal preferences, though its control of public narratives and deft use of supportive political myths presented a powerful façade of stability and competence for mass consumption. The surge of popular support for Putin following the annexation of Crimea in March 2014 seemed to confirm the effectiveness of the new approach.

The legitimation strategies adopted in Putin's third and fourth terms were not mere window dressing, though some have argued that ideas and legitimation matter little for understanding the underlying dynamics of autocratization in Russia. They are not alone, as the comparative study of authoritarianism tends to emphasize coercion and co-optation rather than ideational sources of power. To be sure, the post-2012 shift towards informational autocracy was made possible by the prior centralization of power, weakening of independent journalism and civil society, and the cowing of Russia's oligarchs during Putin's first two terms in office. And yet even these crucial de-democratizing moves benefited from claims to performance legitimacy arising from steady economic growth and the regime's exploitation of the *smuta* myth of the 1990s as a cautionary tale about the dangerous excesses of democracy. Simultaneously, the Kremlin invested in patriotic education throughout the 2000s, reviving a Soviet-style military patriotism fused with conservative and orthodox religious themes that were mobilized in concert with watershed events of 2014, dovetailing with the myth of Russia rising from its knees to regain its rightful place as a great power under Putin's guidance. From the start, then, the politics of legitimation and power politics have been intertwined in Putin's regime.

From a comparative perspective, the challenge in researching the politics of legitimation in autocracies is two-fold: first, one must identify the regime's legitimating strategies and what they reveal about the nature of the regime; second, the effectiveness of the legitimating strategies needs to be assessed, including their implications for consolidating (or enforcing) loyalty among both elites and citizens.

Bo Petersson's book masterfully addresses the first challenge, using public statements, interviews, and other open sources to meticulously unravel the varieties of political myths and how they evolved in response to the existential crisis faced by Putin's regime in 2011-2012. In picking apart the legitimating claims and their roles in contemporary politics, the problem of succession looms large: political myths reinforce Putin's place at the apex of Russian politics but also traps him there as long as his charismatic authority remains non-transferable to other actors. Putin's personal popularity might be genuine, but it does not transfer to other ruling institutions or parties. The 2020 constitutional amendments[1] institutionalized elements of the regime's legitimating myths (not just in terms of their contents, but also the very process of adopting them), but paradoxically they reinforced Putin's personal power rather than routinizing his charismatic authority. It has long been speculated that Putin has the proverbial tiger by its tail. Petersson's analysis demonstrates clearly why this is the case, particularly as illustrated by the challenge posed by Alexei Navalny — though the challenge is intrinsic to Putin's regime, and one could further adduce the 2015 assassination of opposition leader Boris Nemtsov to the Kremlin's inability to find a solution.

The second challenge — that of assessing the effectiveness of legitimating strategies — is no less complicated. The public artefacts

---

1   For a detailed discussion of the amendments and the process of their adoption, see Pomeranz and Smyth 2021.

(in this case, interviews, statements, and public performances) created by authoritarian regimes might reveal the nature of the regime and its limits, but they are not necessarily reliable guides to their inner workings. The pitfalls in analyzing them are many. The intent behind a regime message is difficult to divine, often leading pundits to attempt to analyze Putin's psychology. Whatever the intent of a regime message or claim, it may differ significantly from its effect. When politics are pointedly kept opaque, regime subordinates and citizens, alike, attempt to grasp the meaning behind messages and policies, inevitably leading to misinterpretations and unintended consequences. The mimicking of legitimating narratives may equally provide cover for covert forms of resistance or for bureaucratic incompetence of the sort ruthlessly mocked by Russian satirists from Nikolai Gogol' to Vladimir Voinovich.

Scholars must resist the temptation to infer the effectiveness of a legitimating strategy from a ruler's duration in power or, for that matter, from the absence of overt challenges to a ruler's power.[2] Correspondingly, the notion of *successful* legitimation needs to be unpacked and conceptualized such that it entails more than regime survival. One possibility might be to consider how the politics of legitimation regulate elite competition, determine access to resources, and structure career trajectories. Alternatively, one could examine the range of possible explanations for the absence of open challenges and their points of intersection with the regime's legitimating myths. Still another would be to examine the legitimating narratives that have been abandoned, re-tooled, or held in reserve. Of particular interest in this regard are legitimating fields like gender and nationalism that may be exploited by both regime and opposition.

The difficulty of assessing the effectiveness of legitimation strategies is especially pressing as Putin's regime has reached an impasse. The "Putin predicament," in Petersson's felicitous short-

---

2   At the same time, those who would deconstruct the ideational sources of the regime's power must be mindful of the practical and ethical difficulties posed by autocracies for those who would study them, including for one's respondents, colleagues, and students.

hand, is a multifaceted challenge that is rising to the surface in Russia. Almost immediately following his re-election to a fourth term in 2018, the Russian press was flooded with stories confirming his intent to remain in office indefinitely — a claim that appears ensured with the passage of the 2020 constitutional amendments. While Putin's lingering in power may be a comfort to Russia's elite, Petersson convincingly illustrates that his reputation as a great communicator has suffered with age and the waning of the so-called Crimean consensus in public opinion. In the wake of Putin's handling of the COVID-19 pandemic and the poisoning and arrest of Navalny, the absence of alternatives bears clear implications for domestic stability and even international security that are likely to persist. The materials and analysis in Petersson's book are thus a valuable resource — not just for understanding the politics of legitimation during Putin's third and fourth terms, but also for future research on legitimation in Russia and other autocracies.

J. Paul Goode
Carleton University
June 2021

REFERENCES

Ahram, A. I., Goode, J. P. (2016) 'Researching Authoritarianism in the Discipline of Democracy', *Social Science Quarterly*, 97, 834–849.

Guriev, S., Treisman, D. (2019) 'Informational Autocrats', *Journal of Economic Perspectives*, 33, 100–127.

Kuran, T. (1995) *Private Truths, Public Lies: The Social Consequences of Preference Falsification,* Cambridge, MA: Harvard University Press.

Pomeranz, W. E., Smyth, R. (2021, eds) 'Russia's 2020 Constitutional Reform: The Politics of Institutionalizing the Status-Quo', *Russian Politics,* 6: 1, 1-152.

Schedler, A. (2013) *The Politics of Uncertainty: Sustaining and Subverting Electoral Authoritarianism,* New York, NY: Oxford University Press.

Preface and Acknowledgments

This book has been long in the making. For several years during my academic career, I devoted myself to university management matters, and the little time that I had available for research went into the writing of shorter texts to keep the kettle boiling at least to some extent. This was in a way also a necessity, since my generation of social scientists has had to re-learn, from knowing that it was the writing of monographs that mattered into the new wisdom that only peer-reviewed articles in high impact journals count. Having reached a mature age and being at the stage of my academic career when I can afford the luxury of writing what I want rather than what I should, I have now finally wrapped up this book project. That is a rewarding feeling.

Several people have helped me along the final stretch of the road, and I am indebted to them all. I would like to thank the following colleagues and friends who have read the manuscript, made comments, and contributed to its improvement. Heartfelt thanks therefore go to Anders Blixt, Richard Brander, Derek Stanford Hutcheson, Kalle Kniivilä, Inger Sjunnesson, Andreas Umland, and Carolina Vendil Pallin. Of course, the responsibility for remaining flaws and shortcomings remains solely my own. I would also like to express my appreciation to Jean Hudson for her careful language editing of my text, and to J. Paul Goode for kindly agreeing to write the foreword. Thanks also to Pelle Mickwitz and, again, Richard Brander who have provided regular pep talk and general inspiration during our Thursday night zoom seminars all through the dark and gloomy years of the pandemic. My sincerest thanks go to my family, to Sanja, Teodor and Isidor, who have accepted my reclusive behavior and long evenings in the study without holding them too much against me. Without their moral support and understanding, I would never have been able to finish the book.

I

Introduction

Because princes are of short life, it must be that the kingdom will fail soon, as his virtue fails. Hence it arises that kingdoms that depend solely on the virtue of one man are hardly durable, because that virtue fails with the life of that one; and it rarely happens that it is restored by succession
(Niccolò Machiavelli, *Discourses on Livy*, I 11: 4, 35-36).

I have invariably proceeded from the premise that I need to be doing what I believe to be right for our country. When I do something, I do it not for the sake of pleasing someone abroad
(Vladimir Putin, News Conference, 17 December 2020).

Is it possible to imagine contemporary Russia without Vladimir Putin as its leader? The present Speaker of the State Duma, Vyacheslav Volodin, then deputy chief of staff of the Russian president, was very clear about the answer when he asserted that without Putin there would be no Russia (Moscow Times 2014). For those who are in their early twenties or younger, the question seems justified, as there has simply been no other Russian leader around for as long as they can remember. There certainly was the bracketed president and former prime minister, Dimitriy Medvedev, but not even when he was president between the years of 2008 and 2012 did the public take him seriously. Everybody knew who was pulling the strings, his prime minister at the time, Vladimir Putin.

Since the last year of the 1990s, Putin has held a unique position at the center stage of Russian politics, either as president or as prime minister. His personal popularity may have had some temporary dips, most obviously in connection with the "farcical" (Hanson 2011: 34-35) or even "callous and casual" (Koesel and Bunce 2012: 417) transfer of presidential power from Medvedev and back again to Putin in 2011-2012, but overall, the sustenance of his popularity has been remarkable. Halfway through his fourth presidential period in office it may finally start to wear thin, but there is no doubt that it has proven remarkably sturdy for more than two decades. It is the endeavor of this book to try to find explanations for this durability but also to discuss what dilemmas Putin's unique and total dominance have given rise to and are likely to engender in the future.

In general terms, this book is focused on the concept of legitimacy and its application in the hybrid authoritarian political setting that contemporary Russia represents. More specifically, it will discuss legitimization strategies employed during the Putin era, with special attention to the strategies used from Putin's third presidential tenure onwards. In more straightforward terms the research questions that the book seeks to answer are therefore: How has Putin's legitimacy been constructed and sustained during his third and fourth terms in office? What challenges are there to his legitimacy as a political leader? How is the question of political succession dealt with? What problems may the legitimization strategies employed during Putin's long incumbency bring for his future successor?

There are several reasons for the focus on Putin's third and fourth terms in office. First, the 2011-2012 events brought about an unprecedented legitimization crisis for the Putin regime. Declining approval rates for Putin indicated this. They hit a low and remained at that level until early 2014 when they were boosted again after the support of the insurgency in Ukraine and the annexation of Crimea. The re-legitimation strategies used by the regime during Putin's third and fourth periods in office were a mixture of old and new, but the new elements were so assertive as to warrant the label of "high Putinism" for the political period that they marked.

In view of the content and style characterizing foreign policy actions and domestic politics from 2014 onwards, Putin's third and fourth periods in office can be regarded as qualitatively different from his first two presidential terms between 2000 and 2008. Indeed, in the words of one prominent analyst, Russia at the time of the crisis of legitimation in 2011-2012 and Russia from the time of the annexation of Crimea onwards are "like two different countries, belonging to different historical eras and separated not merely by a few years but by decades, if not centuries" (Sharafutdinova 2020: 4).

In non-democratic systems, legitimacy and issues of succession to the next generation of political leaders are two sides of the same coin (Snyder 2018). This is another reason why the empirical focus of the book is on the third and fourth presidential tenures of Vladimir Putin. Succession issues were not very relevant during his first two presidencies, as the incumbent himself was then relatively young and the constitutional limitations to a prolongation beyond the second term in office were still not overtrodden. Towards the end of his second term in office many observers tended to believe that the two Putin terms were to be followed by two Medvedev terms, whereafter a third actor would enter the stage, much like in democratic systems. These pundits turned out to be deeply mistaken.

As this book nears completion, during the first part of 2021 and halfway through Putin's fourth presidential term, succession issues are still not on the agenda, at least not officially. In 2020, constitutional amendments were hurried through and adopted to get rid of a succession dilemma which consisted in the fact that, on the one hand, the incumbent president due to constitutional regulations would have to leave office in 2024, while, on the other hand, he had no credible candidates to succeed him. The constitutional amendments fixed part of the problem as they made it possible for Putin to stay on for two more tenures, up until the year of 2036, should he and the electorate so wish, and his health so permit. However, this did not change the basic problem, as the succession issues continued to simmer below the surface. Putin, born in 1952, is certainly not getting any younger. Things may happen along the way as they are prone to do in life, and the setup of presidential contenders seeking to fill any political vacuum is still conspicuous by its absence. This is the Putin predicament: It is time for him to go, but there is no one in sight to succeed him. Moreover, as will be made clear in this book, it will be very difficult for anyone to succeed him as current strategies of legitimation have been almost exclusively focused on his person.

The crisis of 2011-2012, when Putin was reinstated as president after Medvedev's first and only term, was so far the greatest challenge to his popularity. Even then, however, he was able to maintain a level of public approval above the 60 percent level. Four times over, he has been elected president already in the first round.

As pointed out by Sharafutdinova (2020: ix): "Putin's appeal to many Russians has been real, and the analysts need to take this reality seriously". What accounts for his success? How long can his personal popularity withstand the wear and tear that a long incumbency and exposure to at least some policy failures would necessarily seem to entail? Are we, due to the year of 2020 that was so rife with formidable political challenges of different kinds, from the ravages of the covid-19 pandemic to the confrontations with the media power and charisma of opposition leader Aleksey Navalny, finally reaching the limits beyond which Putin's legitimacy can be stretched no longer?

The renowned independent Russian sociological institute Levada Center has carried out a series of monthly polls starting at the time when Putin first took office as prime minister in 1999. These polls are studied attentively by analysts all over the world, and the president's approval rates seem to be as much of an obsession on the part of the Putin regime as it is among political observers abroad (Andrews-Lee and Liu 2020, Willerton 2017, Petrov et al 2014: 5). Similar surveys are conducted on a regular basis by the Russian Public Opinion Research Center (VTsIOM) and the Public Opinion Foundation (FOM), both of which are more closely connected to state authorities. Despite this difference, the three polling institutes tend to come up with similar trends, not least since they often use the same methods and indeed fieldwork teams when making their surveys (Yudin 2020: 7).

According to the monthly figures, Putin's approval ratings have by international comparison been uniquely high ever since Levada launched its series back in 1999. As of May 2021, they had since he first became president in 2000 never been below 59 percent, a low point which was reached in April and May 2020. Moreover, the approval rates had always superseded his disapproval ratings by a wide margin. There was a lengthy downturn in connection with the challenges against the Putin-Medvedev tandem in 2011-2012. Despite this severe stress test for the regime, Putin managed to reverse the development. The annexation of Crimea in 2014 was widely popular and in its wake the president's ratings turned steeply upwards again. For almost four years, they stabilized at or even reached above the 80 percent-limit, not sloping downwards until the summer of 2018 when an unpopular pension reform made the figures drop (Logvinenko 2020). The unruly year of 2020 saw both the devastation caused by the corona pandemic and the Russian constitutional reforms, which made it theoretically and legally possible for Putin to go on serving as president until the year of 2036. During 2020, the ratings swung back and forth in an indeterminate manner but sloped anew, approaching the levels of 2011 and 2012 from the late fall onwards.

[1] The negative trend basically continued in early 2021, at the time when this book was finalized.

From January 2021 onwards, the Putin regime seemed to be slated for its gravest stress test since the legitimation crisis of 2011 and 2012. Putin was openly challenged by the opposition leader Aleksey Navalny, who was subjected to an assassination attempt orchestrated by the regime in August 2020 (Bellingcat 2020), survived it, was hospitalized in Germany, openly blamed Putin for being behind the murder plot, and then returned home to Russia in December 2020, only to be apprehended, incarcerated, and sentenced to a perennial prison stretch by the authorities. Through a widely influential film on Youtube about the incumbent president's lavish holiday estate and about his alleged widespread and corrupted business activities, Navalny managed to put more than one chink in Putin's armor. People all over the country turned out to demonstrate their support for Navalny and their discontent with a regime increasingly perceived to be ossified. The jury is still out at the time of writing, but there is reason to believe that this development might imply the onset of Putin's deepest crisis of legitimacy so far.

The ratings problem

It is a main argument of this book that the legitimacy of the regime still largely hinges on Putin's personal popularity and charisma.

---

1   Data were missing for December 2020 so there was an unusual documentation gap between November 2020 and January 2021.

The default position of his incumbency creates a problem for future successors and renders it problematic for the regime to sustain itself, unless a cure is somehow found to restore the charisma that by many signs seems to be in the process of evaporating.

It has become a political priority for the Putin regime to follow approval rates attentively and keep them on a high level (Frye et al 2017). The significance that the Kremlin attributes to the study of the development of popular sentiments is underscored by the fact that substantial amounts of funding go into the regime's own classified surveys administered by the FSO, the President's Federal Protective Service (Pertsev and Solopov 2020). One, slightly anecdotal, piece of evidence of the ascribed importance was when the Russian Embassy in the United States called upon the Bloomberg news agency to apologize for misleading the US public by referring to VTsIOM poll data that indicated remarkably low levels of trust for President Putin (Tass 2020).[2] The logic was simple: since the data reflected badly on the president, they were bound to be wrong. Whereas the episode may seem amusing, it has serious general implications. Polls widely interpreted as truthful and representative have the potential to construct the reality that they represent (Yudin 2020). This fact goes a considerable way towards explaining the Russian regime's interest in the polling industry. Ultimately it makes polling figures a matter of security concern for an increasingly authoritarian regime.

The regime's preoccupation with approval rates is, however, not a unique thing for Russia; other world leaders share the intense desire to maintain ratings on a high level (Frye et al 2017). Such rates are, albeit rough, indices of legitimacy. High approval rates make matters easier for political leaders, regardless of whether they function in democratic or authoritarian contexts. Good showings facilitate the consolidation of power and implementation of policies that the leaders cherish (Andrews-Lee and Liu 2020). The ratings signal whether legitimacy is sustained or whether it needs mending. Trends revealed by the ratings indicate shifts in the societal relevance of the regime and speak to the sustainability of the social

---

2   I thank Carolina Vendil Pallin for bringing this incident to my attention.

contract (Laruelle 2021: 85). It can thus be argued that the ratings are instrumental per se for the construction of legitimacy (Yudin 2020, Frye at al 2017, Rogov 2017). Solid figures may provide people with easily accessible arguments for why they should put faith in their leaders.

To what extent, then, can polling data be trusted when they emanate from authoritarian or hybrid (i.e., authoritarian with some democratic traits) settings? Would it not be easy for such states to cook the data and present fake figures as the truth of the matter? How do the authoritarian characteristics of the political system impact on the responses given in the polls (Yudin 2020, Wilson and Lee 2020, Rogov 2017)? Will respondents not refrain from giving answers from fear of repression, instead articulating the responses that the regime wishes to hear (Nathan 2020, Frye at al 2017)? Or, if the latter is not the case, is it not reasonable to assume that refusal rates will be higher among those invited respondents who have a critical or negative mindset in relation to the regime? This would make the proneness of regime sympathizers to participate in polls greater than that of critics, reinforcing a bias in poll results. It has also been pointed out that refusal rates for the Russian polling industry are very high, around 65-70 percent, and that one therefore should be very cautious in accepting the figures stated at face value (Yudin 2020, Rogov 2017).

These are all highly pertinent questions that need to be taken seriously. However, even if the Levada Center certainly works in an authoritarian or hybrid setting and has since 2016 been labelled "foreign agent" according to the infamous piece of Russian legislation which limits its range of activities (Flikke 2020: 163-165, Yudin 2020: 7)), its series of monthly polls about the president's popularity is very valuable for researchers. The time series display the peaks and slumps of Putin's popularity for every month during more than a 20-year period. It gives a solid foundation for conclusions about his public support during these vicissitudes. Even if, due to the high refusal rates, caution is recommended when it comes to the specific percentages of approval indicated, the trends and changes over time depicted by the series of monthly polls provide a valuable basis for analysis (Rogov 2017).

Throughout this book I maintain that Putin during his first twenty years in power has been largely successful at upholding the main pillars of his legitimacy. Like no other contemporaries, he has been able to get the message across to the electorate that he is the only one out there who is credible and trustworthy enough to hold chief executive power in Russia. The suggested narrative has been that no one else is simply up for the job. Also, Putin's political communication skills have become increasingly honed over the years. Overall, he has managed to tell a convincing story, using a blend of great-power arrogance, pledges to order and stability, and personal charisma (Huskey 2013). According to some, the latter ingredient has above all been added during the third and fourth of his presidential tenures, during "high Putinism". If this picture is now starting to crack, we may be entering a new era in Russian politics with highly unclear implications.

Putin has not created the powerful public discourses about the need for great power assertiveness, stability, and order. Rather, these discourses have created him. They have for a long time had a prominent position in Russian society. Even so, Putin has been markedly successful in making use of master discourses out there, appropriating them and bending them to fit his political purposes (Willerton 2017). His platform of political ideas, Putinism, was not created by him alone, but has emerged out of historical trends, cultural desires, and socially constructed myths (Langdon and Tismaneanu 2020). Again, as if by a sleight of hand, Putin has, for many voters, appeared as the originator and the driving force behind the creation of these societal beliefs. For more than a decade he has been outstandingly successful in this.

This is where we approach the real crux of the matter. The point that prompts careful consideration is that Putin's long-time success may turn out to be a major liability for Russia since the legitimacy of the regime has been, and still is, so intimately tied to his person. What would happen if he were suddenly to pass away? Whoever tried to step in to take his place would encounter major problems of legitimacy, regardless of whether Putin's old magic has started to recede or not. This is the nature of the Putin predicament, the very problem which prompted me to write this book. I shall strive to discuss it further in the following chapters.

Main material

Public addresses by prominent political leaders are always and everywhere indispensable sources for political analysis. Speeches by a political leader function much like the public performance of a national anthem: they become sites where national politics and ultimately states themselves are performed and constructed (Butler and Spivak 2007). However tactical they are at the time of their utterance, words expressed in public tend to live a life of their own. They are made note of, remembered, and kept in store, and in cases of grave inconsistency with other statements or actions, they come back to haunt the originator, with adverse effects on their credibility (Novitskaya 2017). This argument is relevant in most settings, also in non-democratic ones. Words matter. Phrases meant to calm, assuage, deter, or inspire people will be effective if their purposes are met, but may in the end be subversive if they fail to reach their goal.

The analytical focus of this book is on how the Russian regime—the "collective Putin" (Sharafutdinova 2020; Rutland 2017b)—legitimizes Putin's presidential rule. The bulk of the empirical material for the study comes from the official website of the president of Russia, kremlin.ru. The website collects Putin's official statements, such as major addresses, speeches on special occasions, press conferences and interviews.

For several years, there have been certain fixed nodes in the presidential calendar. These are annually recurring and major mediatized events, indeed rituals. The most important ones are the annual address (*poslaniye*) to the Federal Assembly, the speech to the Valdai Discussion Club, the televised Direct Line with Vladimir Putin, and the annual News Conference with major media (Fedotenkov 2020).

These events are important as political platforms from which the president's statements are launched to make an impact. Of the four, the annual address to the Federal Assembly is the one most regulated by form and protocol, as it sets the main policy priorities and defines the most central agenda items for the coming year (Martus 2021, Ambrosio and Vandrovec 2013). The Valdai Discussion Club is a Kremlin-sponsored annual meeting of "experts on Russia in Russia" (Novitskaya 2017). These Davos-like annual meetings are a venue where Russian leaders meet high-level academics and political practitioners from home and abroad who share an interest in Russian political affairs. Putin has met with the participants of the Valdai Club every year since the meetings were initiated in 2004 (Valdai Discussion Club 2021). Current political priorities can be inferred from his addresses to the meeting, even if the format of the discussions is relatively free from protocol. The Direct Line and the News Conference are the media events that by appearance are less structured beforehand. These are occasions when the president meets the press and the public, ostensibly unplugged, to answer their questions on different matters. The shows try to signal spontaneity but there is little doubt that they are strictly regulated in terms of access to floor and microphone. Sometimes they are used to float issues that are introduced through more formal channels later.[3]

Not only do the four major mediatized events differ in terms of form and structure, but they are also different regarding the primary audience for which they are aimed. In the case of the *poslaniya* to the Federal Assembly, national and regional elites listen attentively, regardless of whether their professional affiliation is military, political, bureaucratic, business-oriented, or other. Since the political priorities for the coming year are outlined and presented, the attention of these elites will be guaranteed. Equally certain is that foreign audiences will tune in on these events as the announcement of priorities in foreign and security policies are an important part of the messages sent. Thus, these platform speeches are intended in equal measure for foreign audiences and for domestic ones. Regarding the Valdai Club, the domestic elite audiences are

---

3   In the pandemic year of 2020, the Direct Line and the News Conference were merged into one single event, because the practices of social distancing did not allow the broadcasting of the Direct Line according to the usual format.

again likely to be targeted, not least to cover for the case that trial balloons are sent up or new political initiatives presented. The Direct Line and the News Conference are both events which are more attuned to the public. These are occasions where Putin takes the opportunity to shine and demonstrate his omniscient power and prowess, while using a language that is accessible for his average voters (Kukshinov 2021). He endeavors to speak directly to them.

The kremlin.ru website duly reports on all these major media events, even if the records are not always made verbatim and there are occasional differences of nuance between the spoken word and the written one (Gutterman 2021). The website devotes substantial space to the events, and they are widely noted by the public. Both Russian and English language versions of the documents on the website have been consulted as there sometimes are, again, significant differences of nuance between them. The English versions are frequently shortened and condensed. One kind of source quite often referred to in this monograph is interviews by foreign mass media which are reprinted on kremlin.ru. These texts, which have often proven to be relatively outspoken, should be assumed to be directed primarily to a foreign audience.

Supplementary material has been retrieved on a regular basis from the kremlin.ru website with the use of search terms such as "succession", "constitution", "legitimacy" or proper names of central importance. Aside from the official sources, existing data gathered by the Levada Center, have also been used, primarily in the shape of the monthly popularity ratings. Lastly, I have of course also had the benefit of consulting the works published by colleagues who have visited similar grounds, empirical or theoretical, before me.

Delimitations

Analyzing contemporary developments is always difficult and doing so regarding Russia in a time frame encompassing the eventful years of 2020 and parts of 2021 has been a particularly demanding task. The period has seen dramatic events: the plebiscite on the constitutional amendments enabling Vladimir Putin to serve for another two periods beyond 2024, the regime's assassination attempt on Aleksey Navalny and his subsequent trial and imprisonment, country-wide demonstrations protesting his plight, and not least the devastating onslaught of the covid-19 pandemic. Big things unfold and they do so fast with significant and uncertain implications for the future. One has, on an everyday basis, the feeling of being witness to history in the making. Even so, when writing a monograph and having to meet an agreed schedule of publication, one must draw the line somewhere. There must be a cut-off point beyond which no new information is processed and included. For this book, I have set this point on May 31, 2021. Thus, I have not considered events after this date.

Transliteration of Russian words and names

For the references I have used the transliteration system elaborated by the United States Board on Geographic Names (BGN) and the British Permanent Committee on Geographical Names (PCGN). I have also used this system in the body of the text, except for names where convention suggests another transliteration (e.g Yeltsin has been used instead of El'tsin, Navalny instead of Naval'nyy).

II

Theoretical Points of Orientation

Political succession

As indicated by the introductory quote, the problem of succession of leaders has been a vital concern for political analysts at least since the times of Machiavelli. That famous early political theorist opined that succession by election was preferable to succession by ancestry, and that leaders had to prove themselves worthy of being chosen by election. In a healthy republic, the successor would be elected on the grounds of merit and reputation (Gagné 2011). Machiavelli was, however, not very explicit about the ways in which new leaders would have to prove themselves worthy. Assessed by today's standards, many contemporary observers would consider his recommendations objectionable since he argued that strong leaders, or in his parlance, princes, were those who were prepared to wage war. If the princes were not ready to do this, their city would become "effeminate and the prey of its neighbors" (Machiavelli 1996: I, 19, 52).

Later analysts have continued to grapple with the question of succession and how new generations of leaders are expected to grow with their offices and assume pride of place. Once there, they are in most cases likely to be reluctant to yield the reins of power to someone else. This seems to be close to a natural law in politics, or to use the words of two prominent analysts:

> *Political succession, or rather its avoidance, is at the heart of the decisions leaders make. Except for the rare incumbent who voluntarily steps down, leaders overwhelmingly act as if they want to hold on to power as long as they possibly can* (Bueno de Mesquita and Smith 2017: 708).

From this perspective, executive power is something comparable to "my precious" from Tolkien's *Lord of the Rings*, enviously guarded by its temporary proprietor, always coveted by scheming potential competitors.

In democratic systems, the process of political succession is generally not that much of a problem, since constitutional frameworks and regular cycles of free and fair elections set limits to the rules of political leaders, regardless of whether they are committed and popular, or corrupted and generally estranged from their electorates. In the latter case, they will be more quickly voted out of office. As the saying goes, the rascals will be thrown out. In non-democratic settings, in authoritarian or hybrid systems like in Russia, things stand differently. Most often, there are constitutional frameworks in these systems too, but as practical experience has shown in Russia, constitutions may be altered or amended on the initiatives of the leader or their devout followers (Versteeg et al 2020, Baturo 2019, McKie 2019), and elections do not have the same decisive value and effect as they have in democratic political systems. However, without recourse to the regulating force of constitutional frameworks and regular, free and fair elections, processes of succession will still need to be dealt with somehow, some time, also in authoritarian and hybrid settings.

There will always be some friction in connection with processes of succession in such environments. The core problem is how to hand over power from one individual, government, or regime to another in such a way that "the momentary crisis of legitimacy which inevitably arises is reduced to manageable proportions" (Calvert 1987: 1). There is a need for rules or agreed procedures to make such transitions as smooth as possible, otherwise uncertainty and instability will prevail. Without institutional mechanisms or at least intra-elite agreements in place for how to appoint new leaders, there is a risk of regime fragmentation, infighting, or even civil war and collapse (Kokkonen and Sundell 2020, Stacher 2011). In the worst case, there may be a "Hobbesian struggle for a Leviathan state" (Gould-Davies 2021: 205).

The existence of rules of succession, defined as "clearly specified procedures that govern the transition from one leader to another" (Frantz and Stein 2017: 937) tends to prolong the life expectancy of authoritarian and hybrid regimes. Orderly procedures for implementing succession lower the risk of having contending elites organize coups to grab power (Ambrosio 2015). Nevertheless, even if a roadmap of sorts exists, there is no guarantee for its eventual use, nor that the charted course will ultimately prevail (Meng 2021).

One way to reduce uncertainty in phases of succession is to have an heir identified and appointed by the incumbent leader. For the incumbent there are certain risks involved in identifying a successor before the termination of their tenure in office. This is the so-called "succession dilemma" (Ambrosio 2015) or "crown prince problem" (Meng 2021). The "anointed successor" (du Boulay 2021) can represent both a barrier of protection and a threat to their mentor (Meng 2021, Konrad and Mui 2016). After having emerged as the heir, the crown prince will acquire a power base of their own and may use it to dethrone the incumbent ahead of time. This is what the vice president Aleksandr Rutskoy tried to do against President Boris Yeltsin back in the formative year of 1993 in Russia, and this experience is what accounts for the absence of a vice presidency to this day in Russia's political architecture.

However, if loyal, the named successor will provide additional protection for the sitting president against potentially contending elites. The elites who support the incumbent are likely to be calmed by the relative certainty that the existence of an heir apparent provides. They are prone to continue to support the constellation in power, which in turn reinforces the position of the sitting leader (Meng 2021, Kokkonen and Sundell 2020).

The succession dilemma notwithstanding, the problems associated with naming a crown prince do not eclipse the necessity of safeguarding an orderly transition when the time comes. This would help in avoiding an unstable and uncertain period of political vacuum. The question of orderly succession is of fundamental importance for any state. It concerns the very mechanism that ensures that a state outlives its leader and survives as a political entity (Helms 2020, Snyder 2018, Kailitz and Stockemer 2017, Ambrosio 2015). For an authoritarian or hybrid state, the problem is accentuated, as a non-democratic regime is seldom more fragile and vulnerable than at the time of a change of leadership (Helms 2020, Meng 2021). The perception of the regime as frail has important consequences, as there is a clear correlation between precarious stages of political succession in authoritarian states and the emergence of popular uprisings against their regimes (Hale 2015, Koesel and Bunce 2012). This is when the perceived invincibility of the regime has faded and the kind of legitimacy that the old leader has, after all, been able to construct does not transfer easily to the successor.

Legitimacy

The concept of legitimacy has a long pedigree in political science and social theory (Weber 1978). It refers to a widespread belief that arrangements of power are appropriate, just, and in keeping with agreed-upon rules. On the individual level, legitimacy can be defined as a psychological property expressing such a belief (Tyler 2006).

Because of legitimacy, a popular majority feels that they ought to defer to the authorities' decisions and rules. They follow them voluntarily out of obligation and responsibility, rather than out of fear of punishment or anticipation of immediate pecuniary or other reward. Simply put, legitimacy is "support-worthiness". Rulers who have attained that quality maintain their position without having to use force or bribery (Macdonald and Macdonald 2020).

Social stability rests on legitimacy. Most often, the concept of legitimacy has been applied to the state level of analysis. The logic is that the ideational basis of the state must appeal to the bulk of its population to be sustained in the longer run (Kelman 1969). Political leaders also need the consent of contending elites to stay in power, regardless of whether these represent political, economic, military, or other circles. Unless they are supported, accepted, or at least tolerated by such elites they will not stay on for long, regardless of how popular they may be among the public (Chen 2016). However, the understanding of this phenomenon is better covered by other terms, such as co-optation or clientelism, and should not be conflated with the concept of legitimacy that refers to a social relation between the leaders and the public.

Being able to gain voluntary acquiescence from most people, most of the time, due to their sense of obligation and commitment, allows the state to function even during periods of scarcity, crisis, and conflict. This creates a reservoir of support, which can be drawn upon under difficult circumstances, and is not contingent upon self-interest or coercion. That is why David Easton once defined legitimacy as diffuse regime support (Easton 1975, Nathan 2020). It is diffuse because it does not presuppose quid pro quo deals between the political elites and the populace. The people are content to know that the political system works satisfactorily, and that the government is proper, just, and legal. This foundation may however erode and change. Losses of legitimacy may result in popular discontent and societal opposition. Leaders who have no or dwindling legitimacy will soon find themselves on a slippery slope as the very basis of their government is becoming undermined (Schlumberger and Bank 2001).

Max Weber's classical distinction between three types of legitimate authority — rational-legal, traditional, and charismatic — still has a formative influence on today's literature (Weber 1983: 144–175, Netelenbos 2016). True to his methodology of ideal types, Weber postulated that these manifestations would never appear in pure form or in real life. Instead, all ideal types were likely to blend with the others, albeit often with one sub-type dominating (Eisenstadt 1968, Apressyan 2013). The legitimacy of an individual leader or a group of leaders most often builds on a combination of all three (Weber 1983: 147).

Weber's take on legitimacy has had many critics over the years, most notably perhaps David Beetham (1991). Among other things, he argued that despite Weber's statement that the three forms were ideal types prone to appear in blended form only, followers of his work have come to treat them as real-life descriptions, forcing their empirical observations into narrow theoretical constructs. Bearing this warning in mind, I still believe it to be fruitful to use the classical triad. The lasting value of the ideal-type approach is heuristic. Through its usage, the analyst can discern which approximate type of legitimate authority dominates in a political system during a given period and so assess the degree of vulnerability of the political regime.

Rational-legal authority is the type of Weberian legitimacy that is most intimately associated with established Western liberal democracies. This is the kind of legitimacy deemed most mature and durable by contemporary Western political theorists (Holmes 2016). It builds on the leaders' meticulous adherence to the precepts of the constitution and other national legal frameworks. The loyalty to the legal institutions forms a reliable basis of trust between the leaders and the electorate and makes up the foundations of a social contract between the two parties.

Weber's second type of legitimate authority is the traditional one. Its foundational principle is that a leader or their family has been in power for as long as anybody can remember. In the years of yore power was considered to be vested in those families by the grace of God. In settings where this ideal type still seems to be the most relevant, alternatives are beyond imagination. In this sense, there is legitimacy by default. This is the situation masterfully depicted in Gabriel García Márquez' novel *The Autumn of the Patriarch*. The dictator has been there for so long that no one is able to imagine anything else. His presence is taken for granted and regarded as a fact of life. The people fear him but do not call his rule into question. However, in the novel the unthinkable finally happens. The dictator dies, and the people must face the previously inconceivable period of transition. Regimes with lengthy incumbencies approach this ideal type, even if their reigns have not lasted since times immemorial.

Weber's third type of legitimate authority is the charismatic one, which builds on the leader's personal characteristics and exceptional qualities. Weber had primarily religious leadership in mind here, but secular leaders can also draw legitimacy from these grounds. This is maybe the type of legitimate authority that has been most discussed in the literature inspired by Weber (Helms 2020). It is also the ideal type of greatest interest to this book since I argue that it corresponds to the predominant legitimation strategy in Putinist Russia. I will therefore discuss it in some more detail.

According to Weber (1978: 241-242), charisma denotes a "certain quality of an individual personality by virtue of which he is considered extraordinary and treated as endowed with supernatural, superhuman, or at least specifically exceptional powers or qualities". Charismatic authority is irrational and alien to rules. It does not build on any easily defined, specific characteristics. This makes it difficult to analyze and hard to measure (Andrews-Lee 2019). Charisma does not denote a binary variable which is either there or not there, but a matter of degree determined on a discrete and sliding scale (cf. Gippert 2016). If it is lost, it evaporates slowly. It is not drained overnight.

The literature has long struggled to come up with answers concerning the components of charismatic authority (Mio et al 2005, Chung Yoon-Gun 1993). First, the charismatic leader is an "extraordinary individual with extraordinary qualities and a magnetic personality" (Chung Yoon-Gun 1993: 87). Charismatic leaders inspire their followers, make them believe in their collective abilities and lay out visions of the future. They have unique personal characteristics, are perceived as national saviors or heroes who step in at the very last moment to salvage the nation from crisis and dissolution and are therefore indiscriminately admired by their adherents. The leaders have shown leadership in the initial stage of nation-building and are recognized as capable of accomplishing the great and ambitious goals that they have set out to reach (Chung Yoon-Gun 1993: 85).

Moreover, charismatic leadership relies strongly on oratory and communication skills (Andrews-Lee 2019, Petersson 2017). Charismatic leaders have well developed abilities to get across to the people with stories that matter to them. They own the capacity to sway an audience and tell stories that make a difference. When such political leaders communicate, the audience experiences the illusion of being invited to co-create and co-construct the vision and the world together with them (Kjellgren 2019, Andrews-Lee 2019). The charismatic leaders often enliven their stories by using analogies, metaphor, or political myth (Charteris-Black 2011, 2019; Petersson 2017, Mio et al 2005).

The construction of charismatic authority is, then, more about an "emotional form of irrational relationship" than the work of rational principles and processes (Chung Yoon-Gun 1993: 85). All this suggests a dark side of legitimacy, as charismatic leaders may attract a multitude of supporters and have their commands heeded with consequences that would be deplorable to most other people. This offers an answer to Benedict Anderson's (1983) familiar query about what it is in nationalism that makes otherwise rational-minded people willing to lay down their lives in defense of the national. Historically, sacrifices on behalf of the national have been urged and prompted by charismatic leaders who have managed to gather a large following by manipulation and use of their persuasive skills.

The popularity and support-worthiness of a certain political ruler will only last while the general magic works and widespread perceptions of the leader as charismatic hold sway (Weber 1983: 146). In this sense the concept of charisma resembles the concept of invincibility that some authors prefer to use. The standing of the charismatic leader is so strong that their political misfortune seems inconceivable (Koesel and Bunce 2012). When the ability of the leader to tell a convincing story recedes, so does their authority and the aura of invincibility diminishes with it. When the trustworthy stories end, charismatic leadership also risks vaporizing. The fundamental dilemma for authoritarian regimes is how to follow up a convincing story with credible action to keep it convincing and sustain the orator's legitimacy (Samoilenko 2017).

Legitimacy in non-democratic states

Whether or not legitimacy is a concept that applies in non-democratic settings has been hotly debated over the years. As laconically argued by one proponent of the idea that legitimacy is exclusively relevant for democracies, "only a democratic government can be legitimate" (Buchanan 2002: 689). Other scholars have equally steadfastly argued that the concept is relevant beyond the democratic nation-state context (Omelicheva 2016, Mazepus et al 2016, Heberer and Schubert 2008, Schlumberger and Bank 2001, Holmes 1997, Alagappa 1995, Chung Yoon-Gun 1993, Rigby 1982). To get out of the ideological quagmire, suffice it to suggest that the widening of the applicability of the concept of legitimacy beyond the domain of democratic states becomes possible if the analysis concerns perceived legitimacy, not legitimacy as an absolute or normative value (Arnesen et al 2019: 4). My rationale for accepting the stretching of the concept is simply that it is important for political scientists to analyze what holds states together, short of repression, clientelism, and bribery (Pavroz 2020, Omelicheva 2016, Goode 2012, 2020). This is regardless of whether the legitimizing grounds are democratic or not, since the consequences of the attainment of the societal stability that can only come from legitimacy are profound for domestic politics and the outward behavior of any state. Even if some analysts claim that coercion and clientelism in combination are sufficient to keep non-democratic rulers in power (Orange 2019), I maintain that successful legitimation, in relation to the populace and to contending elites, comes across as the most sustainable mechanism for the political survival of hybrid and authoritarian regimes (Kailitz and Stockemer 2017, Goode 2012).

In such systems, contextual circumstances are fundamentally different from democracies. Factors other than strict legality and adherence to constitutional frameworks, namely, indoctrination, clientelism, and the use of force, play crucial roles (Pavroz 2020, Orange 2019, Feldmann and Mazepus 2017, Mazepus et al 2016). The concepts of legitimacy and regime support therefore mean partly different things, depending on whether democratic or non-democratic states are being discussed (Nathan 2020). Nevertheless, in sheer economic terms, legitimacy comes cheaper than repression, so even an authoritarian regime will gain from achieving acquiescence through non-violent means (Omelicheva 2016). Unless a regime is willing to sustain itself through violence and repression alone, it needs to seem support-worthy to the popular majority. Finding ways of assessing the political dynamics to attain legitimacy is therefore key to the understanding of the relative longevity not only of democratic polities but also hybrid and authoritarian regimes (du Boulay 2020, Goode 2020, 2012).

For the researcher there is a methodological dilemma involved in studying legitimacy in hybrid and authoritarian states, as popular opinions and perceptions are for several reasons difficult or ethically objectionable to investigate there (Omelicheva 2016, Koesel and Bunce 2012). This was briefly touched upon above. Either the respondents to interviews and surveys are reluctant to reveal what they think, or it is irresponsible to put them at risk by asking them in the first place. Several researchers therefore argue that it makes little sense to claim or attempt to study legitimacy in such settings; instead, what one can reasonably do is to study the *legitimation claims* made by the regimes. The focus of study should therefore shift from opinions of the electorate to the ways in which the political elite legitimizes its rule and tries to communicate its claims to the public (du Boulay and Isaacs 2019, von Soest and Grauvogel 2017, Dukalskis and Gerschewski 2017, Omelicheva 2016). Indeed, "[t]o move beyond the inputs and process of legitimation to the output of legitimacy remains the unresolved challenge for all those interested in the study of stability, legitimacy and social change in non-democratic regimes" (du Boulay and Isaacs 2019: 37). So, the argument goes, analyzing the legitimation claims is as good as it gets. This strategy reduces the inherent methodological and moral dilemmas. Official discourse provides the material for the analyst to study central arguments of self-legitimation. Together with polling data and election results, such texts provide grounds for analyses of the effectiveness of legitimation efforts in authoritarian and hybrid systems. These sources enable the analysis of predominant modes of legitimation and the dilemmas that they give rise to.

Charisma and routinization

Weber famously argued that a political system that primarily relies on some type of legitimate authority other than the rational-legal one will have problems sustaining itself. For example, the traditional type of authority would be vulnerable in a situation of political succession when the family wherein traditional authority was nested suffered through death or incapacity. For its part, charismatic authority is the least durable of the three ideal types and is also highly elusive. This authority will be lost as a sitting political leader gradually exhausts their charisma and finds their trust among the electorate to be waning. The more reliant a political system is on legitimacy engendered by charismatic authority, the weaker it will be. Moreover, charismatic authority is not a given. It must be constructed continuously in the relations between the rulers and the ruled. This makes political succession in non-democratic settings particularly difficult. Even if a new incumbent can initially benefit from their predecessor's charismatic authority, the link between the people and the leader needs to be forged anew to complete the transition. At the outset, the successor will probably have difficulties stepping out of their predecessor's shadow and proving themself worthy of taking over the reins of executive power (Helms 2020).

Even if some research has suggested that a successor under favorable circumstances may manage to capitalize on and take over the predecessor's charisma (Andrews-Lee 2019), most authors have argued that this is a difficult undertaking. One contemporary interpreter of Weber's writings expressed the dilemma in the following terms:

> … *pure charisma is liable to collapse with the death of the idolized and beloved leader. In order to survive, it must reverse its valence and be channeled into rationalized secondary forms where leadership is inherited, appointed, or guaranteed by magical signs* (Lindholm 2019).

Even if we may exclude the magical signs from the analysis, charisma is as we saw elusive, unpredictable, irrational, and based on emotions. It does not lend itself easily to the construction of a stable power base, as it may evaporate and desert its master. Charismatic authority may inspire and initiate the foundation of a political system but cannot guarantee its maintenance (Weber 1983: 169, Snyder 2018). It is revolutionary in character and can destroy or transform a political system but cannot sustain whatever it is that it lays the foundations for. Therefore, Weber anticipated that legitimacy primarily built on charismatic authority must be "routinized" to last (Weber 1983, Isaacs 2015). Through the process of routinization of charisma, the legitimacy of a political system can be sustained even after the exit of the current leader, Weber argued. Charismatic authority then transforms into some more durable type of legitimate authority, optimally of the rational-legal kind.

Routinization is never an easy process. The process takes time and is likely to be fraught with conflict as it progresses (Jarbawi and Pearlman 2007). Weber enumerated several strategies of routinization, three of which have continued relevance for how such a transformation can take place in political settings of today. These involve the incumbent's handpicking of a successor, the leader's staff appointing the successor, who will then have to gain popular acceptance, or going down the hereditary path through the identification of someone of the old leader's kin as the successor (Weber 1983, Isaacs 2015). In the first case, the authority still initially rests on the predecessor's charisma, whereas in the second, there are approaches to rational-legal authority. In the third case, charismatic authority will be routinized into traditional authority.

Legitimacy and political myth

Political myth is a central field of political analysis (Bottici and Challand 2013), even if it has not always been recognized as such by social science researchers. It is my contention that charismatic authority is largely constructed through skillful communication and the effective use of political myths. These constructs are "identity-constitutive historical narratives" (Toth 2021), whose contents are largely taken for granted by the public in any given society. The myths express naturalized, taken-for-granted cultural knowledge (Barthes 1993), but they do not arise from thin air. They may be top-down constructs, corroborated and reinforced by "deliberate manipulation and intentional action" (Bell 2003: 75, cf. Toth 2021, Charteris-Black 2011), but they also reflect beliefs that have existed and been widespread in society for generations. Through successful epitomizing of the myths and effectiveness in getting across to the public, legitimacy is bestowed on those leaders who master the game.

Key political actors successfully enact and communicate political myths, which, *nota bene*, are not about falsities in philosophical terms (Bottici 2010). What matters is that a significant number of people believe in them and relate to them as if they were true. Clunan (2014) refers to "fitness tests" that are continually played out in a society. Here, the politicians prove themselves worthy and show that they can deliver on the implementation of cherished political myths. When passed, the fitness tests serve to legitimize the political leaders. When failed, the leaders will find their positions eroding. If they do not live up to the myths and do not deliver on them, the contents of the myths can contribute to bringing the incumbents down. This is "the myth's cunning" (Boer 2009: 26); it can in other words be a treacherous companion (Eatwell 2006).

Like political rhetoric itself, political myth is characterized by the close intertwining of emotive and cognitive elements (Malinova 2015). Unless appealing to people's emotions in a positive sense, no political entity is likely to hold together in the end. At the same time, the construct will not be viable unless it is firmly anchored in widely accepted knowledge. After all, despite its claim of superiority to Western states, the Soviet socialist bloc evaporated as the populace could see with their own eyes that the mythical contention was unfounded and false.

There are strong links between charismatic legitimacy, political myth, and the leaders' capacity to act and live the myth. Political myths concern core values which people feel strongly about. Charismatic leaders convey and recount the important stories that the myths retell. In the process the leaders will see to it that they play a crucial role in the plots of the stories (Isaacs 2015). The term "discourse legitimacy" (Schlumberger and Bank 2001: 65) describes this phenomenon well.

Some political myths reappear in slightly shifting guises, in many settings and across many different countries. They constitute a universal political phenomenon. Radically summarized, such myths are on a very general level about three vital processes in the history or contemporaneity of a nation: glory, heroism, and victimhood (Assmann 2010, in Toth 2021). Similarly, Edelman (1977, in Charteris-Black 2011) enumerated three universally recognized master myths: the omnipresent enemy who conspires against the nation; the valiant and wise leader who salvages the people from that terrible enemy; and the people who in times of great need unite behind their leader to deliver the country from the gravest danger. All three master myths are familiar from the Russian setting and

Vladimir Putin has been markedly successful in exploiting them all. These myths constitute the fabric from which much contemporary Russian nationalism is woven. Their narrative contents are in conformity with the discourse of traditionalism, which over the centuries has been in a constant, antagonistic clash with discourses of liberalism in Russia. The course of Russian political development has been largely chartered out depending on the struggle between these two discourses, famously known as the perennial conflict between Slavophiles and Westernizers (Chebankova 2015, Hosking 2001).

The use of political myth is thus universal political practice. Prominent populist actors have demonstrated its effectiveness in established democracies as well. Together with several other states Russia claims to be "uniquely gifted, accomplished and superior, morally and spiritually, to the West" (Mishra 2017: 164). This corresponds to a powerful and basic political myth about great power supremacy and prowess. Here, non-democratic Russia is certainly not the only setting for such political myths. Corresponding narratives come to mind also regarding democratic great powers such as the United States and France.

Again, charismatic authority is the product of a continuous process of persuasive communication and emotional allegiance which aligns political leaders with the people. It comes into being through interaction with the audience (Hoffmann 2009). Here Vladimir Putin often excels, and his skills at adapting his style of communication to fit the audience, especially when he is addressing the public are well known (Petersson and Sommers 2015, Gorham 2013). His ways of communicating have many faces. In the context of primary audiences of politicians and officials, his presentations are at times bureaucratic and wooden. On other occasions, his way of expressing himself is drastic and vulgar, which in certain contexts seems to be an effective way of making people listen. Having the talent of getting narratives across to the audience, he is in such instances the kind of gifted storyteller that the charismatic political leader is expected to be. Let us ponder one example of this.

The occasion was the Annual News Conference in 2014, the year of the Russian annexation of Crimea. Putin was asked a question about Russia's international role and to what extent current economic difficulties had been brought about by the sanctions introduced by the Western community after Crimea. Putin framed his answer in terms of Russia's national survival and its right to exist as a great power. He conjured up a vivid image of the stereotypical Russian bear losing sovereignty over its habitat:

> At the Valdai Club I gave an example of our most recognizable symbol. It is a bear protecting his taiga. You see, if we continue the analogy, sometimes I think that maybe it would be best if our bear just sat still. Maybe he should stop chasing pigs and boars around the taiga but start picking berries and eating honey. Maybe then he will be left alone. But no, he won't be! Because someone will always try to chain him up. As soon as he's chained they will tear out his teeth and claws... As soon as – God forbid – it happens and they no longer need the bear, the taiga will be taken over. (- - -)
>
> And then, when all the teeth and claws are torn out, the bear will be of no use at all. Perhaps they'll stuff it and that's all. So, it is not about Crimea but about us protecting our independence, our sovereignty and our right to exist. That is what we should all realize... [W]e must decide whether we want to keep going and fight, change our economy – for the better, by the way, because we can use the current situation to our own advantage – and be more independent, go through all this or we want our skin to hang on the wall. This is the choice we need to make... (President of Russia, 18 December 2014, cited in Petersson and Sommers 2015).

This is an illuminating example of a charismatic leader talking to his devotees and colorfully invoking political myth: about Russia's nature-bound greatness, its subjection to threats from powerful enemies abroad, and the need always to be vigilant. It is an effective message, and it bears witness to Putin's skills as an effective political communicator and performer.

III

Legitimizing Putin

The 2011-2012 legitimation crisis

The discursive legitimation strategies used during Putin's third and fourth presidencies can only be understood against the background of the large-scale protests and public frustration in 2011-2012, during the transition from the parenthetical Medvedev presidency to the third Putin presidency. All this led to a crisis in confidence and legitimacy which the regime—"the collective Putin" (Sharafutdinova 2020; Rutland 2017b)—needed to overcome to sustain itself. The crisis prompted the mix of legitimation strategies that is still in use at the time of writing.

When taking up the presidency in 2008, Dmitriy Medvedev appointed Putin his prime minister. Even though high hopes of modernization and relative democratization were originally tied to the Medvedev presidency, it soon became apparent that the prime minister, not the president, was now the de facto power hub in the executive branch of government. This was not least visible in the realm of foreign and security policy. There was speculation that in due time Medvedev would be able to use the presidency to strengthen his power, not least during the second term in office allowed to him by the constitution. If he did try to consolidate his position in such a manner, he was evidently not very successful (Sakwa 2014). There was never to be a second term.

At the congress of the United Russia party in September 2011, Medvedev announced that he was going to forgo his right to run for a second term. Instead, he recommended Putin as the party's front runner. He justified his move by referring to public opinion polls which indicated that Putin was by far the more popular of the two and said that he above all wished to improve the chances of United Russia's success at the upcoming elections for the Duma in December and the presidency in March. In other words, he took a

humble position and ostensibly made his personal ambition sec-
ondary to the goals of the party, and above all, Putin (Tkachenko
2011).

The intensity of the public outcry seems to have come as a surprise to the regime. The tandem deal between Putin and Medvedev
was greeted as evidence of the power elite's cynicism and disregard
of the popular will, as well as contempt for the spirit of the 1993
constitution, which was widely interpreted to prohibit any president to serve for more than two periods all in all. Here, the handy
deal had found a loophole. The official interpretation offered was
that more than two consecutive periods for a president was prohibited by the constitution, but more than two periods all in all was
fully allowed.

Frustration and discontent simmered. In the eyes of many, the
Putin-Medvedev power sharing deal indicated that the Russian political system was little else than "the plaything of Putin" (Gill 2016:
361), and that the terms of the deal had been agreed between the
two leaders a long time ago. This was also later corroborated by a
slip of the tongue by Medvedev (Koesel and Bunce 2012), and indeed also by Putin himself (Stent 2019: 101, Sakwa 2014: 113). Matters came to a head in connection with the Duma elections in December 2011. These were evidently rigged and marred with malfea-
sance to boost the otherwise probably rather weak result of United
Russia. People had had enough and started to take to the streets in
increasing numbers. Demonstrations took place in Moscow, St. Petersburg, and numerous other large cities in Russia, with some of
the manifestations reportedly gathering 100,000 people or more.
The protests were clearly among the most massive and well attended since the fall of the Soviet Union (Koesel and Bunce 2012).

It was during these events that the founder of the Anti-Corruption Fund (FBK), the blogger and activist Aleksei Navalny, in
earnest started his rise to oppositional leadership prominence
(Kniivilä 2021, Flikke 2020, Yudin 2020). Otherwise, the protest
movement was coordinated through social media networking,
which made it hard to control from the point of view of the authorities. Its messages caught on rapidly, and under Navalny's leader-

ship the opposition became skilled at designing one-liners and visual cues which were catchy and increased its social impact. Slogans like "The party of crooks and thieves", "Putin is a thief" and "Vote for anyone except United Russia" became influential. The white ribbon donned as a sign of recognition among the activists had symbolic clout and underlined the kinship with the color revolutions in Georgia, Kyrgyzstan, and Ukraine in the years 2003-2005. White was also a choice of color that could signal innocence and clean slates, especially when compared to the regime which had been in power since the late 1990s and seemed to wish to stay there forever.

Putin made a blunt effort to diminish the symbolic appeal of the white ribbon carried by the demonstrators. He quipped — in a manner in keeping with his populist rhetorical style — that he had mistaken the ribbons for condoms to be distributed by activists in the struggle against HIV (Elder 2011). Putin's crude joke was rapidly turned against him in social media, and photo-shopped images of Putin contained in a huge condom went viral. This seemed to be an occasion when he for once had misread social sentiments gravely.

During the most intense months of the protests Putin appeared to be off-balance. He alleged that the demonstrations had been spurred and funded by the United States to destabilize Russia, and he went as far as to accuse the then US Secretary of State, Hillary Clinton, personally for being a puppet-master of the civil unrest. Angrily responding to a tweet by the Republican Senator John McCain, who had suggested that the Arab Spring had finally come to Moscow, Putin implied that the senator must have lost his mind while held captive in a pit during the Vietnam war (Elder 2011). The emotional reaction on the part of the Russian president indicated that the fear of regime overthrow following the so-called color revolution script was a real one in the Kremlin. Russian leaders have then and later frequently accused the United States of being the invisible hand inciting the turbulence of the color revolutions. In their quest to prevent a similar scenario from playing out in Russia, the authorities took determined action (Petrov 2020). Some observers have pointed out that the lasting democratic effects of the color revolutions were limited in the countries where they unfolded, but that the repressive actions taken by non-democratic regimes in adjacent countries to avoid color revolutions on their home turf were more far-reaching (Koesel and Bunce 2013). We shall return to these dynamics below.

Nevertheless, to initially accommodate some of the demands by the activists in 2011-2012, the Russian authorities installed webcams in polling stations, ostensibly to increase transparency and combat electoral fraud during the presidential elections to be held in the spring. President Medvedev also initiated a return to the system of regional governors being elected by the people, which meant revoking an unpopular reform launched by Putin during his first presidency.

If these measures had been intended to forestall protests at the presidential elections in March 2012, they did not achieve their aim, even if the scale and intensity were somewhat less than at the Duma elections. According to the official results, Putin won the presidential poll by a wide margin, gaining 63.6 percent of the vote. In the evening of March 4, he declared himself as winner at a public event outside of the Kremlin walls. His relief seemed genuine, and big tears were running down his cheeks as he declared:

> We showed that no one can direct us in anything!... We were able to save ourselves from political provocations, which have one goal: to destroy Russian sovereignty and usurp power… The Russian people have shown today that such scenarios will not succeed in our land … They shall not pass! (Heritage and Faulconbridge 2012).

The wording was strong and without doubt chosen carefully, as a key phrase referred directly to Article 3 of the 1993 Constitution of the Russian Federation which made it a federal offence, punishable by federal law, to try to "usurp power". The president indicated that he, as rightful incumbent and guarantor of the constitution, had the privilege to define what amounted to attempts at such usurpation. Harsh measures were to be expected against opponents whose activities fit that definition.

In the same speech Putin said that the battle fought during the presidential race had been "open and honest". Therefore, the sinister forces that he alluded to in the quote were hardly his formal contenders from the within-system opposition, the Communist party candidate Gennadiy Zyuganov, the Liberal Democrat party leader and populist Vladimir Zhirinovskiy, and the billionaire Mikhail Prokhorov. Rather, the wording again insinuated foreign intervention by the hands of the United States. The rhetorical casting of blame was indicative of what was later to come during Putin's third and fourth presidential tenures: an anti-American policy line which would place the blame for all global shortcomings and injustice, as well as all difficulties suffered by Russia, at the doorstep of the United States. With this, the Russian leader laid the foundation for depicting himself and his nation as the staunch defender against US attempts to attain world hegemony. Putin signaled his new hardline approach to the United States clearly, making a trip to China one of his first official visits after his re-election, whereas he cancelled a planned trip to Washington on account of being "too busy" (Stent 2019: 220).

Even if some new elements of the regime's legitimation strategies could be discerned already in Putin's celebration speech on March 4, 2012, it took some time for the regime to regain its posture after the civil protests. The unrest went on for several months and culminated in many ways on May 6, 2012, on the eve of Putin's inauguration as president, with massive demonstrations on the Bolotnaya Square in central Moscow. Violence erupted between activists and the police, hundreds of demonstrators were detained, and court cases opened to be pursued for years afterwards. The square had been a frequent meeting place during the protests, and "Bolotnaya" came to be synonymous with the civil unrest taking place in 2011 and 2012. The clashes that physically took place on the Bolotnaya Square in May 2012 signified a turning point in the regime's response, as in June the same year new laws were enacted that set stricter boundaries on protests and imposed heavy penalties on unauthorized activities (Hinsey 2013). It also ushered in a tougher line against prominent leaders of the protests, such as Navalny, and others.

Even if the public protests abated after June 2012, Putin's popularity ratings remained low throughout 2012 and 2013. It seemed from many of his public appearances that he was lacking in energy (Petersson 2013). He looked listless and devoid of real initiative. The decisive infusion of energy did not come until in 2014, with the annexation of Crimea and the involvement in the war in Ukraine. This was what really turned the public opinion into a direction that was favorable to the president.

Re-legitimization: Ukraine and the annexation of Crimea

In November 2013 large-scale protests erupted in the Ukraine capital of Kyiv following the decision by the president, Viktor Yanukovych, to abandon a negotiated association agreement with the European Union and instead opt for closer ties with Russia and the Eurasian Economic Union eagerly nurtured by Putin from his third term on. The pro-Russian Yanukovych had had a bumpy political trajectory, and this was to continue in the months to come. He was declared the winner of the presidential election in 2004 but never assumed office after having been confronted with massive evidence of large-scale fraud to secure his victory. In what came to be called Ukraine's Orange Revolution there was a rerun of the elections, where the eventual victor was the rightful winner of the original round, the Western-oriented Viktor Yushchenko. Due to domestic scandals and internal squabbles, the latter's presidential tenure did not land well in public opinion, however, so Yanukovych could stage a remarkable political comeback. He served for a while as Yushchenko's prime minister and was elected president in 2010 after a win over Yuliya Timoshenko in the second round.

After the abandoned deal with the European Union, the turbulence around Yanukovych started to grow anew. The agenda of the widespread protests expanded gradually to include mobilization against government corruption and the abuse of power. The allegations were vigorously denied by the authorities. According to some estimations, in December 2013 about 800,000 people had gathered on Independence Square (Maidan Nezalezhnosti), in central

Kyiv, which was to become the center stage of the events known all over the world as Euro-Maidan. Activists occupied the Kyiv City Hall, and protests spread to other major cities in Ukraine.

Clashes between opposition and government forces became increasingly violent, and in mid-January 2014 the Ukrainian parliament adopted strict anti-protest laws to stop the unrest, to little avail as it turned out. Instead, the protests peaked, the prime minister resigned from office, and the anti-protest laws were annulled. In mid-February, activists who had been incarcerated during the protests were released, and the occupants abandoned the City Hall. Lethal violence claimed about 100 lives in the capital as special and Interior Ministry forces attacked people on the Maidan. The parliament voted to remove Yanukovych from office, whereupon he responded by accusing the legislature of staging a coup. On February 22, 2014, he fled the country, later to end up in Russia.

At this point Russia started to act for real, first through armed unidentified "little green men" in combat uniform, who appeared all over the Crimean Peninsula on the Black Sea coast in southernmost Ukraine, especially in the Crimean regional capital of Simferopol where they started to take control over administrative buildings. This surprise move took place as global attention had just been focused elsewhere, at the city of Sochi in southern Russia, where Russia had been hosting the Olympic Winter Games and Putin himself had played a significant role in demonstrating Russia's regained great power position and soft power potential (Persson and Petersson 2014, Petersson and Vamling 2013).

There was little doubt that the green-clad soldiers were Russians, even if the authorities, including President Putin, disavowed any knowledge of their origin or mission. On March 1, 2014, Putin requested the permission of the Federation Council to use military force to protect the interests of Russia and the Russian-speaking population in Ukraine. A referendum was hastily organized in Crimea on joining the Russian Federation. According to the official figures, 97 percent of the voters backed the proposition, but critics argued that electoral fraud had been widespread (BBC News 2014). A few days later, Putin signed a bill to incorporate Crimea into the Russian Federation.

In stark violation of international law Russia thus moved to forcibly change international borders in Europe. This ushered in a new era in global post-cold war politics. Portentously, it seemed as if Russia was aiming for more and did not settle for incorporating Crimea only. In early April, protesters occupied government buildings in the east Ukrainian cities of Donetsk, Luhansk and Kharkiv, calling for a referendum on independence for these regions. In April 2014, armed rebel groups established the Donetsk People's Republic and Luhansk People's Republic (O'Loughlin et al 2017). An all-out civil war unfolded between the secessionists and the government in Kyiv. At this time Putin and other members of the regime started to refer to the whole Donbas area as "Novorossiya" (O'Loughlin et al 2017, Laruelle 2016), i.e., "New Russia", a term originally coined during the expansionist reign of Catherine the Great during the latter part of the 18th century. In the present context the term was used to signal that the region should rightfully belong to Russia, or at any rate, consist of political entities markedly sympathetic and friendly towards Russia.

Eventually, Putin backed down from those ambitions, abandoned the term "Novorossiya" and, to the dismay of hardline Russian nationalists, refrained from giving Luhansk and Donetsk separatists of the Donbas region full-scale support and helping them go all the way to Kyiv. From being hailed for his bold moves on Crimea, Putin was bitterly targeted by radical nationalists for letting the separatists down. Seemingly, however, the vocal nationalist opposition did little harm to his position (Kolstö 2016). Nevertheless, at this stage the leading western powers vocalized their opposition against the Russian actions. Chill came to characterize Russia's relations with the West for several years ahead. The European Union and the United States introduced sanctions which hurt the Russian economy badly. Russia responded with countersanctions which in many cases hurt the population even more as certain imported foodstuffs became unavailable.

New elections for president were held in Ukraine on May 25, 2013, from which Petro Poroshenko emerged the winner. Under his presidency an association agreement was finally signed with the

European Union in late June, reinforcing Kyiv's Western orientation. After a civilian aircraft, Malaysia Airlines flight MH17 from Amsterdam, was downed in July over separatist-held territory by a missile of Russian origin (Dutch Safety Board 2015), with almost 300 lives lost, the Western sanctions were reinforced. The lines of division between Kyiv and Donbas hardened as the civil war raged on. In early 2020 the estimated death toll had reached more than 13 000 persons, a third of whom were believed to be civilian casualties (Reuters 2020, Miller 2019b).

The annexation of Crimea, the insurgency in eastern Ukraine, and the reactions and sanctions by the Western powers came to define much of the political context of Putin's third and fourth presidential tenures. Together with the domestic protests that the Russian regime had faced in connection with the transfer of presidential power back to Putin in 2012, this background offered rough take off grounds for efforts to legitimize Putin's third presidential tenure. However, it also signified opportunities. A strained global climate and demonstrated animosity by foreign Others against Russian actions could justify a strongman rule by a leader believed to be able to take resolute action, lead the country out of the crisis, protect national stability and defeat foreign machinations in one fell swoop. The scene was set for Vladimir Putin 2.0, a stronger and even more authoritative version of the leader who had served as president during the period 2000-2008. The aftermath of the annexation constituted the launching pad for discursive legitimation strategies that would supposedly enable him to continue as president even beyond the end of his fourth term in office in 2024.

Strength and stability

Political legitimacy in contemporary Russia has for a long time been largely built on Putin's personal popularity (Pavroz 2020, Willerton 2017, Sil and Chen 2004). In contrast, the political system as such has little or no legitimacy among the public which significantly reduces the sustainability of the regime. There is little confidence in other political institutions than the presidency itself, be they the Duma, the Federation Council, the political parties, or the judiciary

(Pavroz 2020). This means that if the incumbent's authority wanes, so does the overall legitimacy of the regime.

It is a central argument of this book that Putin's charismatic legitimacy has to a great extent been construed based on an array of successfully communicated and, for a long time, largely well received political myths. Together these myths form a relatively coherent and compelling narrative structure that has been sustained during a long period, forming a mythscape which has been effective in securing the allegiance of a popular majority. In their totality they provide an ideational power basis of the regime and helps to account for its durability (Goode 2012).

The most prominent of these myths will be summarized below, returned to, and illustrated in the following chapters. No single myth may be powerful enough to provide the regime with the legitimacy that it needs. Rather, it is their totality and interrelatedness that produce results, even if individual myths seem to predominate at certain points in time (cf Omelicheva 2016). The importance of effective communication and positive official media coverage for upholding the increasingly authoritarian political system in Russia is in line with the perceived contemporary trend towards a proliferation of informational autocracies. These rely more on propaganda strategies with broad outreach than on large-scale repression to keep popular majorities at bay (Guriev and Treisman 2019).

Showing strength in the international arena, living up to the great power legacy and appearing as the foremost champion of Russia's national interests have always been important for Putin. Sometimes he has come to express this in the blunt, populist style that has become his trademark. At the meeting of the Valdai Club in 2017 he commented on a statement ascribed to the first minister of foreign affairs during the Yeltsin administrations, Andrey Kozyrev. In a conversation with the former president of the United States, Richard Nixon, Kozyrev had been reported as saying that to him there were no national interests, only common human interests. Nixon had seemed confused about the statement and had shaken his head.[6] Commenting on the report about the interaction between Kozyrev and the former US president, Putin remarked dryly:

This shows that Nixon has a head, while Mr. Kozyrev, unfortunately, has not. He has a cranium but no head as such (President of Russia, 19 October 2017).

Never being the great ideologue, nor indeed representing an articulated ideology, Putin has, with his national greatness appeals, filled an ideological void and has emerged as a catch-all president using formulae that are pleasing to many (Sharafutdinova 2020, Petersson 2020). The great power role and its external recognition are of key importance for the public appreciation of the regime's activities. As aptly summed up by Busygina (2019): "in contemporary Russia, foreign policy has become the most powerful of all domestic policy tools". Recognition and respect from abroad have on balance been less important than gaining credit in the domestic arena for actions to the benefit of the fatherland and its glory.

On the other hand, as in all societies, the domestic arena is per se of course vitally important for the legitimacy of Russian political leaders. Unless the regime demonstrates an ability to provide the people with a satisfactory and decent standard of living, its legitimacy is prone to evaporate sooner rather than later (Hutcheson and Petersson 2017, Feldmann and Mazepus 2017, Brusis 2016). Here it is not only the matter of materiality, as the regime's performance at home is also assessed in terms of maintenance of social and political stability (von Soest and Grauvogel 2016, 2017). The latter values have often been in short supply in recent as well as more distant periods of Russia's turbulent past. The longing for stability and for a time with almost no unemployment and low rents helps to account for the nostalgia towards the late Brezhnev period which has often manifested itself in the post-Soviet years (Boele 2011).

The quest for visible performance at home and abroad, as well as stability and predictability in daily life, have provided favorable

---

6   The encounter between Kozyrev and Nixon is described in somewhat different terms by Simes (1999: 19).

preconditions for the successful marketing of the Putin phenomenon from the early years of his presidencies on. During his first two presidential terms in office, economic growth figures served him well. World market prices in fossil fuels hit an all-time high and increased more than tenfold during the period but saw a marked deterioration after the financial crises of 2007 and onwards (von Soest and Grauvogel 2016, Stent 2019). At the time when Putin's third presidency started in 2012, other parts of his achievement record became more important by way of compensation. When economic indicators began to slope, legitimization efforts through other sources became more important to sustain the regime.

From the very beginning, Putin ventured to emerge as a savior delivering Russia from the weak and disorderly conditions that prevailed under Boris Yeltsin. Referring during his first years as president to the dictatorship of the law, he emerged as the prime guarantor of order and stability at home, the anti-thesis of his predecessor in the unruly 1990s (Sharlet 2001). The bringing back to heel of separatist Chechnya became symbolic for Putin's willpower and resolve. The forcing back of the recalcitrant republic into the federal fold was the epitome of the resurrection of stability and order. Putin's hardline policies on Chechnya won him his first presidential election and laid the foundation for his domination of Russian politics for two decades or more (Petersson 2018a). Whereas Chechnya signified the political downfall of Yeltsin, it contributed substantially to the preconditions of Putin's meteoric rise to political stardom (Hutcheson and Petersson 2021).

In the regime propaganda Putin has been depicted as so true to Russian national ideals and strivings that he has become synonymous with Russia itself. In turn, Russia has become synonymous with Putin (Makarychev and Yatsyk 2014). These are significant connotations, as by extension, real opposition to Putin is deemed tantamount to treason (Hall 2017: 175). By design and by default Putin is "the supreme leader" or the rightful "Emperor", under the name of Vladimir I, as the ultra-nationalist Vladimir Zhirinovskiy once suggested (Youtube 2013). Volodin's words cited above say it all: no Putin, no Russia. In the political master narratives that shape the political scene, Putin has assumed pride of place. He is the benefactor, the savior, the dragon-slayer, and there is no one like him.

The great power myth

Putin has, particularly during the early part of his presidencies, repeatedly invoked Tsar Peter the Great as a major source of inspiration among past Russian leaders (Glasser 2019, Bagger 2007). Not only that, but he has also referred to the time of Peter as inspiring for the decisive reforms needed to be made in the present (President of Russia, 16 July 2000). This is significant. Putin has hailed Peter for making Russia an internationally respected great power, while also establishing and maintaining stability and order at home (President of Russia, 27 June 2019). It should be noted that there is a potential point of friction here in relations to radical Russian nationalists who see Peter and the Romanovs as traitors who in complicity with the West, at the time most particularly Germany, in essence betrayed and denigrated Russian traditional cultural and spiritual values (Sheiko and Brown 2014). However, the views of this hardline fringe have not seemed to drain the Putin regime of popular legitimacy. To the extent that they have existed, the main challenges have come from elsewhere.

Peter has suited Putin well as a role model. The suggested analogy is that just as Peter led Russia away from humiliation and defeat by foreign hands—at that time primarily Sweden—so Putin presided over a Russia moving from dissolution, decay, and weakness to become a global power resurrected and respected. Like Peter, Putin is projected as a man of deeds, intent on making use of imported goods when this is useful for reforming the country. Peter was happy to take up Western models of shipbuilding and administration. Putin has favored the entrenchment of market economy and, albeit somewhat less enthusiastically than his longtime sidekick Dimitriy Medvedev, promoted innovation in technology. Just like Peter, he is not much of a democrat. Peter ordered the building of St. Petersburg in the forbidding marshlands on the western fringe of the empire, not shying away from the immense death toll that the project took among the city's forcibly mobilized builders.

Eagerly indicating Peter as his role model, Putin implicitly signals that he too is willing to go far to secure the realization of his objectives.

Over the years, the allegiance to the political myth about Russia's destiny-bound great power status, established and reinforced under Peter, has been the most durable and ever-present part in Putin's self-legitimation toolbox. The idea about national greatness by birthright is a belief thoroughly entrenched in Russian national identity. Tellingly, the myth about Russia's pre-determined great power status was steadfastly adhered to even in the years of weakness and post-Soviet disillusionment during the 1990s (Petersson 2018a).

The great power theme was prevalent during Putin's first and second presidencies in 2000-2004 and 2004-2008 when Russia reasserted itself on the global arena, but it has permeated political and cultural discourse in Russia in general both prior to that and ever since (Wijermars 2019). There is no doubt that Putin has been successful in conveying the image that he is the one who made it possible for Russia to regain its rightful status as a great power and to do so in a very short time.

Getting out of troubles: the *smuta* myth

Since early on, Putin's strategies of legitimation have also relied fundamentally on the invocation of the need to stave off another Time of Troubles, a *smuta*. This refers to another, highly powerful political myth in post-Soviet Russia, which intimately connects with the great power conception. The idea of the repeated emergence of times of trouble is in conformity with a cyclical view on history, which is widespread in post-Soviet Russia (Willerton 2017, Solovei 2004). These periods of ordeal all have common traits: political, economic, and social turmoil, weak incumbent leaders, imposters who aspire to take over the reins of power, foreign scheming and intervention, and ultimately, the risk of dissolution of the Russian state.

The paradigmatic Time of Troubles lasted between 1598 and 1613. It was a period characterized by political disorder, chaos, and foreign military interference by the Polish-Lithuanian Common-wealth. Russia's disintegration as a state seemed imminent. Several false pretenders to the throne had, by posing as the miraculously resurrected-to-life Tsar Dimitriy, Ivan the Terrible's youngest son, tried to take advantage of the political vacuum to seize power. In 1612, a successful popular uprising was initiated under the leader-ship of the merchant's son Kuzma Minin and Prince Dmitriy Pozharskiy. From Nizhniy Novgorod the masses marched to Mos-cow, from where the foreign troops could finally be driven out. The symbolic end of the Time of Troubles was established as 1613 when Mikhail Romanov was crowned tsar (Dunning 2001).

In the aftermath of the dissolution of the Soviet Union the old political script was brought back to life, enacted by contemporary political actors. To replace the Soviet-time holiday commemorating the beginning of the October 1917 revolution on November 7, a new holiday — National Unity Day — was introduced in 2005 to be cele-brated on November 4. This happened to be the same date as Minin and Pozharskiy began their revolt and their march on Moscow (Stewart 2021, Torbakov 2005). On the day that the new holiday was celebrated, Putin expressed his hope that the end of the *smuta* brought about by a united popular effort in the 17th century would also bring inspiration to the contemporary political situation (Pres-ident of Russia 2005).

The narrative about a popular uprising in the past throwing out imposters and intruders, thereto inspired by great leaders, is not the only part of the story that has been applied to contempora-neity. After the paradigmatic Time of Troubles, the new tsar, Mi-khail Romanov, presided over the restoration of stability and order in Russia. In the political mythmaking about Putin the parallels to Tsar Mikhail are easy to discern. The post-dissolution disorder and decay ended thanks to Putin's determination and his strong legiti-macy as a leader. Russia had returned to a position where the coun-try could enjoy respect and recognition. Putin was Minin, Pozhar-skiy, Mikhail Romanov and Peter the Great, all at the same time.

Dynamic interplay: the phoenix myth

Three major periods of *smuta* figure in contemporary Russian discourse. Apart from the paradigmatic one, there is the October coup in 1917, the ensuing civil war and the establishment of Soviet power. The third and most recent example, and most important to the arguments of this book, is the dissolution of the Soviet Union, Mikhail Gorbachev's reign of power, and the Yeltsin presidencies during the 1990s (Wijermars 2019, Mjor 2018, Petersson 2013). The Yeltsin period is described in wholly negative terms as characterized by "instability, moral corruption, populism, and governmental inefficiency" (Ryazanova-Clarke 2013: 115).

According to the cyclical view of history, periods of *smuta* appear from time to time to challenge the fundamentals of Russian statehood. Thereby they inhibit Russia from fully materializing her mission and role as a great power. The great power myth and the *smuta* myth coexist side by side in the public debate, often peddled by the same persons. Herein lies a paradox, for what could account for the fear of recurring periods of weakness if Russia is always predestined to be a great power? As I have argued elsewhere, the two myths live off and nourish each other. Hence, the paradox dissolves (Petersson 2013). The periods of near-fatal weakness are brought to a final halt thanks to the defining characteristics that make Russia a great power: the wisdom of its leader, the greatness of its people, and the vast resources of the country. The periods of *smuta* make it possible for Russia to muster and focus its strengths, develop, and grow stronger. The twin political myths make up two "opposed memory chains" tightly connected to each other (Wijermars 2019). They are symbiotic, not parasitic. The cyclical emergence of political chaos is thus followed by the equally cyclical reinstatement of stability, order, and discipline (Wijermars 2019, chapter 5; Petersson 2013).

This ties in with Malinova's (2020) argument about the myth of Russia as a phoenix, which repeatedly rises from the ashes. This myth has come to be a potent legitimizing tool, particularly regarding Russia's global and international activities during Putin's presidential tenures. It came to be important in relation to the narration about ill-wishers abroad who venture to conspire to prevent Russia from returning to its former splendor and glory.

According to the phoenix myth, Russia has throughout its history been able to defeat all hardships and evil conspiracies thanks to its wise and eminent leaders and to the stamina of its great, united people who have gathered behind them. During his presidencies, Putin has allegedly delivered Russia from the *smuta* of the 1990s, despite the machinations by external and internal enemies. Under his rule, Russia has thrived in conditions of stability and good order, as opposed to the weakness of state institutions, and the permissiveness and chaos that characterized the Yeltsin presidencies. However, there is a dilemma there, as Malinova (2020) notes, because clinging to the stability mantra for too long risks acquiring the hue of stagnation. The history of the demise of the Soviet Union shows that such characteristics are not necessarily of the kind with which contemporary Russian political elites would want to become associated.

The twin strategies of invoking the Russian great power heritage and simultaneously fighting the specter of a looming *smuta* are in their contemporary shape welded together by Putin's individual characteristics as a political leader. In the regime depictions, he is of such stature so as not to have any contenders. He is the chosen one, the embodiment of Russia's great power status, the patron of stability and avoidance of chaos.

According to this mythmaking, Russia is an eternal project (Goode 2021: 121-122). Despite all hardships it constantly proves its ability to endure and grow stronger. For more than a millennium Russia has managed to survive and resurrect itself, and the strongest of links have been forged through the centuries, uniting the people, the leaders, and the land. The paradigmatic example is the Great Patriotic War (the Second World War between the years 1941 and 1945 in Russian parlance), which is depicted as Russia's most trying moment in history but also as its finest hour. Russia was threatened by annihilation but triumphed and came through stronger than ever. As the contemporary representative of a long series of distinguished rulers who have led the country through thick and thin, through difficult times and cataclysms to emerge victorious in the end. Putin is designated as the wielder of the tradition of coming through despite overwhelming odds. If anything, the role of the Great Patriotic War has gained in importance in Putin's Russia. It has a key role in the legitimation efforts of the regime, and the incumbent is the self-evident custodian of the tradition. The additional significance of the War was plainly visible in the constitutional amendments of 2020, which made it a state obligation to "protect historical truth" and implied it to be a constitutional offence to question Russia's role during the War. The authorities wasted no time, as the new paragraph was invoked in one of the legal indictments against Aleksey Navalny in 2021.

For a long time, the Great Patriotic War has been the event in history that Russians in general have felt most proud about (Davis 2018, Petersson 2018a, Malinova 2017, Tumarkin 2003). It is therefore small wonder that Putin tries to link his persona as well as his presidential tenure to this period in Russian history. The underlining of the importance of the War and Putin's recurring emphasis of the vitally important actions of fighting men have also resounded with the machismo that was so prevalent during his first presidential terms in office (Sperling 2014, Goscilo 2013, Wood 2011). The president embodies a Russia that is showing its strength through rational calculation and deeds, not emotional outbursts, and irrationality.

The extent of the emphasis of the Great Patriotic War can be seen as a mirror of other current policies, domestic and external. Scholars have pointed out how Putin's endorsement of Stalin's leadership skills during the War has been congruent with the adoption of more repressive policies at home (Edele 2017). Similarly, shifts in the framing of the celebrations of the War may indicate fluctuations in relations with foreign powers. For example, when Putin in his address to the Victory Parade on Red Square in 2021 claimed that Russia had fought alone in the Great Patriotic War, he was very consciously marginalizing the Western wartime allies, with whom relations were subjected to increasing strain during the spring of that year (Gutterman 2021).

The bulwark and its champion

When returning to presidential power in 2012, Putin faced an acute crisis of delegitimization. The old blend of invoking the great power heritage and the steering clear of a Time of Troubles did not work to sway disillusioned and frustrated masses. This is where a third highly effective political myth rose to prominence: the idea of Russia as a bulwark to the defense of traditional values, with Putin as its foremost champion (Sakwa 2014).

The bulwark idea builds on elements inherent in the two master myths discussed above. Russia, as a great power, is always the subject of envy and scheming from a hostile surrounding. Malevolent forces conspire to bring disarray to Russia, but the nation stands strong, unflinchingly defending its ideals and holding up an example to the outside world. The latter idea is the equivalent of the American exceptionalist conception of the United States as the shining city upon a hill (Restad 2014).

Aside from its interconnections with the master myths about the eternal great power and the recurring *smuta,* this is an idea with deep historical roots. It goes as far back as the 15th century conception of Russia as the Third Rome, standing tall where the other two Romes had fallen, upholding its spiritual values, even if surrounded by a hostile world of decadence and degradation. Depending on the interpretation, these intellectual goods can have different implications when turned into practice, leading to isolationism or to aggressive messianism and expansion (Østbø 2016).

According to this powerful narrative, the Kremlin has with force and energy claimed to be the global leader in the defense of tradition, Orthodox religion, and family values against the perceived Western forces of evil, depreciation and moral decay (Laruelle 2021, Burrett 2020, Terzyan 2020, Oliker 2017, Sakwa 2014, Robertson 2013). In the contemporary version of the myth, Putin emerges as the self-evident leader of this mission of defense. This has made him popular among populist right-wing forces in the West and elsewhere.

The launch of the bulwark myth, particularly from Putin's third presidential term onward, accompanied the heavy anti-US rhetoric articulated from the same time on. The United States were, with the European Union, argued to be the anti-thesis of the traditional values and ideals so vigorously defended by Russia. This surfaced most prominently in connection with the Euro-Maidan and the Russian denouncement of the support and inspiration provided by what was disdainfully referred to as "Gayropa" (Riabov and Riabova 2014).

The man of action

Putin's charismatic appeal is to a significant extent formed upon his reputation as someone who can and will deliver the goods (Wilson 2021, Drozdova and Robinson 2019, Isaacs 2010, Sakwa 2008). Indeed, a poll conducted jointly by the Carnegie Moscow Center and Levada revealed that most respondents believed him to be the only actor who could bring about any major change in the country (Kolesnikov and Volkov 2018). In this sense he has a transactional rather than emotional connection with his electorate, as his devotees are likely to go on supporting him, not so much for his magic appeal but since they can rely on him for getting things done (Burrett 2020).

Putin's reputation as an energetic goal-getter was largely forged during the economically golden years of his first presidencies when Russia, contrary to all expectations, could in just a few years return to the ranks of global powers. His determination to bring back Chechnya to the federal fold served to entrench this reputation, as did his whole approach to politics. As he asserted with great confidence in an interview, "what is important is not to project strength, but to show it" (President of Russia, 10 March 2018). The annexation of Crimea was the epitome of such resolute action. It was immensely popular and signified a miracle cure for Putin's domestic popularity. His ratings hit the roof, or at least went far beyond the 80-percent level according to Levada. There they stayed for four years, while the so-called Crimean consensus prevailed (Nikolskaya and Dmitriev 2020).

The organization of the Sochi Winter Olympics in 2014 was another occasion where Putin excelled at showing what a difference presidential commitment and resolve could make. His support and engagement were key factors for the success of the Sochi candidacy, and the Winter Games emerged as his pet project. He personally headed the Russian delegation to the Guatemala City meeting with the International Olympic Committee in 2007, where the decision on the location was taken. His address to the IOC was believed to have swayed the committee members, not least through his demonstration of top-level political commitment and the powerful state financing guarantee that he offered (Müller 2011).

For the supporters, the maneuvers undertaken in 2020 to adjust or amend the constitutional framework also add to Putin's achievement record, since they testify to the president's ability to get things done (du Boulay 2020). On the other hand, this move may have detracted from his reservoir of legitimacy in view of the loss of rational-legal authority that the maneuvers entailed.

Another component to the action man image is the footage and snapshots generously shared over the years of the energetic Putin, riding bare-chested on horseback, fishing in the middle of a stream, scuba diving in the Black Sea to retrieve an ancient urn from the bottom, practicing judo, or performing countless other tasks bearing witness to his male energy and dynamism. While frequently being a matter of ridicule in social media at home and abroad, these performances have served to underline the contrast with his ailing predecessor, Boris Yeltsin, and to stress the fact that his vibrancy is a force to be reckoned with.

With his increasing age there is, however, some probability that the kind of fitness test mentioned above will be a failure in an almost literal sense. Putin has in recent years, not only during the pandemic, shown tendencies toward scaling down his official duties, working less and spending more time outside of Moscow (Gould-Davies 2021). His energy seems no longer unabated. Youtube footage released in the spring of 2021 conveyed a somewhat ambiguous message. It showed Putin and the minister of defense, Sergey Shoygu, trekking and driving an all-terrain vehicle in the Siberian taiga. On the one hand, the film tried to show an active Putin, just like in the old days. When the couple were driving the vehicle, it was Putin who self-evidently took the wheel. On the other hand, when trailing across the terrain, the president did not strike the viewer as particularly fit. He walked with a stiff and slightly limping gait, like just any other elderly man (Youtube 2021b). The Youtube film could perhaps be seen as an early indication of a new stage in the public imagery of Putin, namely, the president as an elder statesman, a nature-loving, basically benevolent granddad, who is the guarantor of stability and a guardian of all that he has already achieved. Should such imagery turn out to be launched, it comes, however, with certain risks for the incumbent, as stability and calm can again easily be associated with stagnation. As mentioned, the latter turned out to be a significant liability in the last days of the Soviet Union.

Great communicator, benevolent ruler

For the stories about the Putin regime's successes to take root and thrive, it certainly helps that media communication takes place in a setting with strongly authoritarian traits, where the contents of the still highly influential medium of state television are framed to conform to official policies (Kukshinov 2021, Hall 2017). Putin appears consistently in a favorable light, and the policies of his administration are praised or at least presented in non-critical terms. The president comes across as without any credible contenders and as the only leader by default.

With increased experience and confidence, Putin has markedly improved his public speaking skills. He has successively come to master live broadcasts in a way that signals that he owns the stage and does not shy away from dealing with complicated or controversial issues in public (Fredrikson 2019). The annual Direct Line with Putin is a prominent example, as is the annual News Conference. These are marathon events, often with a duration of around four hours, where the president tirelessly answers questions on issues high and low. There is a mixture of everything, from global politics to the ineptitude or abuse of power by bureaucrats in remote provinces. The impression that the mass audience gets is that the president is "omniscient, omnipresent and indefatigable" (Wilson 2021). Despite his four presidential election wins during a twenty-year period, Putin has never participated in a public debate with an oppositional candidate (Kukshinov 2021). That kind of debate format would have been unpredictable, but the televised media shows allow him to excel, as they are very carefully directed and managed.

Even if the shows go directly on air, the people in the audience who get to ask their questions are selected in advance, as are the themes that they will be addressing and the order in which this will happen. This goes also for the accredited foreign journalists. Nothing is left to chance (de Pury 2018). The scale is huge. Already in 2007, the Direct Line received 2.5 million questions for the president, out of which 69 were selected to go on air (Ryazanova-Clarke 2013: 104), and it has hardly diminished in size since.

By seeming to interact closely with the populace, Putin demonstrates a wish to deal directly with them, to care and to listen to their grievances. He conveys the message that he is accessible and reachable when common people have complaints to make (Drozdova and Robinson 2019, Ryazanova-Clarke 2013). This contributes to the perception among his fans that he is a contemporary embodiment of the mythical "tsar-deliverer" (Mamonova 2016). He gives the impression of caring about his people, however insignificant and marginal they may be. As the contemporary counterpart to the tsars of old imperial Russia, he has for a long time been able to keep up his image of a man of action and a benevolent ruler, who can always put things right provided he is adequately informed about the state of the nation and its regions.

Putin the populist

In choosing themes appealing to tradition, religion and family values, Putin shows that it is justified to categorize him as a populist politician. Some might object that the defining characteristic of a populist is above all the pledge to be a supporter of the common people against the political elites, and that Putin during his 20 years and more at the helm of power has come to personify the political establishment in Russia. He is therefore not a populist as traditionally understood. The balance sheet is contradictory. Sakwa (2014: 20) concludes that overall, Putin is "mostly not a populist", whereas

Burrett (2020) holds that Putin is a populist in his discourse, but less so in terms of practical policies pursued.

What makes Putin a populist despite the reservations above is that he has transferred the anti-establishment rhetoric to the global arena. Besides the obvious fact that the audience is vitally important for charismatic leaders, whether they are regarded as populists or not, research has addressed the importance of supporting actors for the legitimation of a leader's position. Joosse (2018) discussed the importance of a cast of "unworthy challengers" and "colossal players" for the evolvement of charismatic authority. In Putin's case, the unworthy challengers are conspicuous by their absence, and the colossal players are primarily structural. They loom large as conspiratorial and devious machinations by foreign countries, most prominently the United States. Their desired result is to prevent Russia's restoration to its former rightful glory. In the national imaginary, there is an ever-present threat to Russia from the outside. If Russia is not alert to the threat, it will be brought to its knees and made to perish (President of Russia, 9 May 2020).

Putin's special brand is populism of the incumbency, which makes it different from populism in its more general sense of a bottom-up movement against national elites. The alleged global elite is in his discourse synonymous with the long privileged United States and its Western allies, against whom Russia purportedly leads the opposition (Burrett 2020, Busygina 2019). The latter argument is a legacy from the Yeltsin period when Evgeni Primakov as minister of foreign affairs and later as prime minister advanced the formula of multipolar diplomacy, according to which Russia had to take a leading role to balance the US superpower aspirations for world hegemony (Sharafutdinova 2020, Ambrosio 2001). An important line of argument consistently nurtured by Putin is that Russia shoulders its global responsibilities in an unruly world in the hope that other powers will do the same. At the St. Petersburg International Economic Forum in May 2018, Putin expressed concern about the toughening tensions in the world and introduced the analogy that the world community had resorted to playing football while using the rules of judo, and that the result was chaos. That was somehow a fitting analogy for a committed judoka such as Putin.

The term "Putinism" denotes a rather vague and general political platform, which stresses state strength and consolidation and expresses adherence to nationalism and traditional values, including those of family, heterosexuality, and Russian Orthodoxy. In broad and general terms, Putinism opposes LBTQ rights, multiculturalism, and the hegemony of liberal values. It is not a distinct ideology, rather a pragmatic summing up of what has characterized Putin's policies over the years. Laruelle (2021: 86) evaluates the ideological components of Putinism as flexible, plastic and dependent on "the regime's needs and its interpretation at a certain time of the world and domestic situations". Fish (2017) has defined Putinism as "a form of autocracy that is conservative, populist, and personalistic".

Putinism is thus not an ideology. Rather it is an eclectic platform of mainstream nationalist ideas, which are appealing enough to garner the support of otherwise contending elite groups and the broader public. Ideationally Putin seems to offer something by way of a compromise to all groups potentially scrambling for power in Russia: the power ministries and the security sector, the nationalists, the Orthodox Church, the nostalgic Soviet romantics, the business elites, and even some Western-style liberals left over from Yeltsin's heyday. All these groups, what was referred to as the collective Putin above, might find him appealing or at least good enough (Chen 2016). Putin emerged originally as a catch-all president, a president for everybody. In several respects, this situation persists, and it is a frequent argument that Putin remains the only figure who can unite the domestic elites (Mazepus et al 2016; FSU Brief 2020c). Putin has been in power for more than 20 years, and these groups have a vested interest in him remaining in power for as long as possible (Dawisha 2015). During these years, the networks have become intertwined, and the elites' own status and guaranteed economic well-being are in many ways dependent on Putin remaining where he is. From their perspective, it is better to play it safe and not rock the boat.

Several characteristics strengthen Putin's populist appeal: the macho image, his sometimes uncouth and blunt way of delivering his speeches and appearing on public occasions, and his alleged siding with the common people against regional political elites at home (Malinova 2020, Busygina 2019, Klapsis 2015). These are all carefully selected elements of strategy where a populist style and approach are used as devices for legitimizing his presidency (Busygina 2019).

It would be an exaggeration to say that Putin is a fiery orator, but he has a way of reaching out to the populace, at times by unexpectedly resorting to colloquial expressions, or even criminal slang. He has, in the words of one commentator, a propensity for sometimes expressing himself in such a way that it makes his interpreters blush (Fredrikson 2019). His penchant for drastic language has long been familiar among Russian political analysts (Gorham 2013). The most famous example was when he, as a newly appointed prime minister, described what to do with Chechen separatist fighters, namely take them out "in the sh-thouse" (Burrett 2020, Wood 2011). This expression is almost impossible to translate into English in an adequate manner, as the remarkable thing about Putin's choice of words was not the vulgarity of the location that he implied but rather that the idiom that he chose normally belonged to the jargon of hardened criminals. Other familiar examples were when he proposed a circumcision to a baffled foreign journalist who had ventured to ask him critical questions (Ryazanova-Clarke 2013: 128), and when he talked about using the law to grab Russian oligarchs "by the balls" (Burrett 2020: 196). One could also mention his flippancy regarding serious themes, such as global warming, which was in line with the general skepticism towards climate change in populist quarters. On one occasion during his early years in power he mused that a warming by two or three degrees perhaps would be good, since that could reduce the need for many Russians to spend money on fur coats[7] (Pearce 2003).

---

7   In recent years Putin has, however, reversed his stance on global warming and recognized it as a major challenge that Russia and the world will have to confront in the coming years (Martus 2021).

Putin the common Russian

The message that Putin's unique and heroic traits make him singularly fit for the highest office of the federation has grown successively stronger during his presidencies. There is something of a paradox here because the branding of the president as unique goes together with depicting him as a man of common background who all Russians can relate to. In line with this framing, Putin endeavors to share, on an individual level, the moments of greatness lived by the Russian nation during the 20th century. Ever since his ascension to presidential power, Putin has emphasized his and his family's linkage to the Great Patriotic War through their residence in St. Petersburg, formerly known as Leningrad (Wood 2011).

The Putin story recounts that his father was seriously wounded in combat during the War and that his infant brother died in the siege of Leningrad (BBC News 2020b). Moreover, Putin's reputation as a hard hitter has been linked to the rough conditions under which he grew up, rat-infested hallways and all. In one famous quote, he said that "Fifty years ago, I learnt one rule in the streets of Leningrad: if the fight is inevitable, be the first to strike" (President of Russia, 22 October 2015). According to this storyline, the less than idyllic conditions during his childhood and adolescence formed him into the resolute and forceful man that he is today (Sharafutdinova 2020, Glasser 2019). Tough circumstances made him into a tough politician who knows how to walk the walk.

Putin's power position is thus enhanced by successful communication of prevalent national political myths and his acclaimed role in them (von Soest and Grauvogel 2017, Charteris-Black 2011). Taken together, the factors elaborated above help to explain the mystery of Putin's widespread and longstanding popularity. No one else could easily step into his shoes, even if the necessity arose. Putin's allegedly unique personal characteristics explain his lingering charismatic legitimacy. This is, however, a problem since such legitimacy, following Weber, will ultimately have to transform and routinize to be sustainable — and there are few signs to suggest that such a process is in motion. A successor would need to work very hard to rid themself from the predecessor's shadow. This is the typical dilemma facing anyone taking up a seat formerly occupied by a charismatic leader (Helms 2020). It is also a significant part of the Putin predicament which this book is all about.

IV

Legitimacy through Othering

Othering and Russia

Othering is a concept familiar from the literature on the construction of social identities (Neumann 1998a, 1998b). In brief, a distinction is made between the Self, on an individual or collective basis, and an Other, which represents everything that is not Self and that the Self seeks to distance itself from. The Self has positive characteristics, whereas negative traits mark the Other. In this manner, the Other has great significance for the construction of the Self, even if it does not always need to be wholly negative. In some respects, it can be e.g exotic, attracting or alluring, even if negative characteristics always predominate. Importantly, in uncertain and insecure times, the presence of a clear-cut Other makes it easier for the collective Self to define what welds it together and remind it what it should fight for. In such circumstances, the Self defines itself as that which the Other is not.

The term has fundamental significance for the study of contemporary Russia, not least in the long Putin era. When Putin won his first presidential election, back in the year 2000, he did so through an intense Othering strategy directed at Chechen separatists who essentially came to represent everything bad that had occurred in Russia during the wild 1990s, be it irredentism, religious fundamentalism, organized crime or weakness of the state. Putin's renewed war effort against the Chechens from 1999 on, as he assumed command as Yeltsin's newly appointed prime minister, was highly popular among the Russian public and essentially won him the election, despite the absence of a coherent political program at the time (Petersson 2018a). The Othering strategy has been an important part of Putin's political arsenal ever since. The targets have shifted over time, from Chechens and, somewhat later, the

Yeltsin-era oligarchs, through post-Soviet state actors, such as Estonia during the bronze-soldier incident in 2007, Georgia during the brief war in 2008, and Ukraine in 2014, up to the explicitly named puppet master and alleged main instigator, the United States, which have been singled out for increasing attacks from Putin's third presidency on (Petersson 2020).

The basic narrative has remained constant. It is a hostile world out there, but Russia stands tall, defending itself against the schemes. Powerful external foes, led by the United States, keep conspiring, at times together with domestic forces, to deny Russia its birthright as a great power and ultimately bring it down. Only resolute action by a powerful political leader can avert the dangers and deny the adversaries their success. According to the regime's legitimizing narratives, the incumbent president is the chosen one who can achieve this.

Relations with the United States

Bilateral relations with the United States seem to be constantly on the mind of Russian policymakers. This is regardless of whether the United States figure as a negative example or as an object of competition and loath admiration. Russian official discourse often praises China, albeit somewhat reluctantly, as a model of economic success, stability, and relative affluence, but compared to the Other which is the United States, it is a reference that is made with "great respect but devoid of passion" (Malinova 2019: 232). The friendly relations with China are praised to stress how the two giant neighboring states work together on global matters and how they oppose the political and ideological, ostensibly universal values espoused by the Western powers. In a way, ties with China serve as a mirror held up to confirm Russia's own strength as a great power (Wilson 2019). Matters stand differently with the United States. Ever since the end of WWII, the US has served as Russia's significant and most often negative Other (Malinova 2019, Neumann 1998b). Whereas good relations with China increasingly serve as a legitimizing device, it is by contrast relations of animosity with the United States that contribute to the shoring up of Russian regime legitimacy.

The 1990s were a glaring exception. After the fall of the Soviet Union, there was a brief period of amicable relations with the United States, prompted by the Yeltsin administration's drive towards democratization and rapid transformation into a liberal market economy. US-mediated international loans and credits prompted the development, and a weak and powerless Russia was eager to get all possible assistance. In his day, Yeltsin did not rule out a Russian membership in NATO, and his minister of foreign affairs, Andrey Kozyrev, symbolized a desire to tie closer and more friendly bonds with the US superpower. Presidents Yeltsin and Bill Clinton were at least for some time on markedly friendly speaking terms, as evidenced by the famous press conference in 1995 when Clinton had a laughing attack after a less than diplomatic comment about the United States press corps by an inebriated Yeltsin (Youtube 2015). However, the relative honeymoon lasted for a brief period only. Even under Yeltsin, there were fluctuations for the worse, not least in connection with the Balkan wars, especially over Kosovo and the scramble for Pristina Airport in 1999.

When the presidency passed to Putin, relations deteriorated gradually even if the new president initially seemed to maintain his predecessor's policy and seek close cooperation with the United States as the leading power of the West. Just like Yeltsin he did not rule out a future Russian membership in NATO. His personal relations with the US president George W. Bush seemed friendly to start with, and on one memorable occasion the US president claimed to have looked his counterpart in the eye, found him to be straightforward and trustworthy and got a sense of his soul (Stent 2019: 305). After 9/11, 2001, Putin was the first foreign head of state to call Bush on the phone, express his condolences and offer to cooperate to combat terrorism. Critical observers maintained at the time that Putin merely pledged support for the US war on terror in return for a carte blanche for Russia's dealing with militant Chechen separatism, which was then the regime's overriding security concern.

Relations turned increasingly chilly over the US invasion of Iraq in the wake of the war on terror. As the world saw a string of so-called color revolutions reach post-Soviet Ukraine, Georgia, and

Kyrgyzstan in the years 2003-2005, Russian leaders increasingly expressed suspicions that US hands could be seen behind the developments. The brief Russo-Georgian war took place in 2008, during Medvedev's presidency. Thorny issues such as US plans for missile defense in Europe and NATO expansion eastwards on the continent further complicated US-Russian relations. By the beginning of Barack Obama's first presidential term in 2009, bilateral relations were so tense that the new US president launched a reset policy, aiming to inscribe US-Russian relations on a clean slate (Deyermond 2013). Part of this strategy relied on focusing on the newly elected president Medvedev as the main interlocutor on the Russian side. Obviously, this failed to consider that Putin even from his prime minister's position continued to be Russia's leading political actor (Stent 2019). On balance, the reset policy did not help bilateral relations much, and the period saw numerous personal attacks, including racist slurs, on Obama by Russian media (Burrett 2020). There seemed to be particular Russian irritation with the high profile of the Obama administration on the global spread of norms of democracy and human rights, which involved pointing out how individual states such as Russia should design their political system and judiciary.

In 2007, Putin made his notorious Munich speech, which due to its confrontational tone created a stir in the international community of observers. Compared to what was later to follow, it was relatively mild, but this was the first time that Putin explicitly singled out the United States as the main adversary of Russia and a threat to world peace. The speech signaled Russia's new and assertive stance in the international arena, and it marked the beginning of a new and decidedly more strained phase in Russia's relations with the West, particularly the US (Stent 2019: 294). The United States had overstepped its national borders in every way, the president claimed. He blamed the United States for not being interested in pursuing disarmament talks with Russia, and underlined, as he would henceforth do in almost every major speech on international and global matters, that NATO's eastward expansion in Europe violated promises made to Russia at the end of the Cold War. The

NATO enlargement would bring military hardware to the very border of Russia and constituted a provocation that reduced the level of mutual trust between the two powers, his argument went (President of Russia 2007).

Charisma in the form of linkages to concrete political action rather than to personal magnetism and messianic traits accords well with rhetoric that pronounces external threats and internal traitors. This is a tendency often encountered in hybrid and authoritarian settings and is visible also in Russia. The great leader arises to counter machinations by the enemies of the state, deliver his country from acute peril, and restore it to its rightful great power status (Charteris-Black 2011), but there will be a price extracted for this by way of increased animosity to the outside world. As mentioned above, Putin has, since the beginning of his third presidency from 2012 on, relied heavily on projecting a dichotomous world order where a morally and spiritually superior Russia is constantly beset by the scheming Western powers, led by the United States and intent on keeping Russia down (Sharafutdinova 2020, Malinova 2015). This rhetoric became especially prevalent during the second Obama administration 2013-2016, when bilateral relations hit a low after the annexation of Crimea and the Russian support for the insurgency in eastern Ukraine.

Unsurprisingly, the Putin administration did not recognize the incorporation of Crimea as an annexation. Rather, it was a matter of reunification, the argument went. Thus, the official discourse had it that a voluntary merger had taken place, based on the will of a clear popular majority in Crimea, as expressed in the local referendum of March 2014. The latter was "the highest form of direct democracy", Putin assured (President of Russia, 22 October 2020). Indeed, the domestic support for the annexation in Russia was so overwhelming that it may have seemed worth the price of strained relations with the West and punitive actions taken by the latter. The move ushered in a long period of favorable ratings for Putin and something close to a nationalist euphoria among broad segments of the population. It saw the emergence of the Crimean consensus in domestic politics which was to last for several years ahead (Nikolskaya and Dmitriev 2020).

In mid-March 2014, when Russia had thus annexed Crimea, supported the separatists in Eastern Ukraine and provoked the worst crisis in relations between Russia and the Western powers since the Cold War, Putin made a general address in the Kremlin, justifying the actions taken. A tough attack unfolded against the United States, for striving for world hegemony and being guided not by international law, but the "rule of the gun". Putin blamed the United States for aspiring to decide unilaterally the destinies of the world and to justify its right to do so by a belief in the exclusivity and exceptionalism of the United States and the American people. He contended that Western powers had the ulterior motive of destroying Russia through their promotion of internal dissolution and decay. He accused the United States of hypocrisy and arrogance and implied that they had acted behind the scenes to plan and produce the Euro-Maidan events and the toppling of President Yanukovych in Ukraine. The aborted agreement with the European Union was just a smokescreen to hide what was to take place, he claimed (President of Russia, 18 March 2014).

The bottom line of the speech was that the United States and its Western partners were simply seeking a pretext to launch sanctions against Russia. Putin typically used the noun "partner", just like the word "friend" at times, in an ironic twist to refer to Russia's perceived Western adversaries, primarily the United States but also the European Union and NATO (Drozdova and Robinson 2019: 818). Again, Putin indicated that their concealed motive was to stop Russia's return to great power status and hinder it from regaining its former economic strength and political influence. Much like the Munich speech before it, Putin's Crimea speech signaled in its harshness a sea change in Russia's conduct and attitude in relation to the world outside. Whereas Putin during his first two presidencies had stressed stability, order, and national unity at home as political priorities, there was from this point on in his third presidency an adjustment towards advancing Russia's positions abroad (Bacon 2015). In the Crimea speech, one could clearly see how the perceived need to stand up against the West in order to defend traditional, moral, national, and religious values was given increased priority. The narrative about the bulwark and its champion grew in importance.

Putin's annual address to the Federal Assembly in December 2014 was equally harsh and bore witness to a thoroughgoing chill in Russia's relations with the Western powers. The address and its somber conclusions marked yet another low point in bilateral Russian-US relations. Again, bringing havoc to Russia was the purported motive for Western engagement in the Ukrainian war. Ukraine was but a stepping-stone on that path. Putin's presidential rhetoric suggested that Russia was next in line and that there was a clear and present danger directed at his motherland. Putin recalled support given by the United States in the late 1990s to the Chechen separatists, and went on to say that "on the other side of the hill" there was a wish to let Russia disintegrate in the same manner as the Soviet Union and Yugoslavia had once done (President of Russia, 4 December 2014).

However, Putin vowed, "talking to Russia from a position of force is pointless" and he praised Russia for withstanding the alleged US plot. In accusing the United States of seeking the breakup and destruction of the Russian Federation, he invoked a parallel to Hitler's attempts during the Great Patriotic War, and issued a stern warning to the United States to stop its alleged scheming or be prepared to face the consequences:

> It didn't work. We didn't allow that to happen. Just as it did not work for Hitler with his people-hating ideas, who set out to destroy Russia and push us back beyond the Urals. Everyone should remember how it ended (President of Russia, 4 December 2014).

During his presidencies, Putin has repeatedly expressed annoyance with the US tendency to lecture Russia on how to implement democracy, human rights, the rule of law, and freedom of speech. The resentment with being taught how to design democracy was already visible in several passages of the Munich address. "Incidentally", Putin said, "Russia — we — are constantly being taught about democracy. But for some reason those who teach us do not want to learn themselves". Putin claimed that the Organization of Security and Cooperation in Europe (OSCE), which had insisted on certain preconditions for observing elections in Russia, had turned into "a vulgar instrument designed to promote the foreign policy interests of one or a group of countries" (President of Russia 2007). At that time Russia's suspicion with the OSCE was so high that the organization was practically barred from sending observers to the general elections in 2007 and 2008 (Hutcheson 2011).

During a heated interview with NBC anchor Megyn Kelly in 2018, Putin expressed his frustration over the self-proclaimed US right to interfere in other states' internal affairs while claiming that this was done in defense of democracy. "You can interfere any-where because you bring democracy, but we cannot (…) [This] is what causes conflicts. You have to show your partners respect, and they will respect you" (President of Russia, 10 March 2018). In the interview, Putin displayed arrogance and annoyance, both against the interviewer and the United States in general. The encounter took place in a tense atmosphere. The president seemed to be in a bad mood and complained that Kelly was impolite cutting him off in mid-sentence. He repeated that the US political establishment was striving to weaken Russia, to halt its progress, in different re-spects, but was adamant that it would never succeed. "They have never managed to contain Russia and never will", he said (Presi-dent of Russia, 10 March 2018).

Over the years, Putin continued to press his argument that the US was forcing its model of democracy onto unwilling recipients, while in essence pursuing quite different goals. At the Valdai meet-ing in 2020 Putin argued that countries that had adopted democ-racy according to models forced on them from the outside had ended up as vassals (President of Russia, 22 October 2020). There were thus security reasons for not accepting and adopting Western prescriptions of democracy, and sovereignty arguments always had precedence over democratic concerns voiced from abroad (Cooley 2016). If the concepts of democracy and internal order would ever turn out to be in conflict, it was clear that the former would have to yield (Willerton 2017). Arguments like these had been the foundation of the concept of "sovereign democracy", that was coined by the then presidential adviser and first deputy head of the presidential administration Vladislav Surkov back in the early 2000s (Surkov 2009), and for some time was used actively by Putin himself. Even if the term was subsequently scrapped, the Kremlin still subscribed to its content: that Western powers, led by the United States, need not bother about trying to inculcate its democratic values in Russia (Casula 2013). During the latter half of the 2010s, however, there was a clear impression that the US were no longer pursuing the Western ideals of democracy equally eagerly. The people of the United States had elected another president, Donald Trump.

Dealing with Trump

In his speech at the Valdai Club in 2016 Putin took his customary criticism of the US tendency to lecture Russia on human rights one step further. Instead of angrily deflecting criticism and arguing that it does not behoove one great power to tell another great power what to do, Putin turned the tables and started to lecture the United States on the deficiencies of its democratic system. Referring to the elections when Donald Trump was elected president, he insisted that the campaign had made it clear that there was a vast distance in views and values between the electorate and the self-proclaimed elites in the United States. The latter were constantly trying to act in their self-interest, he said (President of Russia, 27 October 2016).

With Trump's electoral win, it seemed as if the bilateral relations were at least temporarily to be redefined. Trump had on several occasions during his campaign spoken highly of Putin and stressed his desire to improve US-Russian relations. By many appearances, however, any expectations held by the Putin team about rosy, bright days ahead after Trump's ascension seemed to have been unfounded. What made rapprochement particularly difficult was the lengthy and ongoing investigations by the Special Counsel on Russian hackers influencing the US presidential elections, and the allegations of collusion between Russian actors and the Trump campaign to promote the candidacy of the president-to-be and impede the chances of the Democrat candidate Hillary Clinton.

Because of the constant pressure from the US Congress and the Democrat opposition, the Trump administration was compelled to toughen its policies on Russia. This brought about further US sanctions in the aftermath of the annexation of Crimea, persistent refusal to recognize Crimea as a part of the Russian Federation, and a record-high increase in US military spending. In the words of one prominent analyst, Donald Trump's much-anticipated reset with Russia therefore never happened (Stent 2019: 312). At the same time, Trump continued to express himself in favorable terms about Putin and his political leadership style. In return, the strategy that Putin and his speechwriters seemed to opt for was to depict the actions of the Trump administration as attributable to the US president being held hostage by the US political system. "The swamp" forced the president to act in a manner that he would not have chosen freely.

The actual United States policy on Russia under Trump was not easy to make out. In his State of the Union address to the Congress in January 2018, the US president described China and Russia as rivals of the US, who together with rogue regimes and terrorist groups challenged US interests, economy, and values (Trump 2018). On the other hand, Trump later during the year named its traditional ally, the European Union, a political adversary of the United States. Obviously, it mattered a great deal who was writing his speeches at a particular point in time.

On many occasions after the US presidential elections in 2016 Putin was asked to give his opinions about his US colleague. He always took pains to answer diplomatically and cautiously, not embarrassing Trump but instead giving him the benefit of the doubt. Putin often laid massive collective blame on the United States, but always seemed to offer Trump personally a way out. US foreign policy actions that Putin did not like he held the Congress and the political establishment responsible for.

In this manner, a dilemma could be solved for the Putin administration. In many ways, the legitimization of Putin's presidency built, at least from his third presidency onwards, on identifying the United States as the Other, and Putin's Russia as its most important global counterweight. Should the relations between the two countries look too harmonious and cozy under the new president of the United States, an important legitimizing device would perhaps need to be replaced with something else (Burrett 2020). Depicting a situation where the US President meant well but was held captive by the political establishment of his country served the regime's rhetorical purposes.

The pattern of shielding the US president from the general criticism towards the Western superpower was evident during a meeting at the St. Petersburg International Economic Forum in May 2018. The meeting agenda was dominated by the unilateral US annulment of the Iran nuclear deal and the looming prospect of a major international trade war after the US imposition of protective tariffs on imports of steel and aluminum. Both these initiatives were heavily associated with Trump, but Putin was careful not to level any personal criticism against his American opposite number:

> But of course, we cannot be satisfied with the level and nature of Russia-US relations. We are ready for this dialogue. Mr Trump suggested having a meeting specifically on the issue but we have not had a chance to have it yet, there have been too many issues to address. However, we are ready to have a substantive dialogue on a great number of issues. I think it is high time we did this. Donald has expressed concern over a potential new arms race and I fully agree with him (President of Russia, 25 May 2018).

At the Valdai Club in October 2018, Putin repeated that it was the political establishment in the United States which forced decisions that were negative for Russia and for the bilateral relations between the two great powers. Putin insinuated that the reasons for such moves were to divert the attention of the public opinion in the United States away from domestic difficulties. Probably departing from diplomatic protocol, Putin pointed out that he disagreed with those who claimed that Trump never listened to anyone but himself. Even if the following statement was taken out of context, the way the Russian president expressed himself about his US opposite number was noteworthy: "Of course he listens. And not just listens, I see that he reacts to his interlocutor's arguments" (President of Russia, 18 October 2018). The assessment did not seem laudatory regarding the US president's intellectual capabilities—rather it reminded of characteristics given by someone who had visited an elderly relative at an old folks' home and found that person to be unexpectedly alert.

The organization of a summit meeting between Putin and Trump in Helsinki in July 2018 became major news in Western media. What was to be expected from a meeting between the experienced Russian president and his erratic US counterpart? Could this even amount to a game-changer of global politics for the years to come? At the joint press conference where both heads of state answered questions, considerable attention was given to the US special prosecutor's investigations of alleged Russian meddling in the US presidential elections in 2016 and the collusion between the Trump campaign and Russian actors. Putin denounced the allegations as "rubbish" whereas Trump repeatedly and frantically iterated the mantra "there was no collusion!". In the analyses afterwards, particular attention was given to the US president's pledge to believe Putin's assurance that Russia was not behind any interference in the US election campaign and that he could "not see any reason why it would be" (President of Russia, 16 July 2018). In saying this, he expressed more confidence in the Russian president than in his own intelligence community, which was carefully noted in Western media reports at the time (Yaffa 2018).

At the Helsinki press conference, Trump declared dramatically that US-Russian relations were at its lowest point ever: "… our relationship has never been worse than it is now. However, that changed as of about four hours ago. I really believe that" (Diamond 2018). Whether the Putin-Trump Helsinki summit was such a turning point remains highly unclear, but it did indicate a change in the correlation of forces between the two global powers as well as in the images projected of the power and influence of the two leaders on the podium. The Russian president looked by far the more confident of the two, symbolizing the state that he headed. Putin was advancing his positions in the global arena, whereas his US colleague made a defensive impression, conveying the image that he represented a world power on the wane.

When Putin granted an interview with Fox News on the day after the summit, the impression was further confirmed. Regardless of which topic was addressed, whether it was the matter of the alleged collusion between Russia and the Trump campaign, Crimea and Ukraine, the military involvement in the conflict in Syria, or the

Russo-US arms race, it was evident how the Russian president tried to address the matters from a position of strength. At one stage, the interviewer asked Putin point-blank: "When you were first elected in the year 2000, you were portrayed as a democratic reformer, you talked about the value of European culture and you did not even rule out becoming a part of NATO. What happened?". In his response, Putin reverted to a storyline that he had used many times before. This was not at all about him changing his views, because he had remained the same, but the United States had repeatedly betrayed Russia with regard to the NATO expansion eastwards, promised reductions of the arms race, and the turmoil in Ukraine (President of Russia, 17 July 2018). Putin's message was that the United States had made its bed and would now have to lie in it. The tension in bilateral relations was not of Russia's doing, but now that it was a fact, Russia was not prepared to budge.

Putin also addressed the fact that many worries had been expressed about a deteriorating security situation in Europe, thereby implicitly referring to threats by the Trump administration to scale down its commitments to NATO and European security matters. Here Putin added, not without a hint of sardonic humor, that "Europe depends on the United States in terms of security. But there is no need to worry, we can help with security" (President of Russia, 17 July 2018). The tables had turned since the years of weakness in the 1990s. Russia was back as a global power. Not only that, but Putin also seemed to indicate that Russia was keen to fill any vacuum following a projected withdrawal of the United States from its position of being the prime security partner of Europe. As he said, "we can help". For East Europeans remembering the years of the Cold War this statement may have sent shivers down their spines.

Enter Joe Biden

Approximately one month before the US presidential elections in 2020, incidentally on Putin's birthday, the Russian president gave an interview to a Rossiya 1 TV journalist. After having been asked questions on current events such as the outbreak of hostilities between Armenia and Azerbaijan over the enclave of Nagorno

Karabakh and the unrest following the presidential elections in Kyrgyzstan, Putin was questioned about the upcoming US elections and where his preferences lay. At that point, the journalist referred to the Democratic presidential candidate, Joe Biden, and his accusation that President Trump was "Putin's puppy" (President of Russia, 7 October 2020).

After having answered in the standard way that it would be up to the US people to elect its leader and that Russia had no intention of interfering, Putin went on to develop an argument seemingly indicating that patience with President Trump was wearing thin. He said that Biden's accusation was indicative of the political culture or rather the lack thereof in the United States and that insults like the one Biden had thrown at Trump if anything played into the hands of Russia, as it spoke of its "incredible influence and power". After those preludes, he went on to tell that there had been great expectations in the improvement of US-Russian relations under Trump, and that Russia had appreciated his repeated statements about this from the very beginning of the first campaign. However, Putin made it clear that the expectations had not come to fruition. "We have not accomplished much", as he stated dryly at the Valdai Club meeting a couple of weeks later (President of Russia, 22 October 2020). On the contrary, he remarked that decisions on imposing new sanctions or expanding previous ones against Russia had been made 46 times by the Trump administration, and that the United States had withdrawn from the Intermediate-Range Nuclear Forces (INF) Treaty. This was "a very drastic step" and amounted to "a big danger to international stability and security". Even if Putin noted areas of cooperation where there had been progress, he underlined that there were both upsides and downsides to the relations under Trump. As he had done before, he opined that the frosty relations were due to actions by the US political establishment, but he also made it clear that there was disappointment with the Trump administration itself (President of Russia, 7 October 2020).

At the same time, Putin seemed to hint at having an open mind about what an electoral win by Joe Biden could mean for US-Russian relations. His argument became somewhat strange as he

developed ideas of an ideological kinship between the US Democrats and Social Democrats in Europe, which in turn had been the
environment from which the Communist Party of the Soviet Union
had sprung. According to his argument, the latter still influenced
both political discourse in Russia in general and his own thinking,
and he confessed to having been a Soviet Communist Party member for 18 years. The party had hailed the ideals of equality and fra-
ternity, which he believed to be shared by the US Democrats. Likewise, he noted, again in a somewhat opaque way, that African
Americans constituted a large part of the Democratic stock of voters, and that the Soviet Union had used to support the African
American struggle in the US, believing that this group could be an
asset "in the future revolutionary battle". At this point the viewer
was starting to wonder whether the Russian president was trying
to pull the legs of both the interviewer and the audience, pursuing
a largely irrelevant line of argumentation. However, he then mentioned a reason why an electoral win by Joe Biden could be positive,
namely, that the latter had said that he would be ready to "extend
the New START or to sign a new strategic offensive [arms] reductions treaty". This, Putin concluded, is "a very serious element of
our potential collaboration in the future" (President of Russia, 7 October 2020).

Putin's ambivalence on the outcome of the US presidential
elections in 2020 was later underlined by the long absence of official
response on the matter of who finally won. When the major US media outlets a couple of days after election day in November 2020
called Joe Biden the winner in the presidential contest there were
prompt congratulatory messages sent by world leaders such as Emmanuel Macron, Angela Merkel, and Boris Johnson. Putin, however, remained silent. Nor did he express any support for the allegations made by Trump that the Democratic candidate had appeared as the winner due to systematic electoral fraud. The Kremlin
spokesperson, Dimitriy Peskov, explained the silence on the part of
the president by saying that Russia wished to await the official announcement of the result before commenting on the outcome (CNN
2020). It was not until December 15, six weeks after the elections
and one day after the US Electoral College had affirmed Biden's

win, that Putin finally congratulated his new colleague. "For my part, I am ready for interaction and contacts with you", he assured in his message (President of Russia, 15 December 2020).

Two months into the term of office of the Biden administration Russian-US relations on the presidential level were put to the test. In an ABC interview in mid-March 2021, Biden used strong wording after a US intelligence report had concluded that the Russian government had tried to interfere with the US presidential elections in 2020, promoting Trump's candidacy and denigrating Biden's. Responding to the interviewer's question whether Biden thought that Putin was "a killer", the new US president responded, "Mhmm, I do". He also recounted an earlier meeting where he had expressed doubts that Putin had a soul, thereby referring to the famed statement by former US president George W. Bush. Dimitriy Peskov responded angrily to Biden's comments, arguing that they were unprecedented in history. Putin's own response was calm but condescending. He retorted by using the old schoolyard saying that "It takes one to know one", but also wished his US counterpart good health, subtly indicating that he believed him to be weak, elderly and possibly senile (Chernova et al 2021).

After the incident, Russia recalled its ambassador from Washington for consultations for the first time in 20 years. A stormy period began in US-Russian relations, accelerated by the US expulsion of ten Russian diplomats after the findings of the report about interference in the 2020 presidential campaign and the Russian hacking of US federal agency servers. The Biden administration extended the list of US sanctions and put additional bans on US financial institutions buying Russian government bonds. Predictably, there were countermeasures as US diplomats were expelled from Russia, and high-ranking US officials were barred from entering the country (Isachenko 2021). In mid-May, the Russian government officially designated the United States (alongside the Czech Republic) an unfriendly state. This put severe restrictions on the number of staff the US Embassy was allowed to employ and thus hampered its work considerably.

By April 2021, international tensions had grown for several other reasons. First, there were the alarming reports about the imprisoned Aleksey Navalny's ailing health and his long being denied proper medical care, something that Biden comparatively mildly criticized as unfair and inappropriate. Simultaneously, Russian troops piled up by the border to Ukraine, in concentrations not seen since 2014 and the annexation of Crimea. Sergey Shoygu, the Russian minister of defense, announced later the withdrawal of the troops since they had successfully fulfilled their purpose and taken part in a snap preparation exercise. The purpose of the saber-rattling remained unclear, but it seemed likely that apart from for putting pressure on Ukraine, the Kremlin also wished to test the resolve of the new US presidential administration under Biden. In the next few weeks, the heated atmosphere between the two countries seemed to cool down somewhat as more orderly communications were set up. While relations were still tense, the two presidents agreed to meet for a summit in Geneva in mid-June 2021 "to restore predictability and stability to the US-Russia relationship" (Zeleny et al 2021). There certainly seemed to be a need for this.

No more the underdog

During Putin's third and fourth presidencies, Russia increasingly challenged the Western powers on soft power and the global spread of ideas. Instead of reactively fending off attempts by the Western powers and especially the United States to lecture Russia on what democracy is and should be, Russia opted for another strategy under Putin's fourth term. It emerged more and more as a sender of counter-norms. These were opposed to, or at least far from in harmony with, the precepts of liberal democracy which, after the end of the Cold War, were spread by the European Union and, except for the period 2017-2020, the United States.

According to Cooley (2016), there are three elements, around which global counter-norms to liberal democracy tend to be woven. These are security arguments, concerns about civilizational diversity and, relatedly, concern about traditional values. Putin has emerged as a major spokesperson of all three. The worldwide crisis that liberal democracy appears to have been going through since the mid-2010s (Diamond et al 2016) has seemingly strengthened the attractiveness of the Russian counterexample. Traditional values are nowadays construed as part of the Russian security doctrine. This creates a direct tension with Western conceptions of human rights and multiculturalism as these are said to challenge traditional values. Hence, they are construed as threats to Russia's national security (Flikke 2020: 142).

In interpretations spearheaded by the Putin regime during its third and fourth presidential tenures, Western liberal democracy has become brusquely narrowed down and caricatured. In the Russian propaganda, it has been "reduced to the acceptance of radical minority rights, endangering national identities and traditional values" (Terzyan 2020). Liberal democracy has increasingly become associated with moral depravation, denial of traditional family values and the championing of LGBT rights. This was not least borne out by Russian information warfare during the upheavals in Ukraine at the time of the Euro-Maidan (Laruelle 2021, Burrett 2020, Terzyan 2020, Oliker 2017, Sakwa 2014, Robertson 2013).

By stressing traditional values and the need to defend and advance them in the face of powerful international contestation, Putin has tried to draw legitimacy from sources previously not that heavily exploited by him. He thereby appealed to sentiments that were widespread among the public and influential power elites, not least the Orthodox Church. The hardened rhetoric was combined with stern action to combat protest activity at home, which included the arrest of oppositional figures, violence, criminal prosecution, and hefty fines for participation in protests (Robertson 2013). The legal action taken against the Pussy Riot performance art group for alleged sacrilege was one manifestation of the harsher trends in official policy (Sharafutdinova 2014).

Many experts have observed that the policies of the Putin regime appeal to right-wing nationalist and populist parties across the European space (Makarychev and Terry 2020, Shekhovtsov 2018, Oliker 2017, Klapsis 2015). Considering the memories stemming from the Cold War when the Marxist-Leninist Soviet Union used to be the archenemy of the West, one would perhaps have expected a greater amount of skepticism in these quarters. However, the heavy emphasis on national sovereignty in matters of security as broadly defined creates a natural affinity between the Putin regime and right-wing populists in the West (Stent 2019). Politicians like Marine Le Pen in France and Nigel Farage in the United Kingdom have repeatedly expressed their admiration for Putin's politics and style. The Greek neo-Nazi party Golden Dawn has stated its desire for a Russian-Greek alliance between the two Orthodox states in the areas of trade, energy, and national security (Petersson 2018c), and white power activists in the United States have manifested their admiration of Putin (Oliker 2017). The leaders of the Hungarian Jobbik party praised Russia's annexation of Crimea, advocated Hungary's exit from the European Union and argued for membership in the Eurasian Economic Union that Russia had proposed (Orenstein 2014). In a radio interview, the leader of the populist Sweden Democrat party refused to express where his sympathies would lie if he had to choose between Putin or the liberal French president, Emmanuel Macron (SVT Nyheter 2018). The list can be expanded quite far as the examples are numerous.

Putin's populist condemnations of multiculturalism are attacks on the liberal establishment, which he depicts as a global elite. His fundamental critique of multiculturalism is the ingredient which earns him the particular support of Western populists (Terzyan 2020). Here, Putin shows a convergence of views with those who depict immigration as the most menacing threat against traditional values and the welfare of resident majorities. Putin is there treading a fine line in the multiethnic and multi-confessional Russian Federation. Nevertheless, he is siding with vocal Russian nationalists who are worried about the influx of labor migrants from former Soviet republics in Central Asia and the Caucasus, most of whom belong to the Islamic faith.

In a widely publicized interview with the Financial Times in the summer of 2019 (Financial Times 2019, President of Russia, 27 June 2019, Barber 2020: 416-420), Putin was very articulate. He opined that liberalism was "obsolete", that it had "outlived its purpose", that it was "in conflict with the overwhelming majority of the population", and that it was even in the process of "ceasing to exist". He lambasted particularly the generous migration policies that several European Union countries, above all Germany, had adhered to prior to the so-called migration crisis of 2015. Putin said that Chancellor Angela Merkel had made a "cardinal mistake" in admitting hundreds of thousands of migrants. "The migrants can kill, plunder and rape with impunity because their rights as migrants must be protected", he claimed, and went on to argue that it was primarily this liberal trait that was most out of step with the popular majority and with time. He railed against the liberal argument that hardline policies against migrants had to be opposed since they were against the law: "Well, then change the law!", he exclaimed, in a manner reminiscent of Mr. Bumble in Dickens' *Oliver Twist*.

Liberalism was about to fade out, Putin predicted, even if he did not go so far as to favor its total banishment. Proponents of liberalism simply had to stop trying to dictate the ways and modes of thinking of other peoples, he said. The time of the prime of liberalism was over. However, he continued, the fading of liberalism did not mean that there would be an ideological vacuum left behind. It was time for traditional and moral values, including religious ones, to take priority, because for millions of people such values were by far the most important. The reason why central elements of the liberal idea, such as multiculturalism, were no longer tenable was this incongruence with the popular will. Traditional values were emerging triumphant and resounded with what the popular majority felt "deep inside", he wrote (Financial Times 2019, President of Russia, 27 June 2019).

Paradigm shift and saber-rattling

The launch of the verbal assault against liberalism strengthens the impression that a paradigm shift has taken place in Putin's legitimation strategies. As pointed out repeatedly above, a common denominator of political master myths invoked since the end of the Soviet Union is that Russia is a great power, no matter what the internal and external circumstances seem to suggest. This theme has coexisted with the compelling need to constantly measure up to and compare favorably with the United States, a practice that was already evident in the years of the Soviet Union (Petersson and Persson 2011). As a new element in the Russian great power rhetoric, the assertive wielding of counter-norms to liberal democracy brings in a perspective where Russia is leading the process and forcing its old antagonist to respond.

Clearly, this shift towards greater assertiveness was not about norms and words alone. There was a corresponding toughening of practical policies as words were backed up with tangible deeds. The Russian president was taking the lead in the struggle against the perceived main adversary on the global arena, the United States, and while doing so he did not wait to respond until the antagonist had moved. Under Putin Russia has increasingly come to be "widely seen as a regional or even world innovator in nondemocratic practices" (Petrov et al 2014: 1-2).

The zenith of Russian assertiveness during Putin's first three presidencies was of course the annexation of Crimea and the support of the insurgency in eastern Ukraine. In words expressed to the visiting president and communicated on the official presidential website, a Sevastopol resident in 2018 spoke about the approaching four-year anniversary of the annexation, corroborating the image that the president and his team wanted to convey. According to the praise, Putin was wise, bold, and decisive. His tenure had, according to the devotee, delivered the fulfillment of dreams long held by the affected population: "I would like to tell you that our dreams, wishes, your wisdom and your willpower enabled us to return to our Motherland without spilling a single drop of blood, even though the war was literally on our doorstep" (President of Russia, 14 March 2018).

The military engagement in the Syrian war from 2015 on was a forceful sign that Russia was ready to go global again after having lived through the downgrading hibernation of the post-cold war transition period. Russia's involvement in the Syrian civil war gained increasing significance over time, as the United States under the Trump administration decided to scale down its involvement.

Russia moved in to fill the vacuum left by the retracting super-power. Putin claimed that Russia had moved into Syria to square the bill with international terrorism, something that according to him should have been done by the US a long time ago. He also argued that the Russian military operation was undertaken following the request by the Syrian president al-Assad. This made the engagement legitimate and lawful, as opposed to the Western operations which lacked such a mandate, the argument went (President of Russia, 27 October 2016; Stent 2019).

The long and continuous international discussion on Russian involvement in election campaigns in the United States, the United Kingdom, France and elsewhere contributed to the impression that Russia was back with a vengeance. Putin and the Kremlin routinely disavowed all Russian involvement in the internal affairs of any Western democracies, but while they did so there was, between the lines, a discernible note of contentedness that Russia had finally attained a position where it was perceived as perhaps the most influential actor in global politics.

Putin's address to the Federal Assembly in March 2018 (President of Russia, 1 March 2018) epitomized the shift to increased assertiveness. The address stood out from previous addresses that Putin had made to this forum. The president announced Russia's prepotency in a highly confident and triumphant manner (Youtube 2018). The address showed evidence of his belief that there was a world out there sharply divided between Us and Them, and that Russia had to take immediate and decisive action to fend for itself and advance its positions (Rak and Bäcker 2020).

Using an innovative speech design, Putin showed six videos to his audience. They were all said to depict the most recent advances in Russian strategic arms technology. Putin underlined that Russia had found ways to circumvent the consequences of the US withdrawal in the early 2000s from the ABM Treaty which prohibited the deployment of anti-ballistic missiles. Now, Putin boasted, Russia's top-notch technology had developed missile systems that even state-of-the-art anti-ballistic missile systems in the West could not intercept. Indeed, the technological breakthroughs by the Russian arms industry had made the Western ABM systems obsolete.

Russia was in the driver's seat. It had been forced to take that position because of the intransigence and arrogance of the United States. The new Russian systems were invincible and had unlimited range (President of Russia, 1 March 2018). The US administration was not equally impressed. The then US Secretary of Defense James Mattis indicated his disbelief in the alleged technological advances. These achievements were "still years away", he assured (Watkins 2018).

For every video that Putin showed he took pains to underline that this was world-leading technology, unique and unmatched elsewhere in the world. Whereas he in the beginning of his address had seemed detached and almost bored when bringing up issues such as taxes, infrastructure, and housing, he now appeared remarkably enlivened. "It is really fantastic!" he exclaimed at one point, presenting one example of a technological breakthrough (President of Russia, 1 March 2018; Rak and Bäcker 2020). The president was visibly satisfied with being able to deliver this message. Russia was no longer the underdog. It had acquired both a bark and a bite, and Putin pointed out why this was necessary:

> Why did we do all this? Why did we talk about it? As you can see, we made no secret of our plans and spoke openly about them, primarily to encourage our partners to hold talks. Let me repeat, this was in 2004. It is actually surprising that despite all the problems with the economy, finances and the defence industry, Russia has remained a major nuclear power. No, nobody really wanted to talk to us about the core of the problem, and nobody listened to us. So listen now (President of Russia, 1 March 2018).

At Putin's final remark, the audience burst out in a standing ovation, reminiscent of Soviet time practices (Youtube 2018). In this carefully staged show the weakness after the dissolution of the Soviet Union was reduced to a fading, albeit painful, memory. It should be noted that the address was held less than three weeks ahead of the presidential elections. Even if it was more intended to impress the electorate and lead its attention away from present economic difficulties than to instill fear in foreign powers (Stent 2019: 312), Putin had certainly made a splash.

Coming back to his assertion that the strategic arms technology that he presented for the Federal Assembly was unsurpassed anywhere in the world, Putin ventured to predict that other world powers would scramble for the development of corresponding technology. Not being shy of boasting, the president did not see such emulation phenomena as a problem for Russian security:

> *As you no doubt understand, no other country has developed anything like this. There will be something similar one day but by that time our guys will have come up with something even better* (President of Russia, 1 March 2018).

In Putin's rhetoric, the United States and the political West had maltreated and denigrated Russia for a long time, and now it was payback time. In Putin's words later in the same year: "Dinner is served, enjoy." (President of Russia 25 May 2018, 7 June 2018). He seemed to cherish making the statement. At the Valdai meeting in 2018 the president asserted triumphantly: "We are not afraid of anything". He explained that the reasons for his feeling so secure were the vast territory of Russia, its defense system, the Russian people, and their willingness, if need be, to sacrifice their lives for their motherland (President of Russia, 18 October 2018).

At Valdai in 2018, Putin articulated his view that a global shift away from post-cold war unilateralism had taken place. The United States was no longer the only global power that mattered. It had constantly to consider the actions of global contenders such as Russia, China, Turkey and even the European Union. The United States was a fading empire, on its way to ceding its former global influence. Putin was visibly confident in his role as the guarantor of a great power position according to which Russia was finally on a par with and above the United States (President of Russia, 18 October 2018).

In his address to the Federal Assembly in 2019, Putin developed the theme. The bulk of the address was devoted to domestic issues, such as health, childcare, pensions, housing, education, economy, and the environment. Just like the year before Putin seemed both enlivened and relieved when he could start addressing matters of global politics and security. Prior to this, his voice was "wooden, rushed and without heart" (Sherr 2019). Compared to the Assembly address in 2018, the show was more low-key. No videos were on display, but the communication was brimming with presidential confidence. Putin reported that the development of the weapon systems had progressed as planned, if not quicker. He repeated that the new arms technology was for defensive purposes only, and that Russia still wanted to engage in dialogue about disarmament with the United States, but that it no longer had any intention to "knock on a locked door" (President of Russia, 20 February 2019). There was national pride in this statement. Putin implied that his country had a lead on the United States (President of Russia, 22 October 2020). He suggested that the US, in its continued and erroneous belief in its mission and global supremacy, had failed to consider the shifts in the world correlation of forces:

> *...it seems that our partners fail to notice the depth and pace of change around the world and where it is headed. They continue with their destructive and clearly misguided policy. This hardly meets the interests of the USA itself. (…) We can see that we are dealing with proactive and talented people, but within the elite, there are also many people who have excessive faith in their exceptionalism and supremacy over the rest of the world. Of course, it is their right to think what they want. But can they count* (President of Russia, 20 February 2019)?

A statement tweeted from the president's office in November 2019 underlined that the new weapons—"hypersonic, laser and other cutting-edge"—had no counterparts elsewhere in the world. However, for other countries there was no need to worry, the Russian president's tweet assured, since the arms had been created exclusively to guarantee Russia's security "in the face of growing threats" against it. Russia would not be the one to deliver the first blow (President of Russia, 6 November 2019, 22 October 2020).

One could clearly see the general tendency as Putin's fourth presidential tenure progressed. The old indignation that Putin used to have when talking about the US attitude towards Russia was fading away. There was something else instead, almost a note of sarcasm and amused contempt. In the beginning of 2020, Putin again turned to the Federal Assembly in his annual address. As if in passing he mentioned the innovations in military technology. He was explicit about the shift that had taken place in the relations of strength between Russia and the United States:

> *For the first time ever — I want to emphasise this — for the first time in the history of nuclear missile weapons, including the Soviet period and modern times, we are not catching up with anyone, but, on the contrary, other leading states have yet to create the weapons that Russia already possesses* (President of Russia, 15 January 2020).

At the 2020 Valdai meeting, Putin directed an unambiguous admonition to Russia's competitors abroad. If someone out there still thought that it would be easy to gain the upper hand against Russia in the global power struggle, the president had a harsh, Khrushchev-like message to convey:

> *Consolidating this country and looking at what is happening in the world, in other countries, I would like to tell those who are still waiting for Russia's strength to gradually wane, the only thing we are worried about is catching a cold at your funeral* (President of Russia, 22 October 2020).

Considering the tense international atmosphere developing in the spring of 2021, with its war of words between Putin and the newly installed US president Joe Biden, renewed Western sanctions, massive concentrations of Russian military forces along the border to Ukraine, and a univocal condemnation by Western powers of the regime's treatment of the imprisoned opposition leader Aleksey Navalny, many observers thought that Putin's 2021 annual address to the Federal Assembly would be unusually harsh. Even if the president chose not to continue at the high pitch of the Valdai meeting of the year before and little space was given to international matters, the tone was still tough. Referring to an alleged coup attempt in Belarus, orchestrated from abroad, Putin warned the Western powers about Russia's hard resolve and military might that they had better not challenge, lest they were ready to face the consequences:

> *Those behind provocations that threaten the core interests of our security will regret what they have done in a way they have not regretted anything for a long time (…) I hope that no one will even think about crossing the "red line" with regard to Russia. We ourselves will determine in each specific case where it will be drawn* (President of Russia, 21 April 2021).

Putin seemed to be fully confident about Russia's resilience in political and military terms, and even if he routinely stressed the threats from without and urged the people always to be vigilant and prepared to act in defense of national values, he did not seem to doubt that Russia would stand its ground and even advance its positions in the global arena. As it turned out, however, it was rather on the domestic arena that Putin's legitimacy was subjected to its greatest test since the Bolotnaya events in 2011-2012.

V

Challenges from Within

Electoral authoritarianism in Russia

The literature of recent decades has introduced several different labels for how to best characterize the type of political regime that Russia represents. Oligarchic or personalist authoritarianism are included among the suggestions (Gandhi et al 2020). Soft authoritarianism is a frequent denomination (Sakwa 2014), but the most widespread attribution is that Russia is an example of electoral authoritarianism (White 2017, Gill 2016, Gel'man 2013, Goode 2012 and 2020, Diamond 2002). This is a combination of authoritarian characteristics and shallow traits of democracy and has been characterized as today's most common form of dictatorship worldwide (Lührmann and Lindberg 2019).

The stability of electoral authoritarian states is not secured by repression and co-optation alone. Popular consent is achieved through the application of supplementary formulas, such as elections. These provide the regimes with a "cloak of legitimacy" (Gill 2016: 357), which serves to "confer some minimally sufficient degree of legitimacy on the regime" (Goode 2012: 7). Russia has such a hybrid political system, with the authoritarian traits manifested through the regulation of oppositional and media activities, including elements of harsh repression and violence against individuals who are seen to go too far in challenging the system.

This hybrid political system is thus a crossover between authoritarianism and democracy, but with the heaviest tilt towards the former. Elections with multiple candidates take place within regular and constitutionally prescribed intervals, both for the presidency and for the legislature. The maneuvering space for truly oppositional candidates is severely restricted, whereas the token, within-system opposition as represented by figures such as the eternal candidate Vladimir Zhirinovskiy get considerable leeway.

The political establishment favors its candidate(s) through uneven access to mass media channels, different legislative maneuvers, and, ultimately, repression and violence. Democratic procedures and frameworks are employed without being filled with democratic substance (Pavroz 2020, Gill 2016, Diamond 2002).

Nevertheless, elections in Putin's Russia are hegemonic and competitive at the same time. They amount to more than windowdressing and matter, not least for the signals they send, even if the outcome seems to be a foregone conclusion. On the other hand, organized oppositional and openly critical political activities are barely tolerated, as testified by the murders of journalist Anna Politkovskaya and opposition leader Boris Nemtsov, as well as the attempted assassination, subsequent arrest, show trial and imprisonment of Aleksey Navalny.

If elections had not served a purpose for authoritarian regimes, they would not take the troubles to organize them (Schedler 2013). This goes for Russia as well. The elections offer an opportunity for the regime to co-opt loyal opposition candidates and parties while they also demonstrate regime strength that discourages from challenging oppositional activities (White 2017). In hybrid and authoritarian systems elections take place to ensure that alternations in power will be less likely (Helms 2020). Essentially, they have developed into "a mundane ritual of preserving the status quo" (Pavroz 2020: 459). The official election results signal the incumbent's invincibility, deter from elite defection, weaken existing opposition, dampen popular protests, and relieve the pressure coming from critics abroad (Hall 2017, Tolstrup 2015). Election results minimize the element of surprise from the point of view of the regime as they pass on valuable information about popular sentiments, discontent, and regional patterns of oppositional activity. From the early 1990s up to 2006 Russian voters had the option of ticking a box marking the alternative of voting "against all" (McAllister and White 2008, Hutcheson 2004). Having this alternative on the ballot clearly provided information about patterns of discontent, their development and their geographical distribution. It had forceful signaling value, which may be why the authorities ultimately decided to abolish the option.

Despite White's (2017) premonition that the adjective "electoral" soon will be outdated when describing Russia's brand of authoritarianism, elections hold a significant role in contemporary Russian political discourse and practice (Hutcheson 2018). In this there is clearly a legacy to build on. Regular elections to the Supreme Soviet, the legislature of the Soviet Union, were part of the political routine. Voting in Soviet elections was politically meaningless, but in those years, elections were festivities, reasons for holiday merriment (food, alcoholic drinks, and music at polling sites underlined this), and served a purpose of political control.

Throughout the post-Soviet period general elections have taken place with constitutionally prescribed intervals in between. Voters have been able to choose between different candidates for office, even if the field of contestation has become increasingly limited and the oppositional candidates have had ever more restricted access to mass media and other resources. In this sense, one might observe, as Sakwa (2014: 12), that not a single election in post-Soviet Russia can be considered to have been free and fair.

Overall, the Russian and Soviet traditions of arranging regular elections with an aggregated high turnout provide preconditions for procedural legitimacy. It adds to the president's power base, as it can be argued that he holds his office due to the observance of national legislation and manifestations of popular will (Cassani 2017, von Soest and Grauvogel 2017). Putin can refer to a popular mandate that has brought him to power. After all, he has been elected four times to the highest political office in the Russian Federation. This gives him, in Weberian terms, some rational-legal authority alongside the charismatic one.

While elections thus continue to provide for some legal authority in Russia, there is a theoretical possibility for the electorate not to vote the handpicked candidates into office, however supported and endorsed those candidates might be by the state media and authorities (Cassani 2018, Kendall-Taylor and Franz 2018). Such surprises have taken place elsewhere in history, as in Mexico in 1997 and 2000 (Gill 2016). When Aleksey Navalny ran for mayor in Moscow in 2013 and was finally allowed to stand despite the authorities' reluctance, he came in a strong second with more than a quarter of the vote behind him. Such surprises may occur for as long as the formal possibility to compete for political office is not abolished.

When Navalny as early as the Duma elections in 2011 successfully launched the slogan "vote for anyone except United Russia", it showed that there was a potential for civil disobedience at the polling booth (Yudin 2020). The aim of the campaign was to cast the vote for the opposing candidate who stood the best chance of defeating the candidate representing United Russia.[8] Many voters heeded the call, which contributed to the relatively poor showing of the party at the polls. Navalny continued to develop this strategy under the formula of "smart voting" and turned it into an organized and sometimes markedly successful campaign, which was long a thorn in the side of the authorities (Turchenko and Golosov 2021). Success was perhaps most notable at the elections for the Moscow City Duma in 2019, where the campaign caused the United Russia to lose its majority position in the assembly (Laurén 2021). Duma elections are due again in the fall of 2021, and it was therefore no surprise that the authorities in the spring of 2021 undertook actions to ban the organizations that Navalny had created and to prevent the implementation of the smart voting strategy across the country by labelling Navalny's local branch offices "extremist" and declaring their activities illegal.

For the incumbent regime there is always a calculated risk involved when organizing elections in a hybrid authoritarian setting. Even if rigged they may backfire. Moreover, the progressive hollowing out of election procedures, rendering them meaningless and devoid of democratic substance, may breed disillusionment and lack of societal commitment. It may even engender conflict and unrest as the legitimacy generated by the election procedures goes down the drain (Pavroz 2020). The feasibility of this scenario was fully demonstrated by events in one of Russia's neighboring countries during the fall of 2020.

---

8   This strategy could be applied to half of the 450 seats in the Duma, which are filled using the principle of first- past-the-post in single-member constituencies. The other half are filled through proportional representation with a 5 percent threshold.

When the long-time president and dictator of Belarus, Aleksandr Lukashenko, according to the official results was reelected in August 2020 with 80 percent of the vote against his contender Svyatlana Tsikhanouskaya, the results were so obviously cooked that massive popular manifestations of protest occurred. The activists claimed that the actual results would probably have seen reversed figures compared to the official results with 80 percent voting for Tsikhanouskaya. This flagrant rigging became decisive for the erosion of the incumbent president's authority. Instead of being strengthened by added rational-legal legitimacy, his power basis could only be saved by brute force, repression against the protesters, and the implicit support of the great-power neighbor, Russia. This development could also serve as a memento for Putin, indicating that too obvious vote rigging may turn out to be deeply counterproductive.

The presidential elections of 2018

It took surprisingly long for Putin to declare his candidacy for the March 2018 presidential elections. Speculations about the reasons for the delay abounded, and rumors had it that he might consider not running for re-election at all. Putin had contributed to the rumor-making himself, since he had on several occasions hinted that he may not be willing to run (President of Russia, 24 November 2014, 29 September 2015, 21 July 2017). Not until three months prior to the elections did he confirm that he was going to seek a new popular mandate. Why did it take him so long to announce his candidacy publicly? Maybe it was a deliberate move intended to rub in the fact that had it not been for him the field would have been empty? If so, underlining his legitimacy by default, Putin could depict himself as indispensable.

On the very day when Putin finally made his formal announcement of his intention to run, the following conversation unfolded between the president and his audience at a public event in Moscow:

[Question]: [W]e all want to ask you the following question. Many have already made their decision and announced their plans to take part in the presidential election in spring of 2018. Could you please tell us whether you are going to run for President at these elections?

Vladimir Putin: This is a very responsible decision because it is only motivated by a striving to improve the life of people in this country, to make it more powerful, protected and oriented towards the future. It is only possible to reach these goals if people trust and support you. In this context … I would like to ask you a question. If I make this decision, will you and like-minded people support it?

Response from the hall: Yes!

Vladimir Putin: I understand that this decision should be made soon and it will be made soon. In making it, I will certainly consider our current conversation and your response.

Thank you very much!

(President of Russia, 6 December 2017).

This is Putin the showman talking, enjoying the limelight in front of his loyal supporters. The conversation summarizes the main elements of Putin's legitimation claims. Putin wishes to appear as the guarantor of Russia's greatness and the people's guardian against malevolent forces. Despite, or maybe indeed because of, having been at the helm of power in Russia for such a long time, Putin implicitly depicts himself as the most suitable person to steer the country into the future, and he does so while obviously having every confidence in the trust and support that he enjoys among the electorate.

There was one man who could have been quite a powerful contender in 2018, had he been allowed to run. Aleksey Navalny, who had shown himself repeatedly to have a huge public impact, was barred from running because of suspended court sentences related to financial crimes, which were widely believed to have been dictated by political considerations.[9]

---

9   In one of the court cases, the charge was that Navalny and his brother Oleg had overcharged Yves Rocher Vostok, a subsidiary of the French cosmetics company, for transport services. Even if Yves Rocher insisted that it had suffered no damage, the brothers were convicted by the court in 2014. The sentence was 3.5 years imprisonment for both. Oleg had to serve his sentence at once,

Without Navalny in the lineup, the field of approved contenders for the presidential elections failed to impress. One of the more well-known candidates in the presidential race was Kseniya Sobchak, the daughter of Putin's one-time mentor, the then mayor of St. Petersburg, Anatoly Sobchak, who was one of the forerunners of the liberal sentiments in Russia of the 1990s. The TV-star Kseniya Sobchak, however, had too flashy an image to be credible to the Russian voters. She had fallen out with Navalny on whether to take part in the elections which were obviously to be rigged, and there were suspicions that she had been allowed to run in order to split the rudimentary liberal opposition (cf. Flikke 2020: 213). Old veterans, like the populist and so-called liberal democrat Vladimir Zhirinovskiy and the seasoned and genuinely liberal candidate Grigoriy Yavlinskiy, had both been running repeatedly for president in Russian elections since the early 1990s. They had their political futures behind them and were no longer serious contenders, to the extent that they ever had been. At the polls, Zhirinovskiy came out best of these candidates with about 6 percent of the vote, whereas Sobchak gained 1.4 percent and Yavlinskiy less than one percent.

The most successful runner-up was the Communist party candidate, Pavel Grudinin. He polled rather well and gathered about 12 percent of the vote. Seemingly, Grudinin's relative dynamism during the run-up to the elections had caused some concern among the authorities. Later during the campaign, there were complaints in the Grudinin camp about repeated harassment. Even so, the Grudinin vote landed around the mark where the polling figures for the Communist presidential candidates had usually found themselves at elections in post-Soviet Russia and was perhaps, therefore, not remarkable per se (Petersson 2018b).

whereas Aleksey Navalny received a suspended sentence. In the so-called Kirovles case, Navalny was charged with embezzlement against a timber company in Kirov. The charge was that Navalny had made too much profit from a deal, and he was twice, in 2013 and 2017, convicted by the court to a suspended sentence of five years of imprisonment. The European Court of Human Rights ruled in 2017 that the Navalny brothers had been deprived of their rights to fair trial, but the Russian authorities chose to disregard the ECHR verdict (Palasciano 2021).

Putin sailed through in the elections, gaining over 76 percent of the vote according to the official figures. He comfortably attained the public confirmation of his incumbency, as always already in the first round. About 67 percent of all eligible voters went to the polls, which perhaps was slightly less than expected. Still, the turnout rate was sufficiently high to claim that the people's candidate had won the day and done so because of his widespread popularity and legitimate authority.

The Navalny challenge

At the annual News Conference in 2017, about a week after Putin's official confirmation that he intended to run for president, he got questions about his views on the absence of any credible opposition. His response was that he would indeed have welcomed political competition, had there only been such a thing, but that it could hardly be considered his task to groom an opposition when there was none. Clarifying his point, he added that he was not questioning the abilities of individual oppositional figures but had rather in mind that none of them had a constructive political agenda to offer. According to him, they were all solidly against something — most often his continued presidency — but could not offer any productive alternative platforms. When Kseniya Sobchak was given the floor some time into the press conference, she was at first mocked by Putin as one of those candidates who were against everyone and everything. Then, in answer to her specific question about why Aleksey Navalny was not permitted to run although the European Court of Human Rights had declared the suspended court sentence against him invalid, Putin asked in rather emotional terms whether she would really have wished to condone a [Georgian ex-president Mikheil Saakashvili-like political figure to campaign in Russia. Putin made a reference in the plural but since Navalny's was the only name mentioned by Sobchak, the target for his attack was clear enough:

> *About the figures you mentioned. A question about Ukraine was already asked. Do you want dozens of people like, pardon me, Saakashvili running around here? Those you named are a Russian version of Saakashvilis. Do you want such Saakashvilis to*

> *destabilise the situation in our country? Do you want us to live from one Maidan to the next? Do you wish to have attempted coups here? We have been through this already. Do you want all this to return? I am convinced that the absolute, overwhelming majority of Russian citizens does not want this and will not allow this* (President of Russia, 14 December 2017).

The sheer mention of Navalny's name in the hall obviously touched a raw nerve. Putin went to great lengths to avoid mentioning the apparently detested name. He has turned this non-naming into practice and done so consistently and with a fervor that borders upon the absurd. At a meeting with heads of Russian print media and news agencies in 2017, Putin dismissed a question about why the authorities barred Navalny from running for president by referring to "the character you mentioned" and implying that "this person" would have been the preferred candidate on the part of "the US administration and other nations". Foreign states' criticism of the decision not to allow this nameless and anonymized person to register as a candidate for the presidential elections was nothing but interference in Russia's internal affairs, he implied. The president argued that this amounted to hypocrisy as "certain powerful countries" had accused Russia of having interfered in election campaigns in the West (President of Russia, 11 January 2018).

At the G20 summit in Hamburg in 2017, a foreign journalist asked Putin what his opinions were about Navalny, and why the president took such pains not to mention his name. The answer was curt and barely addressed the question:

> *I think we can engage in dialogue, especially at the level of the President or the Government, with the people who propose a constructive agenda, even if they voice criticism. But if the point is to draw attention, this does not encourage dialogue* (President of Russia, 8 July 2017).

The allegation that Navalny had staged his protest manifestations chiefly because of his strong drive towards self-promotion is an argument that Putin has used several times to underline his dislike. He reverted to it on several occasions long before the G20 meeting, already at the time of Navalny's unexpectedly strong showing in the Moscow mayoral elections, where he, as mentioned, gained more than a quarter of the vote and ended up a strong second after the incumbent mayor, Sergey Sobyanin (President of Russia, 25

April 2013, 2 August 2013, 15 June 2017). It was used again in an almost absurd fashion when Putin, in a leaked conversation with French president Macron, suggested that Navalny had staged his own poisoning in the summer of 2020 to draw attention to himself (Laurén 2021).

A couple of weeks after Putin had been declared the winner of the March 2018 presidential elections, he addressed the Russian people and referred briefly to the opposition articulated against him during the election campaign:

> *Criticism, debates and discussions are necessary and important, but there can be no room for irresponsible populism. The national interests and the wellbeing of the people must be the main guideline for everybody, especially today* (President of Russia, 23 March 2018).

So, this was the red line for the opposition: it had to be constructive, refrain from irresponsible populism, and be in conformity with national interests. Of course, the powers-that-be were to decide what constituted constructive criticism and wherein the national interests lie. There was not much leeway left here, and Navalny for one had obviously overstepped the bounds. Putin's remark was another way of pointing out that the opposition the Kremlin could tolerate was the token, loyal, within-system type represented by familiar and predictable figures such as Zhirinovskiy, but real opposition which fundamentally questioned the regime was a different matter. Such opposition was not to be tolerated, acknowledged, or even mentioned by name.

The main official argument to subvert Navalny's credibility among potential voters was not, however, that he was after self-promotion and that he had no constructive agenda to offer. Rather it was the implication that people who rage against corruption should be spotless, and that Navalny was not (Gill 2016). Putin repeatedly depicted Navalny as a hypocrite and referred to the pending court cases against him for embezzlement and financial crimes. After the mayoral elections in Moscow in 2013, Putin suggested that Navalny did not have much to offer beyond the invocation "Stop the thief". "As a rule, it's people who have stolen things themselves who usually shout like that", he added (President of Russia, 19 December 2013).

Most probably, the campaign against Navalny, including the court cases involving financial crimes, hurt his popular appeal more than the non-naming strategy did. His standing in public opinion evidently took a beating. Besides his record of being a tireless fighter against corruption and the leader of the Anti-Corruption Foundation, he had acquired a reputation of having strongly nationalist views during his early political career, which made him controversial among some quarters of the liberal opposition (Kniivilä 2021, Flikke 2020). This somewhat shadowy past, including an implicit comparison between migrants and cockroaches, backfired at him after his incarceration in early 2021, as Amnesty International withdrew its recognition of him as a prisoner of conscience on the grounds of his previous hardline stances (Amnesty International 2021a). In view of later developments, with the authorities' blatant disregard of Navalny's deteriorating health, Amnesty later revoked its decision and announced its re-designation of him as a prisoner of conscience. While still arguing that Amnesty found some of Navalny's earlier statements "reprehensible" the organization wrote that the Russian state was currently condemning Navalny to "a slow death" and demanded that the maltreatment be stopped immediately (Amnesty International 2021b).

According to a Levada Center poll back in April 2011, only 6 percent of the respondents claimed to know who Navalny was, whereas in February 2017 the figure had risen to 47 percent. On the other hand, in 2011, 33 percent of the respondents who claimed to know who he was indicated that they could consider voting for him in a future presidential election, but in 2017, the corresponding figure was only 10 percent. At the same time, the percentage that was categorically against him had skyrocketed from 19 to 63 (Levada Center 2017).

With somewhat irregular intervals starting in 2017 the Levada Center asked about 1600 respondents in 137 municipalities in 50 regions of the Russian Federation to name those five or six politicians or public figures that they trusted the most. Putin held the uncontested top position, even if his rate fluctuated between a peak of 59 percent in late 2017, when the effect of the annexation of Crimea was still visible, and a low of 25 in May 2020, under the impact of the first wave of the coronavirus. Navalny, on the other hand, never reached beyond modest single digits between 2017 and 2020, and the fraction of those who named him among the most trusted politicians varied between 2 and 4 percent (Levada Center 2020c). However, counterevidence could also be found. In another Levada poll in 2020, Navalny was shown to wield considerable influence and inspiration even among middle-aged people who saw him as a more inspiring person than Putin (Levada Center 2020b). In the fall of 2020 Levada found that around 20 percent of the respondents were positively disposed to his activities, which was twice the corresponding percentage indicated the year before (Kniivilä 2021).

Reverting to the issue of Putin's shying away from uttering the name of his chief antagonist, one certainly needs to ask what the reason might be. In an animated interview in the summer of 2018, an Austrian journalist asked Putin the question twice. He got no answer. Putin again invoked the Saakashvili analogy, insisting that he did not want a "second, third or fourth edition of Saakashvili" on the Russian political scene. Still without mentioning Navalny by name he branded him a "pseudo-politician", even a "clown", and argued that since he commanded only "the trust of one, two, three percent of people or just hundredths of a percent", he was irrelevant and nobody to engage in serious discussion with, especially since he did not offer a constructive agenda about anything (President of Russia, 4 June 2018).

Even after the attempt on Navalny's life in August 2020 became headline news across the world, Putin persisted in his practice. When someone asked him questions about Navalny in public, his response was to refer to "that person" or "the person you mentioned". At the Valdai Club in 2020 he claimed credit for authorizing the decision to allow "the person" to be flown to Germany for hospital treatment (President of Russia, 22 October 2020). At the News Conference in December 2020, he dismissed him as "this patient of a Berlin clinic" and insinuated that Navalny had been far too insignificant for the Russian intelligence service to bother about,

but also added that if they had been after his life, they would probably have succeeded (President of Russia, 17 December 2020). Other
members of the president's administration, such as the Kremlin
spokesperson Dimitriy Peskov, took after the practice of non-naming (Meduza 2020).

The non-naming tactic is exceptional since Putin and his surroundings do not treat other activists and potential dissidents in
this disrespectful way. During the 2020 News Conference, Putin
had for example no problems explicitly using the name of Ivan Saf-
ronov, a former military journalist charged with treason in Russia
(President of Russia, 17 December 2020). The non-naming of Navalny should be understood as a demonstrative and somewhat desperate attempt to diminish the chief antagonist's importance. This
could easily create the opposite impression, like when the evil
Voldemort in the books about Harry Potter is fearfully referred to
as "you-know-who" and the avoidance of his name instills more
fear than the use of the name itself.

Through his command of social media, Navalny has an appeal
among the younger strata of the audience that Putin does not have,
and he wields significant agenda power.[10] As will be recounted in
more detail below, his mastery in the use of Youtube, where he has
run a channel of his own by the name of Navalny Live, is rivalled
by few others.

Navalny's influential campaign against the United Russia
party before the Duma elections in 2011 was the first striking evidence of his agenda power. His hard-hitting one-liner of not supporting "the party of crooks and thieves", and, as mentioned, his
exhortations to practice smart voting so as to "vote for anyone except United Russia" played a significant role for the poor showing
of United Russia, both at that time and later (Gill 2016). He then

---

10   In a partly discrepant survey, Levada Center presented poll data from late April
     2020, according to which Navalny had more popular appeal than Putin in the
     age cohort between 40 and 54 years of age, and had an equally large appeal
     among the members of the 24-39 year-olds. Putin, however, dominated strongly
     in the categories 18-24 and 55 plus. The number of respondents was 1608
     (Levada Center 2020b).

developed the "smart voting" idea from a catchy slogan to an organized campaign to coordinate and bolster the support of candidates
not representing United Russia across the country. Navalny
worked hard and successfully to build a national grassroots net-
work for his anti-corruption campaigns with nodes in about 40 Russian regions. Even if he has had most of his followers in the traditionally liberal capitals of Moscow and St. Petersburg, he has been
able to build an organization that has manifested its presence in
other major cities, such as Yekaterinburg and Novosibirsk but also
in more rural areas (Flikke 2020).

Navalny being 24 years younger than Putin, time would seem
to work in his favor if there are no further attempts on his life and
the effects of his detention in a penal colony from 2021 on are not
too detrimental for his health. In view of the deeply worrisome
news trickling out from his prison in the spring of 2021, great
doubts arose about the latter. His physical survival seemed highly
uncertain. Considering Navalny's command of social media, the
impression is in any case that the future belongs to the likes of him,
not to those of Putin. This might go at least some way towards explaining Putin's recurring discomfort whenever Navalny is referred to (Gill 2016). Navalny has posed major and unresolved
problems for the Putin regime for more than a decade. Regardless
of whether Navalny himself survives his prison camp, the protest
momentum that he mastered and initiated is likely to live on and
remain challenging to the Kremlin in years to come.

Medvedev's downfall

In March 2017 Navalny demonstrated his formidable media power,
in connection with his vitriolic criticism of Dmitriy Medvedev for
extensive corruption. In a follow-up to his earlier critical scrutiny
of the long-time prime minister and former president, Navalny's
video exposed Medvedev's lavish holiday abodes at home and
abroad, which had cost close to 100 million Euro of funds, all supposedly gained by dishonest and shadowy means. The Youtube
video clip, "Don't Call Him Dimon" (Youtube 2020), hurt

Medvedev's credibility badly. Its posting coincided with a disastrous, continuous, and accelerating dip in the then prime minister's popularity. A month after its release, 45 percent of those surveyed in a poll requested Medvedev's resignation (Samoilenko 2017). In late 2019, the video clip had been viewed more than 36 million times. In connection with the publication of Navalny's video, thousands of people in 95 cities all over the country took to the streets in rallies coordinated to take place simultaneously. The mobilization evoked a harsh reaction from the authorities. Over 1600 participants in 47 cities, many of them young people under 18 years of age, were detained (Semenov 2020).

The effect of the video clip was lasting. Medvedev was unable to recover politically from the blow. Ever since March 2017, the month of the release of Navalny's scathing clip, more people disapproved than approved of Medvedev's activities as prime minister (Levada Center 2021c). Medvedev's image was already weak before, but he found himself in a hopeless position after the release (Fredrikson 2019). His position kept deteriorating, and in August 2018 there was a confidence gap of minus 43 percent, with 71 percent disapproving and 28 percent approving of him (Levada Center 2021c). This was a crushing verdict.

Medvedev had not always had an image problem. In the autumn of 2008, he had, as a newly elected president of the Russian Federation, an all-time high approval rate of 83 percent according to the Levada Center. Since then, his ratings went steadily downhill. The comparison with Putin and his continuously high level of approval was unavoidable. According to the Levada Center, Putin had in August 2018, at the time when Medvedev's popularity curve hit an all-time low, an approval rate of 70 percent, whereas 30 percent disapproved of him, which gave him a net approval rate of 40 percent (Levada Center 2021c).

In January 2020 Medvedev was finally relieved of his duties as prime minister and was moved sideways to the position of deputy chairman of the Security Council, which is chaired by President Putin. The previously little-known Mikhail Mishustin, up to that point the head of the Federal Tax Service, replaced him as prime minister. Public opinion seemed to give the successor the benefit of the doubt. During his first year of service, Mishustin could enjoy a positive net approval rate, with at best 60 percent approving and 36 percent disapproving in August 2020 (Levada Center 2021c). When the change of cabinet took place, there was thus an abrupt shift from negative to positive approval rates for the prime minister. Since Mishustin could hardly be said to have wielded much personal charisma during such a short time, these fluctuations were telling for how deeply unpopular Medvedev was.

As one caustic observer wrote with reference to Navalny's clip, one could perhaps argue that character assassination does not work when there is no apparent character to assassinate in the first place (Samoilenko 2017). Charismatic legitimacy obviously needs charisma to be sustained, and when there is none, other foundations for legitimacy are needed. Medvedev's dilemma was that he no longer seemed to have any alternative sources to draw upon. When he was elected president in 2008, his legitimacy stemmed from legal authority, but he lost it all when he conceded to the deal of handing the reins of presidential power back to Putin in 2011. No longer being the first in command, he could remain in the prime minister's office only for as long as his boss permitted. Moving on to the commanding heights again after his demotion in 2020 would seem difficult given his poor showings in the opinion polls, and it is doubtful whether he could improve his position from the deputy chairmanship of the Security Council, to which he was relegated after the cabinet reshuffle.

In view of Medvedev's lack of popular appeal, it seemed surprising to many that Putin, at the beginning of his fourth presidential tenure in 2018, again chose to nominate him as his prime minister. There may have been several rational explanations for this, however. As will be developed later, Medvedev's weakness may well have been an asset for Putin, as it contributed to the reinforcement of his own strongman brand. Even more importantly, removing Medvedev soon after the release of Navalny's video clip could have been interpreted as giving in to the demands of "you-know-who", acknowledging the legitimacy and influence of the latter's views. There was a struggle for public opinion going on between Putin and Navalny, even if it was a battle that unfolded on very unequal terms (Flikke 2020). The Putin team had certainly realized Navalny's social media power. What Navalny could do to hurt Medvedev he could potentially do against Putin too.

Navalny vs. Putin

Against this background the assassination attempt on Navalny in August 2020 was perhaps only to be expected. According to forensic laboratories in Western Europe, he was poisoned with the infamous nerve agent Novichok while travelling in Siberia. Once developed in Soviet military high-security labs, this lethally toxic substance is today probably only available within the Russian state security sector. Someone, somewhere, had apparently decided that Navalny finally needed to be dealt with and taken out of the way. The aircraft that he was on made an emergency landing after which he was taken to hospital in the city of Omsk. With some delay, the Russian authorities permitted his onward transportation to a hospital in Berlin where his life was rescued. He recovered relatively quickly, resumed his oppositional activities, and declared his intention to return home to Russia to resume the struggle on site. So he did, and in mid-January 2021 he boarded a plane from Berlin, bound for Vnukovo Airport. The aircraft was redirected to Sheremetyevo Airport, presumably to evade his followers and the foreign press who had gathered at Vnukovo to meet him. Upon arrival he was promptly arrested by Federal Penitentiary Service personnel under the pretext that he had violated the terms of the suspended sentence passed on him at a trial about financial crimes some years before.

After Navalny's return to Russia, January and February 2021 saw several clear illustrations of Navalny's media power. Navalny had not been idle during his convalescence but produced a one-and-a-half hour long Youtube documentary where he subjected Putin to the same treatment as he had once bestowed on Medvedev. Navalny chose to release the film, "A Palace for Putin", two days after his return to his homeland, ostensibly to avoid accusations that he had published it while being safe in Germany and afraid of encountering the authorities at home. Fear is not Navalny's most characteristic trait, however. The film went viral and had an enormous impact. Five days after its release, 81 million viewers had watched it, and after just two weeks, it had reached the 100 million mark (Youtube 2021). The estimations were that every fourth Russian adult had seen the film a month after its release (Levada Center 2021a).

Building on drone films and evidence leaked by construction workers who had built and furnished the estate, Navalny focused on details of Putin's palace-like mansion near the town of Gelendzhik off the Black Sea coast. The estate, which had allegedly cost 1 billion Euro, presumably coming from kickbacks and graft, took up an area 39 times the size of Monaco. It contained the bare necessities of life — such as an underground hockey rink, a casino, a theater, an aqua disco, and a vineyard. The furniture was exquisite and luxurious. Giving away one particularly catchy detail, Navalny pointed out that the toilet brushes for the president's bathrooms alone had cost about 700 Euro each. This exceeds the average monthly salary in Russia, which is about 550 Euro (Nokhrin 2021). Navalny's adherents immediately picked up the detail.[11] In the demonstrations that took place across the country after Navalny's arrest, people started to brandish toilet brushes, to underline their incantations such as "Shame!" and "Putin is a thief!". This was evidence of Navalny's ability to inspire the launch of visual, humorous cues that are highly efficient in the struggle against the increasingly authoritarian regime. Putin did not really have much to match this. In the sport of using humor and satire to make an argument, there are few who can equal Navalny, and the president is not one of them.

It is hard to see Navalny's release of the film "A Palace for Putin" as anything but an outright declaration of war against the incumbent. Surely Navalny must have suspected that he would be arrested upon his return, but still he chose to go back. The new film

---

11   This was not the first time that Navalny's visual cues developed into memes for the opposition against the regime. After the film "Don't call him Dimon", the yellow plastic duck came to symbolize Dimitriy Medvedev's exorbitant spending of illicit funds (Flikke 2020). In the film, the drone zooms in on a house in a pond that was built for Medvedev's ducks and which Navalny did not miss the opportunity to inform the audience about.

created such attention at home and abroad that he may have seen it as a life insurance of sorts. Through the film Navalny challenged Putin to the fullest. He went as far as depicting him as mad and out of touch with reality. Towards the close of the documentary, he urged people to take to the streets, saying that if only 10 percent of those who felt maltreated by the authorities went out to protest, nothing and no one would be able to hold them back. On January 23, 2021, for the first time in a planned series of weekly demonstrations, people heeded the call. The genie seemed to have slipped out of the bottle. The following week there were peaceful protests in some 80 cities across the country, gathering tens of thousands of people. Overall, the demonstrations were perhaps not as well attended as the manifestations in 2011 and 2012, but they seemed to be more widespread. The regime was doubtless concerned, and around ten thousand people were estimated to have been arrested during the demonstrations.

When clamping down on the manifestations, the authorities had a trump card. The protests were unauthorized and had not been granted due permission. Hence, they violated the law. Putin himself addressed the theme in January 2021, asserting that everyone had the right to express their opinion, provided it was done "within the legal framework". When it was not, such unlawful protests were both counterproductive and dangerous and had to be put down by the authorities. To justify this, he cited the example of the riots in Washington DC on January 6, 2021, when a mob stormed the Capitol. Those riots had taken place for political reasons, had been prompted by political slogans, and the perpetrators were legitimately hunted down and punished for federal offences. So, why should not the Russian authorities take corresponding actions against lawbreakers, he queried (President of Russia, 25 January 2021).

In early February 2021, Navalny stood trial on charges of having violated the conditions of parole while undergoing medical treatment in Germany. What was on the agenda was his old, suspended sentence of three and a half years' imprisonment for alleged embezzlement. The international attention paid to the case was considerable and the pressure continued to rise on the Putin regime. It is conceivable that this added to a figurative insurance policy for Navalny but as he headed for years of imprisonment in a penal colony 100 kilometers distant from Moscow his prospects were nonetheless unclear.

When the court case about Navalny's break of probation rules took place in February 2021, and foreign media filmed the interior of the courthouse with Navalny locked up inside a cage of glass, the defendant was seen forming a heart with his fingers, passing on a greeting to his wife who was outside, on site to follow the proceedings. While deeply touching, the gesture was also indicative of Navalny's communication skills, and his instincts about how to make his messages and his personal aura appealing to the wider audience. In terms of the media contest between him and the incumbent president—"the old man in the bunker" as Navalny had taken to referring to him, responding in kind to Putin's non-naming strategy—it was clear who had won the day. The young, handsome, and mercurial opposition leader was pitted against an increasingly bureaucratic, wooden, and listless president. Being a man of action might not help when the action is perceived as prompted by self-interest and the drive to defend increasing stagnation. Putin's charisma-based legitimacy was bound to take severe hits from this.

The strength of Navalny's challenge to Putin's charisma was made apparent at the trial as the defendant, referring to the assassination attempt against him in the summer of 2020, suggested that the incumbent would go down in history as Vladimir the Poisoner of Underpants. The epithet was chosen in view of the way in which the poison had been applied and administered to infiltrate the opposition leader's body. As always, Navalny's instincts were well developed regarding what would catch on among his followers. Already during the first demonstrations after his incarceration in January 2021, people had been seen brandishing blue boxer shorts of the kind that Navalny had worn when he was poisoned.

Moreover, Navalny mocked the president as "just a petty bureaucrat who was accidentally appointed to his position" (Navalny 2021). For the president trying so hard and so consistently to appear as the guarantor of greatness, the savior from the unruly 1990s, and the warden of stability in a hostile world, these epithets were a mockery with less than glorious connotations. If the expressions went viral in the public space, they could in the long run lead to an erosion of Putin's image as the great and invincible leader. Ultimately, this could on a slippery slope lead to the incumbent increasingly being perceived as an "embarrassment", as a "source of mortification" where he previously used to be a source of national pride (Galeotti 2021).

In the spring of 2021, alarming news broke about Navalny's state of health. Considering the statement attributed to Putin, that Navalny would come to "regret that he stayed alive" (Lönnqvist 2021), there seemed to be reason for concern. The opposition leader was suffering from severe back pain caused by herniation and was generally weakened since he was woken up every hour at night due to his being labelled prone to escape by the authorities. His health deteriorated badly. As he was denied his request to see a medical doctor to receive proper treatment, he went on hunger strike at the end of March, which led to further worsening of his condition. In mid-April, a physician warned that Navalny suffered from impaired kidney functions and ran the risk of cardiac arrest. In fact, the doctor claimed, his health was so bad that he might die any day, unless he was promptly taken care of by medical experts. After a substantial delay, he was transferred to a hospital within the penal colony, and somewhat more than three weeks after he initiated the hunger strike, Navalny announced through his Instagram account that he had ended it.

Navalny's sympathizers called for country-wide demonstrations, determined to organize powerful manifestations in his support. The aim was to do this as soon as the organizers were assured that half a million people would take part. When they finally took place, the turnout was significantly lower, but even so people took to the streets in many locations across the country. There was a vast difference, however, between the protests in April and the demonstrations that took place in January and February 2021. Then the objective was to have Navalny freed, now it was about saving his life.

Meanwhile, the Moscow prosecutor's office suggested that Navalny's Anti-Corruption Fund, FBK, be labelled an extremist organization, which could lead to ten years' imprisonment for active members. The authorities were evidently trying to force the genie back into the bottle from where it had come. They had succeeded in doing this in 2012, but the question was whether they would be equally successful in 2021.

The fall guy function

Let us now return for a while to the story of Putin's perennial sidekick, Dimitriy Medvedev. Paradoxical as it may seem, his receding image over such a long period of time may have contributed to the consolidation of Putin's own brand. The weak Medvedev made Putin's strengths more visible. Where Putin wielded charismatic legitimacy, Medvedev had precious little to offer (Apressyan 2013). Where Putin came across as the uncompromising guarantor of Russia's increasingly stronger global role and the maintenance of domestic order and stability, Medvedev was never able to convey an image even remotely like it. In comparison with Putin, Medvedev had the more "modest personality" of the two (Sakwa 2014: 44). Maybe it is enough to recall Medvedev's publicly underlined preference for the sport of badminton. It is a great sport and a fabulous pastime activity, but when it comes to conveying a strongman macho image, it is a poor substitute for Putin's judo (Youtube 2011a).[12]

Conversely, it can also be argued that, as he was situated next to power, Medvedev's weakness was his main strategic asset. He could never compete with Putin on the strongman stage and showed no ambition of doing so, he was always a loyal team member who could be trusted to toe the line, and he was simply not the kind of threat to the incumbent that the crown prince problem anticipates. All this is likely to have contributed to keeping him in the position of the formal second in command for such a long time. His

---

12   In the curious Youtube clip, Medvedev takes on a seemingly unengaged Putin in a low-pace badminton game, but it is Medvedev who argues for the great merits of the sport.

weakness played out to mutual benefit for himself and his president.

Here one should, however, recall that the projection of Putin's macho image has had its weaknesses, too. At the time of the biggest crisis yet to the legitimacy of the Putin regime, in 2011-2012, the then prime minister Putin entered the ring of an international martial arts contest in Moscow to congratulate the Russian winner (BBC News 2011). An amateur video posted on Youtube showed how Putin was jeered at, booed, and heckled by the spectators (Youtube 2011b), indicating that his standing was decreasing among the audience with which he most of all seemed to want to become associated: the strong, fit, male, and macho (Koesel and Bunce 2012). Putin's image was restored after the annexation of Crimea in 2014, but Medvedev never underwent a similar recovery.

It has been suggested that Putin's experience as a judoka is reflected in his way of doing politics. Rather than representing the classical image of the calculating statesman as a chess player who thinks several moves ahead before doing anything, Putin has the judoka way of circling around his adversary, ready to seize the moment and use whichever weakness the opponent happens to display (Galeotti 2019a, Fredrikson 2019: 43, Stent 2019: 4): "A brief moment of disbalance on the part of the enemy can be used productively. It may even be sufficient to cause his fall" (Umland and Klimkin 2020). Badminton-style competition does not translate equally well to the international arena.

As the contemporary counterpart to the tsars of old imperial Russia, Putin has for a long time been able to keep up his image as a formidable force, a man of action, who can always put things right provided he is adequately informed about the state of the nation and the regions (Mamonova 2016). This is the aforementioned myth of the "tsar-deliverer", which may help shed some light on the question of why Medvedev was kept in his position for so long. Having a head of government who can serve as a fall guy during a crisis could be an asset for someone in Putin's position. In case of need, the president could sacrifice a pawn, continue the game and, without harming his own legitimacy, go on appearing as a doer and the people's benefactor. It was indicative that Putin handed over the announcement of the unpopular pension reform in the summer of 2018 to Medvedev (Fredrikson 2019). This gave himself opportunity to take credit for sweetening the pill and introducing cosmetic changes to the originally proposed scheme (Busygina 2019). Likewise, Putin's outsourcing of the main responsibility for combating the covid-19 pandemic to the regional heads of government in 2020 provided him with the opportunity to let other persons take the fall, should there be major setbacks in the handling of the crisis. There are several other such examples, albeit of somewhat lesser magnitude. One of them was the abrupt dismissal, after the disastrous fire at the Kemerovo entertainment center in 2018, of the long-standing governor Aman Tuleyev. More about this will follow below.

From 2018 on there were several signs of growing dissatisfaction with the Putin regime. The public discontent over the pension reform was as evident as it was deep and increasingly put the social contract between the president and his electorate in question (Pavroz 2020, Sharafutdinova 2020). The reform increased the pension age for both men and women, setting the limit for men at 65 years of age, which is only two years below the average male life expectancy in Russia (Wilson 2021). In the spring of 2019, there were also massive protests against the Moscow city authorities' refusal to allow popularly nominated candidates to run for office in the local elections. In the late summer and early fall of 2020 large demonstrations, gathering tens of thousands of people, rocked the Far Eastern city of Khabarovsk and spread to locations such as the Primorye Territory, Sakhalin, Kamchatka, and the Magadan Region. The reason was the removal from office of the popular governor of Khabarovsk Krai, Sergey Furgal of the Liberal Democratic Party. This followed upon his incarceration due to murder charges, widely regarded as fabricated. Demonstrators took to the streets for several weeks in a row. Support for the dethroned governor was the immediate reason, but the manifestations quickly took on an anti-Putin hue (Laurén 2021, Dik 2020).

In the spring of 2020, a slump in Putin's popularity figures was exacerbated by the public discontent with the authorities' handling of the corona crisis, not least that of the president himself. The dip below 60 percent in the popularity ratings was the first ever in the 20-year history of the monthly Levada surveys and seemed to bode ill for the president[13] (Pavroz 2020). In the fall of 2020, after several troubled months of the corona pandemic and other wear and tear, the curve turned upwards again, reaching 69 percent in October, but then sloped anew to settle on a plateau until the first quarter of the year in 2021 (Levada Center 2021c).

Stability and order

As was shown above, Putin on several occasions referred to the non-named Navalny in the same context as Mikheil Saakashvili, the former president of Georgia who held that position at the time of the Russo-Georgian war in 2008. Putin has repeatedly linked these two persons with the Euro-Maidan events in Ukraine. The coupling of these names and events in public statements is perhaps more significant than it appears to be at first glance.

At the annual News Conference of 2017, Putin elaborated what efforts the Russian government would be prepared to make to prevent Russia ending up in the same kind of political turmoil as Ukraine during Euro-Maidan. He expressed himself very graphically:

> *I assure you that the government has never been afraid and is not afraid of anyone. But the government must not be like a bearded peasant idly picking at cabbage pieces in his beard and watching the state turn into a muddy puddle where oligarchs fish out goldfish for themselves, like it was here in the 1990s or in Ukraine today. Do we want a replica of today's Ukraine in Russia? No, we do not want it and will not allow it* (President of Russia, 14 December 2017).

While having a self-evident ring to it, and despite the graphic choice of words, a critical interpretation would have it that Putin seemed to be looking at power as something that it was his indisputable

---

13   Due to the general prescription of social distancing during the corona crisis, the Levada surveys from April 2020 on were not undertaken in the standard way through face-to-face contact with respondents. Instead, the interviews were made by telephone. To some extent this may have reduced the comparability of these surveys with earlier polls (cf. Swedish Center for Russian Studies 2020:4).

right to keep. He was obviously not willing to share it with people he perceived as usurpers.

Even if Putin says that the government is not afraid of anyone, this does not seem to be entirely true. One can often sense in his public statements that there is a nagging fear in the Kremlin, maybe not of someone, but of something. In the paragraph cited above, there is an allusion to the heyday of the oligarchs in the Russian 1990s, but above all to Ukraine of the Euro-Maidan, which is a specter seemingly ever present for the regime. Along with the color revolutions in Georgia, Ukraine, and Kyrgyzstan in 2003-2005 and the Arab Spring in 2011, the Euro-Maidan is in Putin's public imaginary a clear-cut and warning example of the dire consequences of domestic turmoil, instability and the alleged and devious instigations by the rival global power, the United States. Here, the *smuta* myth is being invoked again. There is no doubt that authoritarian regimes the world over have dreaded the scenarios of the color revolutions and their followers. They have equated them with violence, instability, foreign intervention, and forced regime change, and have studied carefully countermoves that could be taken, lessons that could be learnt and unsuccessful actions that should not be repeated by the ruling elites (Hall 2017).

For Russia, as for many other hybrid and authoritarian states, these events signified two things. First, in geopolitical terms, the color revolutions meant that states previously belonging to a perceived Russian sphere of interest moved closer to the leading Western powers, at least temporarily. Secondly, they were also a memento for the Russian regime itself (Omelicheva 2016). As in the old Cold War scenario in the United States about a row of falling dominoes, there was a fear that one's own regime might be the next to fall. Therefore, the regime deemed it imperative to take precautionary action such as to limit the sphere of activities of domestic NGOs, restrict their chances of receiving foreign funding, mobilize the support of the younger generation and see to it that no surprises were sprung at election time to the legislature and the presidency (Wilson 2009). One prominent example was the establishment of the Nashi movement, a youth league highly devoted to Putin, which was set up in 2005 to stem the threat of young people engaging in oppositional activities (Hemment 2012).

There is little doubt that the massive demonstrations in 2011-2012 created some anxiety in the regime that the bells now tolled for Russia. It was after these events that the law on foreign agents was adopted, that is the regulation that any NGO that received funding from abroad had to register as "foreign agent" (Martus 2021, Hall 2017). Putin's angry and emotional reaction to John McCain's tweet that the Arab Spring had finally reached Russia becomes more understandable when interpreted in this light. There was a real fear, and the explicit mention of the dreaded outcome touched a raw nerve.

The Kremlin's references to Euro-Maidan are presumably there to insinuate what the United States were hoping to achieve through covert action in Russia itself. This theme was manifest in connection with the protests in 2011-2012, when, as we saw, the United States in general and Secretary of State Hillary Clinton personally, were accused of inciting the unrest. After the announcement of the official results of the presidential election in 2012, Putin shed large tears of relief and spoke about forces that had been intent on usurping power in Russia (Busygina 2019, Rutland 2017a, Hutcheson and Petersson 2016). He clearly had external influences in mind.

The upheavals in Belarus in the late summer and early fall of 2020 added another example to the Kremlin's fears of foreign-induced unrest which could ultimately topple authoritarian regimes, even in Russia itself. Following upon the fraudulent tabulation of the August 9 election results in Belarus, people took to the streets to express their anger. Putin's enthusiasm with the discredited president Lukashenko was already lukewarm, but on several occasions, he reiterated that Russia would honor its obligations according to the Collective Security Treaty Organization (CSTO) and the Union State Treaty between Russia and Belarus. He indicated that he saw foreign interests at work, and that these were acting to aggravate the situation in Belarus (President of Russia, 27 August 2020).

In a bilateral meeting between the two leaders in Sochi in September 2020, a desperate Lukashenko begged Putin for help to remain in the presidential seat. Frantically trying to bolster his case, he invoked parallels both to the outbreak of the civil war with Chechnya in the 1990s and to the Nazi German attack on the Soviet Union through Belarusian territory at the outset of the Great Patriotic War. He continuously alluded to sinister foreign forces that conspired to wreak havoc. Overall, Lukashenko made an unstable impression, trying hard to please and flatter his host, but also mistakenly suggesting that the latter had already been the president of Russia in 1998. For his part, Putin was acting the stern master, promising a large-scale loan and joint military exercises, and even offering Belarus to be the first foreign country to receive the Russian pioneer vaccine Sputnik V against covid-19. In view of its limited trials, this may have seemed like a mixed blessing at the time. In return, Putin demanded things of Lukashenko, urging the need for constitutional reform and dialogue with the opposition but also maintenance of the present level of bilateral economic interchange with Russia. Importantly, he promised that Russia would honor all its commitments to Belarus and described it as Russia's closest ally (President of Russia, 14 September 2020).

At a follow-up meeting about five months later, the two leaders endeavored to send the message that the situation had returned to normal. There was no mention whatsoever of the still ongoing social unrest in Belarus. Neither was there even a tacit reference to the demonstrations in support of the imprisoned Aleksey Navalny, which had unfolded in Russia in January and February 2021. The images of the two leaders, showing them both beaming in the wintry sun, were supposed to suggest harmony and calm. The question is whether the receiving audience was particularly convinced by the imagery.

Indeed, the depicted tranquility soon gave room for other, more somber, nuances. As Putin in April 2021 delivered his annual state of the nation address to the Federal Assembly, he again brought up the specter of foreign intervention in Russia and its allies with the aim to sow unrest and bring instability. He accused foreign powers of having instigated a plot to assassinate

Lukashenko and to bring havoc to the country through power cuts and cyberattacks (President of Russia, 21 April 2021). Belarusian authorities claimed to have thwarted the coup attempt in its early stages and to have detained two Belarusian citizens involved in the preparations.

The president claimed that this was not only about Belarus. In his address to the Assembly, Putin argued as was mentioned above that unfriendly moves against Russia continued unabated, and he warned foreign powers not to cross the "red line", the exact location of which it was Russia's own privilege to decide on. If the foreign powers did not heed this, they would come to regret it "in a way they have not regretted anything for a long time", he warned (President of Russia, 21 April 2021).

It was against this political backdrop that the Moscow Prosecutor's Office announced its intention to designate Navalny's Anti-Corruption Fund and his regional branch offices as "extremist organizations". Ostensibly, they were "creating conditions for changing the foundations of the constitutional order, including through the scenario of a 'colored revolution'" (Roth 2021b). The rationale was spelled out clearly: Navalny and his organizations had to be stopped, since they were allegedly supported by the West to undermine the regime. The Kremlin seemed to harbor a concern that Navalny could be instrumental in triggering a color revolution scenario that might ultimately lead to its overthrow. Action was taken, connecting to the mythmaking about the necessity of upholding order and stability in the face of foreign plots. Repressive measures were undertaken against Navalny and his organization, supposedly with a desire to restore cracking regime legitimacy at least somewhat, but if this did not come to pass, the Kremlin seemed willing to rely on repression alone.

The good tsar

After the presidential elections in March 2018, Putin initially kept a low profile in his public appearances. No tears were shed in public this time, and no allegations were made of attempts by his opponents to undermine Russia's statehood and usurp power. Neither was there any need for such a reaction at that point in time. Even if some scattered protests took place there was nothing like the massive civil unrest that had rocked the country in 2011-2012. One thing that the two post-election years of 2012 and 2018 had in common, though, was that Putin seemed compelled to stress the fact that he was still the man of action to whom there were no real alternatives.

Soon after the elections in 2018, a minor but highly indicative opportunity arose for Putin to demonstrate his unabated energy and dynamism, and to show that people could still rely on him to get things done. In comparison with the annexation of Crimea, the involvement in Donbas and the armed actions in Syria, the event may seem insignificant, but its unfolding provides some insights into how Putin's legitimizing strategies work.

In late March 2018, there was a devastating fire in a shopping mall and entertainment center in the Siberian city of Kemerovo. More than 60 people, many of whom were children, perished. It quickly came to light that there had been gross violations of local security regulations. The fire escapes had been blocked, leaving the people trapped and without any chances to fight their way out to survival. Soon after the catastrophe, the president visited Kemerovo to pay his respects. The mayor of the city accompanied him at a meeting with angry and grieving local activists. Putin cross-examined him about the reasons for permitting the entertainment center to continue its activities, despite its clearly deficient fire safety precautions. The president not only subjected the mayor to tough interrogation but also to public humiliation. The discussion seemed most of all like the third degree in front of a live audience:

> *President of Russia Vladimir Putin: (To Ilya Seredyuk.) How long have you been mayor?*
>
> *Kemerovo Mayor Ilya Seredyuk: Since 2016, or two years as mayor. Before that, I was deputy mayor for six years.*
>
> *Vladimir Putin: How come you issued the permit?*
>
> *Ilya Seredyuk: <...> I was head of a municipality and then returned to the city. During that period, in 2014, the permit was issued for commissioning the section where the tragedy happened.*

Vladimir Putin: Nothing was checked for two years.

(…)

Vladimir Putin: There were no inspections for two years.

Ilya Seredyuk: Mr President, there was an inspection.

Vladimir Putin: When? In 2016?

Ilya Seredyuk: The State Fire Inspection issued instructions.

Vladimir Putin: In 2016. Now is 2018.

Ilya Seredyuk: Instructions were given and then the building was sold.

Vladimir Putin: Selling has nothing to do with it. Safety must be ensured. Sold or not sold, what does it matter? Safety must always be ensured, right? What difference does it make who the owner is? Services must operate properly to provide security. Where are these services?

(…)

Vladimir Putin: An investigative team of 100 people is working here. They will look at every link in the chain, from those who issued permits to those responsible for monitoring safety and security, the private security companies whose staff were there and did not push the panic button in time, and so on and forth. They will follow the chain starting from the re-registration of the building and the permit that allowed a factory to be turned into an entertainment centre, to those who permitted those materials to be used in a facility of this purpose. This is a disgrace, no doubt about it.

Remark [from bystander]: Can we have your word that the investigation will be strictly under control and we will find out the truth?

Vladimir Putin: Do not even doubt it.

Remark: And that it will be as transparent as possible?

Vladimir Putin: Rest assured.

Remark: And those guilty will be punished?

Vladimir Putin: There's no need to doubt that.

Remark: The people want them to be punished.

Vladimir Putin: That will be so.
(President of Russia, 27 March 2018).

Here Putin attains several things. He demonstrates that he is a man of action who stands by the people in their struggle to exert their rights against local authorities. He shows firmly who is in command, and that legal and uncompromising action will follow against those who have fallen short. Just a few days later, it was announced that the long serving governor, Aman Tuleyev of Kemerovo, who himself had lost a niece in the fire, had been immediately relieved of his duties. Due to issues of health and old age, Tuleyev, who had served as governor for more than 20 years, was probably on his way out anyhow. However, this does not alter the fact that Putin grasped a chance to demonstrate how attentive he was and always is to the demands of local people. The man at the top, the good tsar, had listened, made a firm statement, and acted accordingly.

There was a world of difference between Putin's uncompromising handling of the Kemerovo tragedy and the event that troubled the early part of his first presidency, namely the disaster in 2000 when the nuclear submarine Kursk perished with all its crew of 118 people. That time, Putin chose not to interrupt his holiday and elicited harsh criticism for going into hiding when the country needed him most. The criticism that he earned for his late action on that occasion "signified the first serious public opposition Putin had faced in his entire career" (Barany 2004: 490). In 2018, he seemed to have learnt his lesson thoroughly and there was no faux pas. He deftly distributed the blame to his cronies, like the poor mayor of Kemerovo and the governor, Tuleyev.

This modus operandi is consistent with the "myth of the tsar-deliverer", which was referred to earlier: "the regime ably reconstructs the myth of the tsar-deliverer to justify its autocracy and to guarantee the existing order" (Mamonova 2016: 326). Regardless of whether the citizens believe in the contents of the myth or use it strategically to address local grievances, the myth of the benevolent leader who can put things right, if only he is informed, is an important part of the toolbox for constructing the legitimacy of the Putin regime (Ryazanova-Clarke 2013). Malinova makes a similar point, referring to the pattern set by the old myth about the good tsar and the bad boyars, where the expectations are that the former will always side with the people (Malinova 2020). This is a further reason why it is justified to label Putin a populist, albeit a populist of the incumbency. His populism is about protecting the "real folks" from "bad elites" and the "oligarchs", be they domestic or foreign (Busygina 2019).

The annual Direct Line with Putin offers a display window for these kinds of presidential intervention, where the incumbent can show that he cares about his individual subjects. He promises to rectify wrongdoings committed by local and regional authorities and acts like a stern master in overseeing those authorities, making sure that they put things right. In the 2018 version of the Direct Line, the examples were prolific. Regional governors, key federal ministers, and deputy prime ministers all over the Russian Federation had been instructed to be on stand-by to appear by video link on the live broadcast, should the president wish to get in touch with them to clarify an issue or ask them questions (Reevell 2018). There were several instances of local or regional politicians or executives being called on to explain themselves. Sometimes they received encouraging words from the president who had been assured that things were moving in the right direction, but equally often they had to put up with being publicly snubbed by him for actions done or, equally often, not done, even if things seldom went as far as with the unfortunate mayor of Kemerovo. In one case, the president, markedly unimpressed with the regional authorities' actions, rebuked the governor of Tomsk for referring to a woman who had complained about a local grievance as "she" and not by name:

> *Here is what I would like to say. It is not "her" or "she." It is "Natalya Nikolaevna".*
> *This is the first thing* (President of Russia, 7 June 2018).

At the annual News Conference of December 2020, which due to covid-19 had to be amalgamated with the Direct Line of that year, Putin started the event by elaborating on why these medial events were so important. What he said was a vivid illustration of the myth about the good tsar who always cares about his people and therefore needs be informed of how they live and what worries them. The whole point of this media exercise was to provide a platform where the citizens could pass on this information to the incumbent:

> *Even though I have a vast flow of information about what is happening in the coun-*
> *try reaching me through various channels, still, there is nothing more valuable than*
> *direct communication with the people, with Russian citizens, there is nothing more*
> *valuable than hearing their opinions about their lives and concerns, and again, what*
> *we need to do in order to have a better life* (President of Russia, 17 December
> 2020).

The Direct Line with Putin is a primary outlet for the display of the
tacit alliance between the benevolent autocrat and his people. To
show the wide audience that Putin can always help, these ritualized
media performances contain, as a rule, at least one example of an
individual citizen who is being helped by the president's direct and
personal intervention. Such demonstrations can be read symboli-
cally to underline that direct rule by Putin is more effective than
any abstract model of representative democracy out there in the de-
praved West (Kukshinov 2021). Charismatic authority is shown to
trump rational-legal authority. To use another normative yardstick,
Western-style good governance is proven insufficient. Instead, it is
traditional, patrimonial "bad governance" that wins the day
(Gel'man 2017).

The alliance between the "tsar-deliverer" and the public, or
the public's "naïve monarchism", as Mamonova (2016) prefers to
call it, goes back a long time in Russian and Soviet history (Fredrikson 2019). It was widespread practice in Imperial Russia but was
frequently used also during Stalin's rule. If only the good ruler had
known, he would have put things right. If only the good ruler had
known, repressions would not have taken place and would not
have hit one's own family. Therefore, such matters had somehow
to be brought to the ruler's attention. Due to the unpopularity of
Boris Yeltsin, especially during his second presidency, the practice
seems to have been rather dormant during his time, even if Yeltsin
also used it during the more dynamic first years of his presidential
tenure. Clearly, it acquired a new lease of life during Putin's presidencies. As Mamonova writes, the myth about the tsar-deliverer
has traditionally been a phenomenon nurtured by the rural population. This goes some way to explaining Putin's strong standing in

the countryside, as opposed to the urban centers, where considerable segments of the population are more skeptical about his long rule.

Naïve monarchism may not be as naïve as the expression indicates. Mamonova explains how the apparent manifestations of loyalty towards the president (or the tsar, or the general secretary of the Communist Party of the Soviet Union) serve both parties well. For the president, the phenomenon adds to his support base and helps him to become re-elected. For the rural population, it provides a way to put pressure on intransigent local and regional officials, at the same time as the invocation of the president's name gives protection against harassment by local authorities. This is not to rule out that some people sincerely believe in the contents of the myth, but the instrumental element of the arrangement is evident. The president does not get the yeomen's support gratis.

Mamonova (2016) describes three basic manifestations of naïve monarchism in contemporary Russia: the signing of petitions to the president, marches to bring grievances to the president's attention, and finally the naming of certain places and localities after the president. To illustrate the latter, she recounts the rather amusing story of how a forest in the Kholodniy Rodnik settlement near Stavropol was named after Putin to protect it from being cut down after a decision by the local authorities. The local population went to the lengths of attaching posters with Putin's portrait to tree trunks but could obviously not cover them all. The lumberjacks did not dare to cut down trees that bore Putin's image, so those trees were spared from the chainsaws, whereas trees that were not so adorned were cut down. Moreover, lo and behold, a few days later a decision was taken by the local authorities to save the remaining trees of the newly named Putin Forest from destruction.

No item seems too mundane for Putin to underline that he stands on the side of his rank-and-file citizens against the local or regional authorities. His 2019 annual address to the Federal Assembly provided new examples, such as the pension reform, the unpopularity of which he acknowledged and seemed to blame on his underlings, and also the problem of garbage treatment and overuse of landfills, which had become increasingly acute during the past few years:

> *I am also interested to know how you issued permits for the construction of residential neighbourhoods next to these dumps and landfills. Didn't you think of that? You should have. I urge the representatives of the authorities at all levels: pretending that nothing is happening, turning away, brushing aside people's needs is absolutely unacceptable. These issues are difficult, of course, but difficult issues must also be addressed* (President of Russia, 20 February 2019).

The good ruler seemed shocked to hear about the grievances of his suffering people. Putin's tacit claim that up to this point he had known nothing about the shortcomings in garbage collection was noteworthy. The president has been synonymous with the political establishment for 20 years or more but still pledges to have been unaware of this widespread problem. The issue of malfunctioning and dislocated landfills and dumps has been prominent on Russia's environmental agenda for several years and has repeatedly prompted policy action on the part of the president himself. Not least, it was given a top position on the agenda for the Year of the Environment declared for 2017 (Martus 2021). The argument that the incumbent president had known nothing about the problem may therefore not have much credibility to it. Even so, it connects to the old tradition of the benevolent tsar speaking to his people, giving them hope that he will try to put things right, now that he finally knows about the situation.

In a paradigmatic example set in December 2020, when the coronavirus was raging in Russia, Putin seemed to opt for a diversionary maneuver that would permit him to show that he was now, as always, on the same side as his people who were suffering under the pandemic. He chose one of the areas closest to the average citizen, namely, the rapidly rising food prices (Blackburn and Petersson 2021). To do this he went against his own government, which he accused of doing nothing, and he commanded them to act within a week. Whereas average net incomes had decreased by about four percent, retail prices of sugar had for example risen by more than 71 percent. Railing against government inaction and the growing profits of the middlemen, he expressed himself indignantly to show with whom he sided:

People impose restrictions on themselves because they have no money even for basic food. Where, where are you looking? This is the question! This is not a joke (RIA Novosti 2020).

In a sunshine story unfolding at a public meeting towards the end of 2020, the contemporary and compassionate tsar again showed how much he cared for even the smallest of his subjects. A participant of the meeting conveyed the wish of a 97-year-old lady who wanted nothing more than to talk to her president. The woman who conveyed the greeting had no telephone number to the lady, only her name, family name and patronymic, as well as her area of residence, which was in the Stavropol region. In what was certainly a stark demonstration of power, Putin immediately tasked the director of the federal security service or the minister of internal affairs with finding the elderly woman's contact data, saying that "I believe that our colleagues are listening". Towards the close of the meeting, the president had received the necessary information together with the old woman's biography, so he called her up, chatted with her, and congratulated her on the outstanding contribution that she as a nurse had rendered to Russia during her active working life (President of Russia, 10 December 2020). The woman was presumably made happy, the president had managed to pose successfully as the good and benevolent tsar, and an image of harmony was projected to the audience. However, the world outside was stricken by a pandemic, the country was unruly and the image of harmony was deeply flawed.

VI

Challenge from Without

The corona crisis: devolving power

In 2020 it turned out that there were limits even to what the good tsar could deliver to his people. The handling of the corona crisis from the spring onwards did little to enhance Putin's overall legitimacy. Besides the direct political action taken or not taken to combat the virus itself, the oil-and-gas-export dependent Russian economy suffered from the prolonged crisis and its global reverberations, testing the limits of Putin's reputation as a man who almost guarantees a certain level of national affluence. In fact, it has been suggested that the year of 2020 may have amounted to "an annus horribilis for Russia, and perhaps Putin's most challenging year to date" (Hodge 2020).

In his initial statements on the corona issue during the spring of 2020 Putin downplayed the significance of the virus and the threats that it held to Russia and its people. He was too quick to state that Russia had been successful in slowing the spread of the virus. By international comparison, there was nothing remarkable in this since many other leading politicians in authoritarian as well as democratic countries took the same initial and flawed stance. Even so, according to some analysts, the Russian government was "woefully underprepared in March of 2020" (Sokhey 2020). After a substantial period of prevarication, Putin some weeks later started to take the floor more regularly to address the issue (Åslund 2020). His most tangible action was when he in early April 2020 declared the whole of that month to be a period of non-working days to keep people at home and off the streets. The period was later extended to cover the national holidays in early May up to the date of May 11. In all fairness, Putin was certainly not the only world leader to waver and vacillate in the face of the advance of the virus, but it was contrary to his image as a man of hard resolve to do so.

Early on Putin issued an executive order conferring additional powers on the regional heads to undertake any preventive action they deemed necessary to combat the virus. This was a strategy of outsourcing responsibility (Duleba 2020). It was ironic that Putin since his early days as president had been a champion of the strengthening of the vertical of power, but now when Russia was hit by an acute global crisis, this forceful tool was hardly used at all. Instead, policy was decentralized to the regions in an "incoherent fashion" (Åslund 2020). This open dodging of responsibility was uncharacteristic of Putin. It was almost as if his lacking visibility harked back to the disastrous handling of the Kursk catastrophe in his very first year as a young president, where he learnt some hard lessons about the dos and don'ts of crisis management. In any case, it appeared to be risky to transfer the bulk of decisive action to the governors, even if it offered the opportunity to shift the blame for shortcomings to the regional heads. Many governors were more accustomed to receiving orders and implementing them than to coming up with initiatives of their own (Blackburn and Petersson 2021, Åslund 2020).

Entering center stage — and exiting again

In practical terms, Putin delegated the day-to-day handling of the crisis to the Moscow mayor Sergey Sobyanin and the regional governors, coordinated by the new prime minister, Mikhail Mishustin. When the latter in April 2020 tested positive for the coronavirus and headed into self-isolation and care, the graveness of the threat to Russia was underlined (Rainsford 2020a). Other highly profiled politicians in the Russian Federation similarly fell ill with the virus, including the Chechen hard-core regional strongman, Ramzan Kadyrov (Hutcheson and Petersson 2021).

The fact that Putin devolved executive responsibility to the regional level of state power also meant that he gave up some space at the political center stage, which meant that regional actors could grow into prominence. It was above all Sergey Sobyanin who tried to use the opportunity. Even if Mishustin headed and co-ordinated the government's task force on the handling of the coronavirus,

Sobyanin played from the beginning a very important role and was also appointed head of a working group on corona in the president's State Council. This led to some strain in relations to Mishustin, who as a newly appointed prime minister found himself eclipsed by the more experienced Sobyanin. Apparently, Sobyanin wanted to model the capital's coronavirus lockdown on the tough measures rolled out in China and Singapore, closing the subway, deploying troops, and declaring a curfew, but in all this the president ultimately overran him (Meduza 2020). Most importantly, Putin went against Sobyanin in his wishes to enforce a lengthier lockdown. The president pushed through a quick opening of the economy ahead of the July 2020 plebiscite vote on the constitution (FSU Brief 2020a).

There was another weighty reason why the president wished to avoid a lengthy lockdown of the capital. 2020 was to be the year of the Victory Parade on Red Square, marking the 75th anniversary of Russia's victory over Nazi Germany in the Great Patriotic War. In mid-April Putin had declared that the parade, scheduled for May 9, must be postponed. Putin testified that this had been a difficult decision to take. He explained, however, that the "risks associated with the epidemic, whose peak has not passed yet, are extremely high", and "this does not give me the right to begin preparations for the parade and other mass events now" (BBC News 2020a).

Given the centrality of the memory of the Great Patriotic War for Russian national identity (Davis 2018, Petersson 2018a, Malinova 2017, Tumarkin 2003), the parade could be considered a sacred component of the Russian national imaginary, and therefore it was a unique undertaking to postpone it. When the parade was finally held on June 24, the date of which was hardly coincidental as it marked the 75th anniversary of Stalin's Victory Parade in 1945, Putin said that the victory in the Great Patriotic War was "a triumph of unprecedented scale, the triumph of good over evil, of peace over war, and life over death" (President of Russia, 24 June 2020). The memory of the War and of Russia's ultimate victory after immense suffering and hardships contains the mythological stuff of which legitimizing strategies are made. Such trump cards were not to be discarded lightly, particularly not by the incumbent president, who regarded himself as the custodian of tradition. The parade was a risky undertaking, given the continued magnitude of the corona pandemic. Over 14 000 people participated, not counting the spectators (BBC News 2020b).

All this apparently went against Sobyanin's wishes. He had quickly realized the public health disaster looming and wanted correspondingly strong measures to combat the virus. Some actions that were taken in Moscow cost small and medium-sized enterprises dearly, as the mayor's efforts prioritized saving lives over saving businesses. Meanwhile, certain measures were not very effective, reportedly due to miscommunication inside Sobyanin's team. One such was the issuing of digital passes required for using the city's public transportation system which led to overcrowded entry points to the subway as the passes were scanned and checked (Pertsev et al 2020). Such missteps along the way seem to have hurt Sobyanin's public image. A nation-wide Levada poll indicated in the early fall of 2020 that his ratings had receded somewhat during the year (Levada Center 2020c).

Even so, Putin was reportedly unenthusiastic about Sobyanin's rise to celebrity status during the spring, when many regional heads followed his lead in the combat against the virus. This center stage position could potentially have meant a springboard to the position of emerging as Putin's successor, and it is very likely that the incumbent president wanted to have a say in the matter. The bad vibrations seemed to have been felt by Sobyanin, who toned down his public profile and fell into line (Pertsev et al 2020).

At a publicly reported meeting with Putin in the early fall of 2020, Sobyanin appeared to be aware of the risks. The bilateral talks were largely about the actions that the Moscow city authorities had taken to combat the pandemic. In describing the measures, the mayor took pains to attribute as much of the credit as possible to the president, be it due to compensatory support packages, instructions, or general inspiration. The polite nods to the president were so many as to be servile. The reader might naturally suspect that they had been included to placate an incumbent who might otherwise have sensed upcoming rivalry and could turn against his underling. The list of such references by Sobyanin was long, and when reading the excerpts from the conversation between the mayor and the president one could not help getting the impression of an anxious jester trying to please his king at a court somewhere and some time during the Renaissance:

> *... all the decisions that we took were coordinated with you.../ you helped to transfer.../Following your instructions...../...you were absolutely right when you set us a fairly serious job at controlling the situation.../We received instructions from you and the Healthcare Ministry.../ You are absolutely right.../...the measures taken by the Government pursuant to your instructions.../Your instructions to introduce mortgage concessions [produced a positive result]* (President of Russia, 14 September 2020, quoted in Blackburn and Petersson 2021).

The images on the website accompanying the official report of the meeting were telling. Three images were on display in the posting about the bilateral talks. Two of the images were snapshots of Putin only, and the third one showed Putin sitting by his desk facing a huge TV screen during the digital corona-style meeting. To the far right one could glimpse Sobyanin on the screen but only from a perspective that made him look flat, one-dimensional, and highly marginalized. There was clearly no room for anyone else but the president on center stage (President of Russia, 14 September 2020).

While it was uncharacteristic of the president to leave a vacuum concerning who was exercising executive power during the corona crisis, this still suggests a familiar pattern in Putin's legitimation game. Always wishing to appear as the man of action who ultimately guarantees that things will be done, he lets regional front men take the hit if they go wrong. Entering a rostrum before an audience of ministers and regional governors in early May 2020 to address the struggle against the coronavirus, he expressed himself in terms that must have been received by some as ominous:

> *Any negligence or haste can lead to a breakdown or a backlash. The cost of even a minor mistake is the safety, life and health of our people. This is why our colleagues from the Government and the regional governors bear extremely high responsibility for each adopted decision. We can never forget this* (President of Russia, 6 May 2020).

The president continued to hammer in this message throughout the year of 2020. At a meeting of government members in November he was again very clear that the executive responsibility and onus were on the regional governors:

> Colleagues, you have received broad powers for implementing anti-pandemic measures. And nobody has relieved you of personal responsibility for the adopted measures– I really do hope that they were adopted on time – or, unfortunately, the non-adopted ones in some cases (President of Russia, 18 November 2020).

The threatening messages to the regional heads were repeated many times over. Putin warned them of "rosy reports and attempts to hush up the truth" and asserted that it was their task to "promptly and consistently resolve the emerging problems on a daily basis, and I would say, even hourly basis", which was a tall order. "If there are setbacks, please respond immediately and remedy the situation without any further delay", he commanded. If the federal funds allocated for the purpose of combating the virus were not used promptly, this was "absolutely inexcusable" (President of Russia, 18 November 2020). The good tsar was talking tough to his misbehaving boyars.

The Sputnik V vaccine

Putin's disengaged approach to the issues broached by the pandemic was further suggested at a meeting with Sobyanin in September 2020, when he referred to the corona infection as an "issue that everyone is tired of hearing about but which we must discuss" (President of Russia, 4 September 2020). There was, however, one aspect of the combat against the pandemic that seemed to engage Putin more than others. This was the matter of the vaccine, which, hopefully and ultimately, would end the iron grip of the virus. In several public appearances, Putin mentioned that Russia was at the forefront of developing a vaccine. In a meeting with government ministers in mid-August 2020, the minister of healthcare, Mikhail Murashko, reported that the Russian Gamaleya Centre had, as the first research institute in the world, managed to develop a vaccine. Putin thanked the minister for his report and tried to make sure that no-one had missed the information that the Russian research team was the first one globally to develop a vaccine. The minister confirmed this, whereby Putin again, apparently content, repeated the information: "Which means we have the first registration" (President of Russia, 11 August 2020). He again referred to this fact during the United Nations General Assembly in September (President of Russia, 22 September 2020) and the G20 summit meeting in November (President of Russia, 21 November 2020).

There was great national prestige involved in the worldwide scramble for being the first to develop a corona vaccine (Yatsyk 2021). The Russian project had taken several shortcuts, and so reduced the number of human tests involved, down from the customary quantity of a couple of thousand to less than a hundred, including one of Putin's daughters and Mayor Sobyanin (President of Russia, 14 September 2020). Unruffled by the limited number of human test persons and its possible implications regarding effectiveness and side effects, the Russian authorities named the vaccine "Sputnik V", signaling that the project had the same importance for Russian national identity and global prestige as the Soviet space program once had during the Cold War. In those days of glory, the Soviet Union had beaten the United States to being the first nation to put a man in orbit in space. Now, in an equally stiff and prestigious international competition, history had repeated itself. Russia was first again. There was no absence of criticism from abroad, however: "I would hope that other countries are not drawn into such 'pork barrel' vaccine nationalism . . . The less that vaccine development looks like this, the better", one medical researcher opined (Mahase 2020). However, the global race was on, and Russia was an eager participant.

In addition to the Sputnik V vaccine, Putin revealed, there was another project going on in Russia, a vaccine developed by the Vektor Institute in Novosibirsk, expected to be fully ready for use by the early fall of 2020 (President of Russia, 27 August 2020). In October he announced that this second vaccine, EpiVacCorona, had been registered by the authorities (Medical Xpress 2020). At the G20 meeting in November, he declared that a third Russian-developed vaccine, the CoviVac, was also coming up (President of Russia, 21 November 2020).

As the US pharma giant Pfizer and the German firm Biontech in early November announced that their vaccine had proven to be 90 percent effective during the third and final round of trials, the Russian Gamaleya Institute rose to the challenge. In the week after, its representatives declared that during their third round of trials, which had now been carried out and comprised 16 000 volunteers, the Sputnik V had proven to be more than 92 percent effective (Radio Free Europe/Radio Liberty 2020). The bidding was on also in other countries. Only a couple of days later the US-based pharmaceutical company Moderna claimed that its vaccine was 94 percent effective. Outgoing US president Trump was quick to credit the successes of Pfizer and Moderna to his administration's Operation Warp Speed. Not many weeks elapsed before there was a second bulletin from Gamaleya, claiming that a second round of large-scale trials had surpassed the first one and reached the conclusion that Sputnik V was 95 percent effective (Medical Xpress 2020). Putin himself asserted that according to his information, the first two Russian vaccines were approaching 96 or 97 percent effectivity, and no serious side effects whatsoever had been reported about them (President of Russia, 17 December 2020). No other vaccines offered an equally high degree of protection, he vouched (President of Russia, 22 March 2021).

Even if trials of the Sputnik V vaccine had been made in other countries, at least the Kremlin press spokesman Dimitriy Peskov was very clear about which nation was to enjoy the benefits of the vaccine first: "The absolute priority are Russians... Production within Russia, which is already being developed, will meet the needs of Russians" (Al Jazeera 2020). Putin took up the same theme during the News Conference: "Our task is to carry out vaccination inside the Russian Federation", he said (President of Russia, 17 December 2020). With time, however, the export dimension seemed to acquire increasingly greater importance.

Despite considerable skepticism abroad against the Sputnik V vaccine when it was first registered for use in the late summer of

2020, the tables turned rather quickly, and the vaccine was with increasing eagerness embraced by a surrounding world in dire need of a panacea. The vaccine was labelled "Russia's biggest scientific breakthrough since the Soviet era" (Bloomberg and Meyer 2021, Gulina 2021). Putin reported in March 2021 that 55 countries had authorized its use (President of Russia, 22 March 2021), and in his annual address to the Federal Assembly later in the spring he said that it reflected Russia's "growing science and technological potential" (President of Russia, 21 April 2021). The supply shortages encountered in many countries waiting for deliveries of the Pfizer, Moderna and AstraZeneca vaccines made the Sputnik V attractive, especially since peer reviews in the authoritative medicine journal The Lancet confirmed its effectiveness to be on a par with its Western competitors. While being more expensive than the AstraZeneca vaccine, it had proven to be more effective. Sputnik V was not only an increasingly important export commodity. It was also an emerging tool of Russian soft power and a pawn in the game of geopolitics (Gulina 2021). The Kremlin clearly seemed to hope that the Sputnik V vaccine would both pay dividends abroad and improve its reputation at home (Gel'man 2021).

Towards the end of 2020, Russian authorities embarked on a sales pitch. Apart from securing markets in the countries of the former Soviet Union, Latin America and Africa, Russia endeavored to have Sputnik V accepted for use also in the European Union. Efforts were made to negotiate the co-production of the Russian vaccine together with AstraZeneca, and a medicine factory in Italy was to be used as a production facility for the vaccine in Europe. One EU member, Hungary, purchased the Russian vaccine ahead of formal EU approval. Similarly, during the early months of 2021, in view of the devastating spread of the virus in the country, the Czech Republic expressed interest in acquiring the vaccine. In March, the German state of Bavaria struck a deal to purchase 2.5 million doses of Sputnik V.

The phenomenon of vaccine nationalism was rather amusingly illustrated in February 2021 during the unofficial meeting between Putin and his Belarusian colleague Aleksandr Lukashenko in a wintry Sochi. The Russian presidential website showed images of the two casually dressed men standing closely and shaking each other's hands so firmly that it seemed as if the coronavirus and recommendations of social distancing had never existed. During the exchange of initial niceties, the two presidents came to touch upon the mutually beneficial cooperation between the two countries on combatting the virus. Lukashenko had in 2020 gained notoriety for arguing that the Belarusian public would be able to keep the virus at bay by relying on the prophylactic use of vodka, sauna, and tractor-driving, but now he had come round to seeing the pandemic as a threat of common concern. The Belarusian president thankfully acknowledged the support that Belarus had received from its great neighbor, not least through the deliveries of the Sputnik vaccine. As the conversation unfolded it was almost painfully clear how Lukashenko enacted the role of a servile yes-man, studiously praising his host and the great nation that he represented:

Vladimir Putin: (…) As to our joint efforts on fighting the coronavirus, this is progressing successfully. We delivered the first batch last year, and the next deliveries are due in February and March. But most importantly, in my view, is that we are launching it at your company…

Alexander Lukashenko: We began production with your technology in March.

Vladimir Putin: Absolutely correct. What is important is that the technology has been transferred. So far, we have not closely cooperated this much with anyone…

Alexander Lukashenko: It is substantial support. Without it, we would have had trouble with vaccination. We have already vaccinated almost all doctors, and now we are vaccinating teachers and retail workers – those who have the most contact with people. This is why it is such substantial support.

Vladimir Putin: And the overall result is, to put it modestly, satisfactory. According to an objective indicator, we recently had 12 new cases a day per 100,000 people whereas now the number is smaller, I believe, around 10.

Alexander Lukashenko: The Russian vaccine is the most efficient one; it is acknowledged throughout the world. It is the most efficient vaccine, no matter how they troll and dig at it.

Vladimir Putin: This is true.

Alexander Lukashenko: Two or three people of every hundred of those vaccinated can experience a mild illness. We had one person, I will not mention his name, who fell ill after being vaccinated with the Russian vaccine. He was sick for a day and a half altogether.

Vladimir Putin: *Right.*

Alexander Lukashenko: *There was just one case.*

Vladimir Putin: *It comes as a mild infection. But I meant to say that we have about 10 new daily cases per 100,000…*

Alexander Lukashenko: *That is very little.*

Vladimir Putin: *Whereas in the south of France there are over 70 cases per 100,000 people. This is a disturbing number.*

Alexander Lukashenko: *Of course.*

Vladimir Putin: *You see, this is objective data, which says that we should join efforts with our European colleagues, among others. We are trying to do that; we are open to cooperation. Our Gamaleya Centre has a contract with AstraZeneca. I am pleased to note that we will be joining efforts with our European partners as well, we will be working together. And with Belarus – that goes without saying. Let me repeat, the technology has already been transferred, and according to the reports I receive, production is being rolled out.*

Alexander Lukashenko: *You promised that Belarus would be the first country, and you did this.*

Vladimir Putin: *And it happened like that.*

Alexander Lukashenko: *Thank you for this.*
(President of Russia, 22 February 2021).

In this revealing conversation Putin achieved several things. Through his faithful but beleaguered henchman he argued that the Russian vaccine is the most efficient in the world. He also said that Russia had largely overcome the desolation of the pandemic and was doing much better than leading Western powers such as France. He reminded his Belarusian colleague of the dependent situation of his nation in relation to Russia. During the recorded part of the conversation no mention was made of the social unrest characterizing developments in Belarus during the second half of 2020, not to speak of the demonstrations in Russia in support of the imprisoned Aleksey Navalny in early 2021. This was also part of the message. There was an evident intention to signal the sustaining of status quo in the civil arena and the stabilization of the situation on the corona front. The images of the two men, unmasked, clasping their hands in the wintry sunshine, and with confident smiles on their faces, served to underline this. A critical-minded outside observer might however have concluded that the message was slightly overdone and be rather prone to suspect that the idyllic surface maybe served to hide something from public view.

In the beginning of December 2020 mass vaccinations with Sputnik V started in Russia, with two million doses being distributed to the prioritized categories of doctors and teachers. During a televised government meeting Putin instructed the minister responsible to start the vaccinations during the week after: "Let's agree on this—you will not report to me next week, but you will start mass vaccination … let's get to work already", he said, again playing the role of the tsar-deliverer (President of Russia, 2 December 2020). There certainly was more than one element of vaccine nationalism in the scramble for being the first nation to start vaccinating on a massive scale. During the first week of December Russia managed to be the very first, beating the United Kingdom to it by a couple of days, the United States by more than a week, and China by roughly the same amount of time.

Despite the authorities' enthusiasm over the vaccine, the Russian public was hard to sway. A series of surveys conducted by Levada showed that remarkably few were willing to take the vaccine. In March 2021, 62 percent of the respondents declared themselves unwilling to do so, and 64 percent believed that the virus had been manufactured artificially as a new kind of biological weapon. The most prominent reasons for not wishing to take the vaccine were fear of side effects, coupled with the belief that the vaccine had not been sufficiently tested (Levada Center 2021b).

It also did not seem to help much that Putin himself was wavering for a long time before he took the shot, and when he did in late March 2021, he did so off camera and without the expected media fanfare. Seldom missing a good photo opportunity, this modesty was not anticipated, especially since other world leaders, including US president Joe Biden, had taken the jab with considerable publicity. Putin also refrained from revealing which of the three

Russian vaccines he had been taking, ostensibly to underline that all of them were of equally high quality (Roth 2021a), but inevitably breeding speculation that he may even have taken a foreign vaccine. Coupled with the Russian public's lacking enthusiasm for taking the vaccine, the president's wavering about the matter would seem to have taken some of the steam out of the Sputnik V global sales pitch campaign.

Faring better than the West?

In August 2020, Putin answered questions on the pandemic on an evening program shown by the TV channel Rossiya. He held that Russia had fared better than most comparable countries during the pandemic and had among the lowest mortality rates in the world. Reaching out to the past and the feats that Russia had been capable of performing in difficult times and circumstances, Putin saw a pattern of heroic stamina, which the current ordeal confirmed:

> In general, it is a tradition of all people in Russia, including Russians and other ethnic groups, to marshal their resources at the time of trouble. This is what happened this time as well (President of Russia, 27 August 2020, also 17 December 2020).

The president opined that Russia had proven its superiority compared to other countries, and he hinted that the lifestyles and the political systems of Western countries were to blame for the new outbreaks. He implied that they would have some things to learn from Russia's handling of the crisis. Putin used the pandemic as an illustration of Russia's moral lead on the West, which purportedly was suffering much more badly from the disease (President of Russia, 22 October 2020, 17 December 2020, 21 April 2021). Connecting the pandemic to the wider picture and to the metanarrative of Russia's superiority to the degenerated and individualized societies in the West, Russia was better at weathering the storm, Putin suggested. Russia's people excelled at exercising discipline and not letting the desires of individuals get the better of the common good. Russia was leading the way and had again showed itself capable of doing so on a global scale (President of Russia, 27 August 2020).

This was a theme that Putin returned to many times, not least in his annual address to the Federal Assembly in 2021 (President of Russia, 21 April 2021).

In October 2020, Russia was hit by the second wave of the pandemic (President of Russia, 28 October 2020). At a meeting with the Speaker of the Duma, Vyacheslav Volodin, Putin was informed that out of the 450 Duma deputies, 91 had contracted the virus, 38 were hospitalized and one had died from the infection. There was one conspicuous image accompanying the posting. The two politicians had a physical meeting, facing each other across a desk no more than a meter wide. Neither of them was wearing a face mask, which sent the strange signal that Putin did not take the recommendations to use one very seriously (President of Russia, 26 October 2020). Nor did Putin ever seem willing to wear a face mask in public. However, his administration apparently took no chances in shielding him from the contagion. This included the installation of a special "disinfectant tunnel" for visitors to his residence outside of Moscow and in the Kremlin itself (Hodge 2020). Aleksey Navalny mercilessly alluded to the protective measures as he referred to Putin as "the old man in the bunker".

At a meeting with government members in late October 2020 the tone was grim. Between 90 and 95 percent of all available hospital beds were reportedly taken either by covid-19 or other patients (President of Russia, 28 October 2020). At another meeting with government members in November 2020, Putin conceded that the situation was "far from simple". On the one hand, he asserted that it was "certainly not easy but under control", but on the other, he referred to severe shortages of medication, equipment, and supply of medical services (President of Russia, 18 November 2020). Using a typically Russian bureaucratic euphemism, he conceded during the News Conference in December 2020 that "not everything has been resolved" (President of Russia, 17 December 2020). The statistical agency Rosstat reported a death toll for December 2020 amounting to more than 44 000, which made it the worst month since the pandemic started (Meduza 2021).

In January 2021, Putin asserted that the situation was stabilizing in the country and conceded that "we should thank the Moscow authorities for this", thereby granting some belated recognition to Sobyanin, and diverting from the pattern of casting blame on others while reserving the praise for himself (President of Russia, 25 January 2021).

Skewing the statistics

Already in early June 2020, Putin had announced that the spread of the virus had reached a plateau in Russia and that the struggle against it had been successful. Official figures supported this at the time. However, persistent rumors told a different story and claimed that the official figures were cooked. Contending statistics showed that in the first half of 2020, Russia had lost more than 265 000 people from all causes, which was about as many as during the whole of 2019. The mortality figure was so high that it had to be related to unreported covid-19 deaths (Baev 2020). Critical reports claimed that by April 2020 the capital of Moscow had a death rate about 20 percent higher than the 10-year average for a whole year (Hodge 2020).

In the very last days of 2020 the Moscow Times reported that Russian officials had admitted that the death toll from the pandemic was gravely underreported. The Russian statistical agency Rosstat concluded that during the period between January and November 2020 the number of deaths from all causes recorded had risen by 229 700 compared with the previous year. A Russian deputy prime minister estimated that more than 81 percent of the increase in mortality had been due to covid-19 (Moscow Times 2020). If correct, the official figure related to the pandemic should be increased more than threefold (The Guardian 2020). In February 2021, Rosstat largely confirmed the assessment. The agency's figures showed 162 429 "coronavirus related fatalities" occurring in Russia in 2020, which was almost three times higher than the Russian health ministry's official figure for 2020 of 57 019 (BMJ 2021). The adverse effects of such misreporting on the legitimacy of the Putin regime could be monumental.

In his address to the Federal Assembly in the spring of 2021, which despite the raging pandemic was delivered to a hall crammed with representatives of the country's federal and regional elites, Putin conceded that the average life expectancy in Russia had decreased due to covid-19 (President of Russia, 21 April 2021). This was doubtless a setback for the country as well as for his administration.

The pandemic and the image

For Putin's general image, there was another potential side effect of the corona crisis, which was hard to assess amid the pandemic challenge, but which might nevertheless turn out to be important. Throughout his presidencies, Putin has been eager to emerge as hyperenergetic and omnipresent, always on the move, inspecting, meeting admirers, briskly power walking in the lead of delegations, riding bare-chested on horseback, practicing judo, scoring eight goals in a single hockey game, escorting endangered cranes to their natural habitat, shaking hands with prominent world leaders. The presidential website has displayed ample evidence of this. During the pandemic, the image of the president mediated through the kremlin.ru website changed abruptly, however.

The typical photo illustrations now showed the president barricaded behind his desk, facing a huge screen, and participating in a seemingly endless row of virtual meetings. Pictures of Putin wearing a face mask were painstakingly avoided, but the image was still conveyed of a leader who had become less active and less energetic, older, and possibly weaker. Since this impression corroborated the epithet of the old man in the bunker that Navalny tried to pin on him, the image change may in the long run add negative effects to his popular standing (Blackburn and Petersson 2021). Footage such as the one from the spring of 2021, showing Putin and defense minister Shoygu trekking and driving through the taiga was probably released to balance this impression, but as mentioned above the imagery failed to convince, since Putin moved in a way that certainly did not signal youthfulness, vigor, and boundless energy.

VII

The Succession Issue

Looking to the East?

Russia has a long tradition of rulers who have nurtured cults of personality around them. Within such cults there is not much space for discussing principles of succession, and this is maybe also where part of the problem lies today. Even if Putin's Russia is far from subjected to the kind of personality cult that characterized Stalin's Soviet Union, Kim Il Sung's North Korea or Saparmurad Niyazov's Turkmenistan, there have since the latter half of the 2000s been ample signs of Putin developing a personality cult, albeit modest, around him (Sperling 2014, Goscilo 2013, White and McAllister 2008). While this is not the kind of cult that is characterized by semi-religious devotion or unconditional submission instilled by massive fear, Putin is the only person allowed on center stage and no one else is let into the limelight. Even if social media have used and referred to these manifestations with a good measure of irony and satire, central aspects of the emerging cult have long appeared to be taken seriously by considerable segments of the population (White and MacAllister 2008).

Outside the historic experience of royal dynasties where power was inherited, there has been no Russian tradition of securing orderly processes of political succession. Perhaps therefore inspiration for finding solutions to the dilemma need to be sought outside the borders of Russia. Dukalskis (2017) and Cheng (2016) endeavor to explain the solid grip on power by the Chinese Communist Party regime after the end of the Cold War. They find that from the late 1990s and well into the 2010s the political elite cherished a leadership culture where no individuals stood out as unique. This made successions easier to handle. Openly manifested regime splits could be avoided, and an image of unity could be projected to the people. In March 2018 this changed after the decision of the Chinese National People's Congress to make it possible for the incumbent Xi Jinping to serve as president for an unlimited period (Helms 2020). Nevertheless, for twenty years or more, the relatively faceless and collective leadership style in China facilitated transitions from one political leader to another. As a matter of fact, Putin's constitutional reform activities in 2020 provide evidence in the direction charted out by Xi two years before. Russia is therefore not heading for a collective leadership like China before Xi; it is rather going for a prolonged incumbency of an aging president who seems to be intent on tightening his grip on power rather than loosening it.

Guarantor of the constitution?

For reasons provided by the political turbulence of the 1990s there is no vice presidency in the Russian political system. The Russian authorities had the chance to change this in the spring of 2020, when the package of constitutional amendments was suggested to the Federal Assembly and the people, chiefly to secure extra tenure time for the incumbent. However, at the time there was no suggestion about reintroducing the formal position of vice president. Even if some scholars would argue that a vice-presidency is not necessarily a natural springboard to the presidency (Helms 2020), the opposing viewpoint has also been made (Meng 2021). Nevertheless, it can rightly be assumed that the position could have been instrumental in securing smooth transitions in the short-term perspective. With the absence of a vice presidency, there is no natural position for grooming a political heir who is destined to take over in the future but for the time put in the situation of having to watch and learn.

Instead of there being a formal position of vice president, there is a provision in the Russian constitution that if the president resigns or dies, the prime minister becomes acting president. Presidential elections are then to take place within three months. This means that the prime minister will be put in pole position in the ensuing presidential campaign. As of spring 2021, this would mean leaving the prime minister, Mikhail Mishustin, with that advantage. Appointed in January 2020, when the loyal henchman Dimitriy Medvedev was relegated to the wings, Mishustin has yet to build his platform and reputation to prove his status as a serious contender for chief executive power. In case of an unexpected mishap involving the current president, the prime minister would have to work hard to fill his predecessor's shoes. Even so, it should be noted that Mishustin has a respectable standing in the opinion polls. Levada has had him on solid approval figures above 50 percent ever since he took office, which is around 20 units higher than the rating Medvedev had before stepping down in January 2020. He has a positive net approval rate, whereas Medvedev consistently suffered from a negative rate after March 2017 when Navalny's "Don't Call Him Dimon" was released. However, in the spring of 2021 Mishustin's approval rate was sinking which may perhaps indicate that his honeymoon with the electorate had come to an end and that the times of pandemic and social unrest had backfired on him more than they did on the president (Levada Center 2021c).

At the meeting of the Valdai Club in 2016 Putin was asked by a renowned historian at Berkeley, Yuri Slezkine, about his administration's strategies for political succession. The professor underlined that there had never been a mechanism in Russian history for an orderly succession of power. Therefore, he was wondering what was being done in the face of this to facilitate the inevitable future transition to the period after Putin. For his part, the president tried to give an impression of not understanding the question or at least not caring much about it. What followed was the standard answer that it would be up to the Russian people to elect the next leader and work together with the new government that would come into power at that time (President of Russia, 27 October 2016, Petersson 2017). When confronted with similar questions later, regardless of whether they were asked by Western news agencies or loyal followers at home, he repeated the formula. During the four-hour News Conference in 2019, someone asked him about the prospects for a completed State Union with Belarus and to what extent the construction of a new subject under international law would give him an opportunity to stay on beyond 2024 as the president of a newly formed, amalgamated state (President of Russia, 19 December 2019). The news media had seen several speculations about this at the time (Miller 2019a). Putin ignored this question too, thereby perhaps indicating to suspicious minds that there was substance to the rumors.

On another occasion, Putin displayed a certain sense of rugged humor when the subject was broached. In an interview with British journalists on the eve of Boris Johnson's elevation to the prime minister's office in 2019 after the change of leadership in the Tory party, he retorted that Russia was a democracy, which in contrast to the United Kingdom, was in the habit of letting the people elect its leaders (Financial Times 2019, President of Russia, 27 June 2019).

Several times, when the question of succession came up, Putin answered that the thoughts about how and when to identify a political heir apparent had been on his mind ever since he first assumed presidential office in 2000 (President of Russia, 10 March 2018, 27 June 2019). He even claimed never to stop thinking about the matter (President of Russia, 7 June 2018), but did not reveal any details concerning in what direction his deliberations had taken him. On one occasion, he answered ambiguously that when looking around the world one could see several political leaders who were older than him (Financial Times 2019). With hindsight, this was an early indication of his intention to prolong his occupancy of the president's chair beyond the formal close of his fourth mandate in 2024.

The year of 2019 was full of rumors regarding the succession issue. On the one hand, there were signs that persons within the Putin circle started to claim space and make statements indicating that they might be available for the highest office, should the people so wish, and the opportunity arise. The minister of defense, Sergey Shoygu, made veiled declarations in such a direction, as did the CEO of the industrial conglomerate Rostekh, Sergey Chemezov (Galeotti 2019b). On the other hand, several of Putin's closest collaborators, such as Volodin and the very same Chemezov, sent up trial balloons to the effect that constitutional amendments could be considered to address the succession issue. Among the suggested amendments were measures to allow an incumbent president to serve for more than two consecutive periods or redressing the balance of power between the executive and the legislature. The latter should be done in favor of the cabinet, presumably to prepare for a future move to the prime minister position by Putin after the expiration of his current presidential mandate in 2024 (Eckel 2019).

In a frank interview with an Austrian journalist in the summer of 2018, Putin was asked whether he would be willing to follow the Xi Jinping formula and have a limitless extension of his mandate. The interviewer asked him directly whether there was anything behind the speculation that he might arrange a referendum on such an extension for life. Putin retorted that it was beneath the dignity of the president of the Russian Federation to comment on speculations, but repeated, just like many times before, that he had never violated the constitution and implied that he did not have any intention of doing so in the future either (President of Russia, 4 June 2018). He repeated the promise many times over during his third and fourth terms in office (President of Russia, 24 November 2014, 29 September 2015, 1 September 2016, 21 July 2017, 1 March 2018, 10 March 2018, 4 June 2018). To pick one example out of several, his answer had seemed convincing and sincere when, midway into his third term in office, an American journalist had asked him how long he desired to serve:

> The period of my service will depend on two conditions. Firstly, of course, there are rules stipulated by the Constitution, and I surely will not infringe them. But I am not sure whether I should take full advantage of these constitutional rights. It will depend on the specific situation in the country, in the world and my own feelings about it (President of Russia, 29 September 2015).

Two years after this event, he expressed himself even more clearly at a meeting with a student organization in Sochi. His words could hardly be misread or misunderstood and the pledge to be true to the constitution was crystal clear, as he answered a question from a young student, who wished to know if Putin ever desired to be relieved of the burden of the presidency:

> *[T]here is nothing special that I would like to do if I relieved myself of this burden, as you said. But still, I will have to do it some day as there are term limits for the President, which are set by the Constitution (…) You are all young people, but you probably know, should know, that I had a possibility, and they even begged me at the time to amend the Constitution. I refused to do it, nor do I intend to do it in the future. All is written in the Constitution* (President of Russia, 21 July 2017).

There was no ambiguity here; President Vladimir Putin pledged not to change the constitution. In this respect, he had been at least somewhat truthful until the spring of 2020. The agreement about the switching of positions between him and Medvedev before the 2011-2012 elections violated the spirit of the constitution, not its letter. There was admittedly a decision to prolong the period of the presidential terms from four to six years, benefitting Putin from his third presidential term on, but that legislative action was taken during Medvedev's presidential interlude, not during his own incumbency. However, Putin's record of scrupulously observing the constitution was somewhat sullied by his and Medvedev's slips of the tongue as they conceded that the terms of the tandem deal to switch offices had been agreed long ago (Stent 2019, Koesel and Bunce 2012). This made them both look like tricksters.

Considering Putin's repeated assertions, any tinkering with the constitution on his part had for a long time seemed to be out of the question. The author of this book had to rewrite substantial parts of it after Putin's spring surprise in early 2020. At that point in time, there were still no major indications that the Xi Jinping precedent was on Putin's mind. The rational-legal part of his legitimation strategies appeared to weigh heavily in his deliberations. As Sakwa (2014: 3) put it a couple of years into Putin's third presidency, serving the constitution was made into "a key part of his political identity". Loyalty to the constitution was considered one of the most steadfast pillars of his legitimacy as president. The constitution was the epitome of the Russian state and the president was its foremost guardian (Hall 2018, Hill and Gaddy 2015). End of story, at least that was what many were thinking at the time.

Successions in the Russian post-Soviet past

Halfway through Putin's fourth period of incumbency, the unavoidable question arises about how to handle the charismatic authority that has been upholding the political system for so long.
How to sustain this brand of legitimacy in a situation where Putin
chooses to or is forced to leave office abruptly?

Despite some formulations in the first draft of the constitutional amendments of 2020, there are no provisions in the final version that substantially expand the influence of the parliamentary
branch of government. The legislature has been given a somewhat
greater role in government formation, as the formal confirmation of
the State Duma will be required to appoint the president's candidate for prime minister. However, in essence, it is the president's
powers that are enhanced by the amendments, not those of the legislature (Teague 2020). In the final analysis, therefore, no routinization into rational-legal authority is to be expected as a strategy to
convert receding charismatic authority. Moreover, Putin has refrained from elevating any of his two daughters, or any other rela-
tives into a political career (President of Russia, 5 September 2016).
He has in other words made no attempts to routinize charismatic
legitimacy into the traditional type of authority either.

If one goes by Weber's routinization strategies as enumerated
in an earlier chapter, the remaining alternative is to try to transfer
charismatic authority to a handpicked successor. As of spring 2021
there was still no single person in the president's inner circle who
was given enough confidence to be publicly slated as his crown
prince. Post-Soviet Russian history has otherwise seen three attempts at handling the succession problem this way, essentially the
first occasions in Russian history when there has been a voluntary
handover of executive power. The first time was in 1999 and the
second in 2007-2008, both with endeavors to transfer legitimacy
that had been engendered by the preceding Russian president, i.e.
first Yeltsin and then Putin. On the latter occasion, Putin was about
to round up his second presidential tenure—which at the time was
mistakenly believed to be his last. Then there was of course the
third occasion, when Medvedev handed the baton back to Putin in

2011-2012, but that move can hardly be discussed in terms of trans-
ferring legitimacy. Rather, it signified a breach of legitimacy and a
cunning bending of rules.

In 1999 the ailing Boris Yeltsin had to hand over presidential
power, partly for health reasons, and partly since he had already
used up the two consecutive periods of presidential tenure allowed
to him by the 1993 constitution, which was adopted during his first
presidential tenure. He had once enjoyed considerable charismatic
authority, but towards the end of his second presidential term in
office it had waned considerably (Shevtsova 1998). Even so, he was
the first president ever of the Russian Federation, and this fact alone
awarded him legally based legitimacy. The handpicking of his immediate successor, Putin, became the strategy of his choice.

Putin was the successor whom the political system had produced and elevated. Outside the narrow circle of Russia specialists,
he was practically unknown abroad. His biggest initial asset was
that all major political camps could accept him. A corresponding
scenario remains the most likely to appear at the end of Putin's
terms in office, whenever that may be, provided that it takes place
in an orderly fashion and not during an acute crisis. It would seem
most probable that the political system at that time will try to identify a candidate within its own ranks to save and sustain itself.

Before the second presidential transition, in 2008, it seemed for
quite some time as if two favorites of the political establishment, the
then deputy prime minister Dimitriy Medvedev and the former
minister of defense, Sergey Ivanov, would face each other in the
presidential elections. If two visibly equal contenders had run
against each other in the polls, this would have been an interesting
contest. If the run-up to the elections and the polls themselves had
been fair and beyond democratic reproach, the emerging victor
would have been able to wield substantial rational-legal authority
(Hanson 2011). The position of the emergent winner would have
been strong. This was however not the way that it turned out to be.

United Russia, Putin's supporting political party, and the
president's "personal political machine" (Gill 2016: 359) nominated
in December 2007 Medvedev as its candidate, choosing not to en-

dorse Ivanov. Putin was quick to pledge his support for the nominee. Medvedev returned the courtesy by nominating him as his candidate for the prime minister's office. If this was an attempt to routinize Putin's charisma and transfer it to his successor it was not very successful. As has been made clear above, Medvedev did not manage to uphold the presidential magic. Crucially, the arrangement made it possible for Putin to hold on to power by wielding it from the position of prime minister which he had first served as back in 1999. It paved a legal way for him to return to the presidency for a third and fourth term in office, since the formulations of the 1993 constitution left a loophole which did not explicitly rule out the possibility of having more than two periods of presidential tenure in total. The fact that Medvedev obediently left the presidential chair after one single term in office made it possible for Putin to return before reaching a very old age. Medvedev, for his part, lived up to the mocking epithets of being Putin's "servant" (Judah 2013), "receptionist" (Gel'man 2015: XIII) or "placeholder" (Koesel and Bunce 2012: 413).

Even if Putin was re-elected by a broad margin in the presidential elections of 2012, there was as recounted above widespread social discontent with the glib power-sharing deal between him and Medvedev. The legitimation crisis hit, and Putin's popularity ratings did not recover until after the annexation of Crimea. Then his approval ratings skyrocketed, passed the 80-percent threshold, and remained there until the slump following in the wake of the pension reforms in 2018 (Levada Center 2021c, Burrett 2020). Acknowledging all this, one could still argue that it was in 2012, at the time of Putin's return to presidential power, that Russia's crisis of political succession began in earnest (Snyder 2018: 50). It took some time for it to develop and mature, and as of spring 2021 it has still not reached an acute stage, but the day when it will do so is approaching without much mercy.

Post-Soviet precedents

Most certainly, Putin's administration has attentively studied processes of political succession taking place in neighboring countries, not least in the former Soviet republics of the so-called Near Abroad. For scholars looking into principles and policies of political succession in authoritarian and hybrid settings, post-Soviet Central Asia is an interesting field of inquiry. From having been an area with petrified government structures with four out of five heads of state serving since the gaining of independence in 1991, the Central Asian region has seen a series of successions during the first two decades of the 21st century: Turkmenistan in 2006-2007, Uzbekistan in 2016, and Kazakhstan in 2019. In Tajikistan there has been no change of president since the time of the civil war in the mid-1990s, and Kyrgyzstan has seen a row of turbulent power transitions since its Tulip Revolution in 2005. This makes these two countries less interesting to discuss from the perspective of potential precedents for Russia.

During the long rules under the same presidents in Turkmenistan, Uzbekistan, and Kazakhstan, charismatic legitimation was an important component in securing popular consent, most often through supplementation with repressive means. One could also argue that these three Central Asian presidents had served for so long that their rule started to rely on Weberian traditional legitimation. In none of the three cases were there any crown princes groomed in advance. At least nothing to that effect was publicly communicated.

Turkmenistan basically held on to its closed authoritarian political system with a blazing personality cult, and in Uzbekistan and Kazakhstan within-system candidates replaced charismatic strongmen, retaining the authoritarian systemic traits. In Turkmenistan and Uzbekistan, the transitions took place after the death of the incumbent, whereas in Kazakhstan the former president chose to leave center stage voluntarily, while retaining considerable informal influence.

Turkmenistan was an extreme case in all respects of the word. There was an exorbitant personality cult around its longtime leader, the Turkmenbashi (Head of the Turkmen), Saparmurad Niyazov. When he died in 2006 the harshly repressive regime faced the risk of an evolving political vacuum with all its implications of spreading insecurity in society. According to the national constitution, which played some role despite the totalitarian traits of the country, the Speaker of the parliament was to serve as interim president, cushioning the time between the death of the almighty president and the emergence of his successor. The stipulated procedure never took place, however, since the interim presidency was, after a non-transparent process, transferred to the vice president of the ministerial cabinet, Gurbanguly Berdymukhamedov, who had previously held a marginal position in the government. The Speaker was prosecuted and sentenced to five years' imprisonment on presumably trumped-up charges of abuse of power and immoral conduct (Peyrose 2012). In the elections that followed the year after, Berdymukhamedov received a suspiciously solid 97.7 percent of the vote, suggesting that the personality cult had been retained, albeit transferred to another person.

In Turkmenistan, physical intimidation has continued to be used to uphold the regime. The post-Turkmenbashi path would hardly suggest a scenario for Russia post-Putin. In the 21st century, Russia is too vast and too closely linked to social media and the internet to have its borders sealed and its citizens subdued in a manner comparable to what has been taking place in Turkmenistan.

Uzbekistan suggests a different picture. In the fall of 2016, there was the sudden demise of the long-serving and authoritarian president Islam Karimov. Political instability could largely be avoided, even if no clear rules of political succession had been presented in public prior to the incumbent's death. Some parliamentary reform had been instituted in advance with a strengthened role of the legislature. This looked like a proactive strategy to lessen transition problems once Karimov was gone (von Soest and Grauvogel 2016). Even so, there were similarities with Turkmenistan concerning the way that constitutional rules of transition were transgressed or at least bent to adapt to the circumstances. According to the constitution, the Speaker of the senate was to serve as interim president for a period of three months until new elections were held. The Speaker was, however, quick to relinquish his position in favor of the prime minister, Shavkat Mirziyoyev, who could now enter the presidential campaign in pole position as acting president (Blackmon 2020, Horak 2018).

The Speaker seems to have acted proactively not to have his destiny repeat what befell his Turkmen colleague ten years earlier. The constitutionally prescribed order was followed in some sense, even if it was modified. As in the Turkmen case, there was little transparency in the process of identifying the emergent leader (Horak 2018). In late 2016, Mirziyoyev was formally elected president with 89 percent of the vote. He proceeded quickly to consolidate his position and hamper the ambitions of the members of Karimov's family to strengthen theirs. This presumably created a stir among incumbents in nearby authoritarian states who wished to see a more managed succession in their states to safeguard the political future of their allies and kin (Blackmon 2020).

After the elections, the new leader in Uzbekistan undertook some liberalizing reform and, among other things, released political prisoners incarcerated on religious grounds (Human Rights Watch 2018). Economic reform was launched, mainly benefiting the rural population (Blackmon 2020). Despite pledges to reform, corruption and nepotism continue to plague the state apparatus (FSU Brief 2020b). Even so, the first years after the transition suggested that the Mirziyoyev regime was considering relying less on charismatic legitimacy, and for that matter of repression, and instead tried to have charisma routinized into more rational-legal forms of authority. However, routinization of charismatic legitimacy through the strengthening of parliamentary power and liberalizing reform is at least for the time being not the path that the Putin regime has chosen to take.

Kazakhstan may suggest a scenario for a managed succession in Russia. The perennial rulers of both countries have relied on a threefold foundation of legitimation: economic success, vows to honor traditional values, and patrimonialism. The latter term connotes that the incumbents have considered themselves above the law in key respects and therefore not subject to the same legislative restrictions as ordinary citizens. One obvious example would be the glibness with which Putin arranged his return to presidential power in 2012, despite the constitutional limitations (du Boulay 2020). Even more glaring was the fact that Putin, despite all his promises to abide by the constitution, opted for changing it in 2020, making it possible for him to serve for two additional presidencies beyond that which expires in 2024.

Nursultan Nazarbayev, the ruler of Kazakhstan since its gaining of independence in 1991 and the object of an accelerating personality cult (Orange 2019, Orange and Petersson 2017), formally stepped down in a surprise move during the spring of 2019. In doing so, he formally designated his preferred choice as successor, the Speaker of the senate and former prime minister, Kasym-Zhomart Tokayev, as interim president pending the presidential elections to take place some months later.

The move was "eerily reminiscent" of Boris Yeltsin's elevation of Vladimir Putin to the equivalent position in Russia back in 1999 (Blackmon 2020). It was a surprise announcement as Tokayev had not been given that kind of official recognition before. Presidential elections took place in June 2019, widely seen as rigged to produce Tokayev as the winner. The result was the expected one, and Tokayev received more than 70 percent of the vote. The elections were held amidst widespread demonstrations and arrests extensively reported on in social media. This suggested that even if the state had not been willing to quench the civil unrest totally through repressive means, there was still a distance to go before the charismatic legitimacy bestowed on Nazarbayev was transferred to the regime of his designated successor.

There can be little doubt that authoritarian and hybrid regimes study each other's experiences and learn substantial lessons from each other. Kazakhstan had learned from Russia and Yeltsin's promotion of Putin, and it is conceivable that Russia in turn will learn something from Kazakhstan. For its part, the script of an undisputable leader who formally retreated but continued to wield power from backstage was clearly inspired by the strategy used by former Singapore strongman Lee Kuan Yew, who in the early 1990s formally stepped down after more than 30 years at the helm (Gould-Davies 2021). All available evidence shows that Nazarbayev intended to retain a strong and decisive influence from behind the scenes. He was to keep the formal position of chair of the crucial national Security Council, remain leader of the all-dominant political party Nur Otan and continue holding onto the epithet of Elbasy, "the leader of the nation". For his part, from the very beginning To-kayev turned out to be very loyal to his predecessor, practically vowing not to change anything at all (Pannier 2019).

Speculation abounded that the new president was only a transitionary figure. This was especially so as the Elbasy's daughter, Dariga Nazarbayeva, was elevated to the office of Speaker of the senate and thus identified as the person to become interim president should anything befall the new incumbent president (Roth 2019). Had this happened, Kazakhstan would have represented a case of routinization of charisma through a hereditary path. In May 2020, there was a slight change of scenery. Amid the turmoil of the corona pandemic and the general economic downturn in its wake, the new president demoted Nazarbayeva from her post as Speaker. She lost her seat in the senate at the same time, even if she later gained a seat in the lower house of the parliament. While Nazarbayev himself did not seem to be directly affected by his daughter's demotion, Tokayev appeared to strengthen his position, presumably constructing a more independent power base of his own (Putz 2020).

Developments in early 2020 notwithstanding, the Nazarbayev solution may still be appealing to Putin (Gutterman 2019). The two leaders were reported to have had lengthy phone conversations prior to Nazarbayev's decision to step down (Pannier 2019). The idea of continuing to wield influence from backstage as an elder statesman comes close to what Putin did during the Medvedev presidency 2008-2012. Would he perhaps be inclined to use the same formula again? In early 2020, however, it turned out that the president had other plans. Instead of turning to Kazakhstan for inspiration he chose to adopt a formula that had already been tested in Belarus in 2004 by its autocrat president Lukashenko. In that year, the latter had managed to bring about constitutional changes that permitted him to serve longer than allowed by the existing constitution (Silitski 2005).

Postponing the succession: the constitutional reform

Before the presidential elections in 2008, prior to the nomination of Medvedev as the establishment's preferred candidate, there were already discussions in Russia about whether the best solution might be a constitutional change allowing the incumbent, Putin, to continue to serve as president (Hanson 2011). In fact, similar discussion had taken place towards the end of Yeltsin's second term in office, despite the latter's ailing health and waning popularity. One can easily perceive a pattern here. The ruling elites of the establishment are not interested in the kind of change and uncertainty that a newcomer might bring.

Had there been a referendum on the matter of extension of Putin's presidential mandate before the elections in 2008, there is little doubt that he would have gained the approval of a popular majority (Sakwa 2014: 34). A provision where the incumbent could be entrusted with serving as president for life, as in the example of China and the limitless extension of Xi Jinping's term in office, would perhaps also have been within reach.

After the Duma elections in 2017 Putin's supporting party, United Russia, commanded a supermajority of three fourths of the seats (White 2017). In view of this qualified majority, the constitution could be changed or amended without difficulty. Analysts speculated about different ways in which this could happen, including by prolonging the presidential term in office further from the current six years, or by abolishing the limitation that barred any incumbent from the possibility of serving for more than two consecutive periods at a time (Kendall-Taylor and Franz 2018). The latter was also what took place through the amendments of 2020. This was manifestly not a solution to the Putin succession predicament but the wholesale denial of its existence. Even more ominously, the removal of the limitation to two consecutive periods of presidential tenure for the incumbent brings the country significantly closer to autocracy (Goode 2021: 127, Flikke 2020: 17).

At a meeting with Russian and foreign journalists soon after his win in the presidential elections in 2018, Putin expressed himself ambiguously on the issue of the constitution: "I do not plan any constitutional reforms yet" (President of Russia, 18 March 2018). This could be read as a subtle hint that a change of position was in the offing. However, on the same occasion when someone asked him if he would be willing to run again for the presidency in 2030, provided that the constitution remained unchanged, he joked:

> *Listen to me. I think what you are saying is somewhat ridiculous. Let us count. Am I supposed to be President until I am 100 years old? No* (President of Russia, 18 March 2018).

From late 2019 on Putin made a volte face in his publicly expressed position on the prospect of changing the 1993 constitution. At the annual News Conference of 2019, he indicated unexpectedly that it should be possible to change it if the people so wished. He declared as his opinion that the first chapter of the constitution, on the fundamentals of the constitutional system, was sacrosanct and unchangeable, but opined that other parts, including the ones on obligations and rights of the parliament and the president, should be amenable to change. As a concrete example, he suggested that the provision that no president may serve for more than two consecutive periods be changed so that the word "consecutive" was dropped (President of Russia, 19 December 2019).

In mid-January 2020, Putin followed up on the theme in his annual address to the State Duma. He suggested several amendments to the 1993 constitution (President of Russia, 15 January 2020). In contrast to the procedures stated by that constitution it was, according to the originally proposed draft amendments, the Duma, not the president, who would have the prerogative of nominating a prime minister, even if the candidate would still have to be endorsed and accepted by the president (Kommersant 2020). The proposed provision of preventing any future president from sitting for more than two periods in office in total limited the possibilities of having future incumbents reaching the same singular position of prominence as Putin currently has. This could also be interpreted as a way of preventing any future successor from becoming too powerful, thereby threatening the interests of Putin and the elites favored by him once he has left presidential office (Teague 2020).

On the very day of the president's annual address in 2020, Prime Minister Medvedev declared the immediate resignation of his whole cabinet to make room for a new government, which would lead the process of constitutional review. In an unexpected move, Putin appointed Mikhail Mishustin as the new prime minister.

During the further process of preparations there was a most crucial change in relation to the original draft amendments about the maximum tenure allowed for the president. It took place when the constitutional changes were debated in the State Duma at a second reading on February 10, 2020. The parliamentarian and former cosmonaut Valentina Tereshkova took the floor, saying that she wished to add the suggestion that the incumbent president, Putin, be allowed to run again in the next presidential elections due in 2024, and likewise to do so in the regular presidential elections due in 2030:

> *I propose either to remove the restrictions on the presidential term, or to write in one of the articles of the bill the provision that after the updated Constitution enters into force, the incumbent president, like any other citizen, has the right to be elected to the post of head of state* (MEMRI 2020).

In re-setting the clock in this manner, it would become possible for Putin to continue as president until the year of 2036. This, stated Tereshkova, would effectively be a new constitution, so therefore it was logical to wipe the slate clean, so that no one, not even the incumbent, should be discriminated against. The sitting president should have as much right to run for the presidency as any other citizen, and in Putin's case there would be an additional factor to be considered for the common good, Tereshkova argued: "Given his enormous authority, this would be a stabilizing factor for our society". When the suggestion had been made, there was, as one observer put it, a "quick cascade of developments that seemed to be carefully planned to carry a patina of spontaneity" (Troianovski 2020).

After her intervention at the State Duma meeting, Tereshkova was subjected to a harsh campaign from oppositional quarters, including from Navalny who tweeted mockingly that Tereshkova was the first woman who "bravely traveled into cosmic cold and darkness, and then brought the entire country there" (Balmforth 2020). Other social media voices suggested that it would have been better if she had remained in orbit after her space adventure. Trying to back Tereshkova up and defend her from her critics, Vyacheslav Volodin, Speaker of the Duma and a known Putin devotee, underlined his support for the process that she had set in motion:

> *Today, facing the current challenges and the threats that exist in the world, oil and gas are not our advantages. As you can see, both oil and gas can fall in price. Our strength is Mr. Putin, and we must protect him* (State Duma 2020).

Putin seemed surprised at the proposition to re-set the clock to his benefit, but few doubted that the scheme was planned in meticulous detail (Higgins 2020). The president said that he was willing to consider the offer, provided that the State Duma accepted the proposition in its third reading of the amendments and that the Constitutional Court had nothing against it. Unsurprisingly, both instances turned out to agree. The Duma vote was dealt with already on March 11, the Federation Council (the upper house) voted in favor on that day, and when it convened on March 16, the Constitutional Court had no problem accepting the proposal (Teague 2020). As required, all regional parliaments also voted in favor. Following Putin's explicit request, the remaining hurdle in this scheme was to be cleared in a plebiscite on the constitutional amendments, to be held on April 22, 2020.

Just as a date was set for the popular vote, the corona crisis hit the world and Russia. After a period of prevaricating Putin decided to postpone the plebiscite for public health reasons. Since there was a lockdown in both Moscow and St. Petersburg, and Putin had declared the month of April as a non-working month to force people to stay at home, it would clearly have been untenable to hold the vote on the date originally suggested.

Much of the process toward the constitutional changes so far had been swift as a smash-and-grab operation. Had the electorate been given the time to reflect, matters might have turned out differently. Now, the pandemic brought uncertainty to the scheme.

Putin would need to consider that his overall popularity might recede because of the handling of the corona crisis and the death toll covid-19 would take. In the final analysis, there might be a risk that the main onus would fall on Putin himself.

Ultimately, the new date set for the vote was July 1, even if one could scarcely say that the pandemic was under control at that time. To make it possible to carry out the vote, the procedure was spread out during one full week to avoid crowding in and outside the polling stations. The proposed amendments sailed through comfortably, according to official figures gaining 78 percent of the vote with an overall turnout of 68 percent (Goode 2021, Rainsford 2020b). Judging by a poll carried out by the Levada Center (2020a) the figures were exaggerated. According to their survey, only 60 percent voted in favor of the reform package. If the poll results were representative on a national level, less than half of the eligible voters would have cast their ballots in support of the proposed changes, which in turn would have lowered their overall legitimacy significantly (Baev 2020).

The package of amendments had already been passed by the Duma, the Federation Council and the regional parliaments and, therefore, the vote did not qualify as a referendum in legal terms. Nor was it formally required to have a referendum to make a constitutional change. However, it was important for bestowing legitimacy on the constitutional reforms as well as on the persona of the president himself. The project needed popular endorsement.

The package to be confirmed did not only contain the provisions of exempting Putin from the rule that no president may serve for more than two periods in office, and the new rights of the Russian parliament regarding the formation of government and the appointment of the prime minister. It also held a batch of other amendments. Among these were new provisions to protect the institution of marriage as a union between a man and a woman; vows about the inviolability of Russian territory; a declaration that Russian law always eclipses international regulations; the barring of any future presidents or senior state officials from office in case of their holding or having held foreign passports or permanent residency permits or overseas bank accounts; the index-linking of pensions; and the setting of the minimum wage at no less than subsistence minimum income (President of Russia, 17 December 2020, Teague 2020). This was a sly move by the Kremlin as several of these items concerned social or patriotic themes which the public evidently cared about, as opposed to the political or institutional amendments which left them unconcerned at best (Goode 2021). Holding all amendments together in one package therefore increased the likelihood of the plebiscite approving the possible extensions of Putin's term in office (Rainsford 2020b). The barring of future presidential candidates was also significant, as the formulations even covered residence permits once held for studies abroad, which would inhibit candidates such as Aleksey Navalny from running for office in the future (Spiegelberger 2020).

When asked at the 2020 News Conference about the constitutional amendments, Putin tried to give the impression that the inclusion of components such as the index-linking of pensions and the minimum wages, the pledge to inviolability of the territory of the nation and the assertion of the supremacy of Russian constitutional law over all international norms were the most important changes. He did not even mention the extension of his own right to act as president among the most crucial amendments adopted through the plebiscite (President of Russia, 17 December 2020). In fact, he tried to argue that the changes that allowed the incumbent president to run for two more periods after 2024 were just epiphenomena. Most important, he argued, were the amendments that strengthened Russia's national security, stability and reinforced the constitutional foundation for economic development (President of Russia, 17 December 2020). Notably, however, he did not gainsay the moderator's argument that the changes in the presidential tenures reduced the risks of future bureaucratic intrigue when people in his surroundings started to look around for possible successors. As for what would happen in 2024, Putin added cryptically, "we will see when the time comes" (President of Russia, 22 October 2020, also 17 December 2020).

The factor touched upon by the moderator on that occasion stands out as one of the most important drivers behind the constitutional maneuvers in 2020. The amendments to the constitution do not guarantee nor necessitate that Putin will stand for a fifth or even sixth presidential tenure if biological factors so permit. The mere fact that it is possible for him to do so, however, will prevent him from ending up in a lame-duck position halfway through his fourth tenure where he would increasingly be looked upon as someone on his way out, a has-been soon to give way to an anointed successor (Teague 2020). With the new legal instrumentation as basis, he will remain a force to be fully reckoned with and his authority will not be disputed on the grounds of his being an outgoing president. Other factors permitting, this situation will prevail up until January 2024 when he is legally bound to announce whether he intends to run for a fifth time or to stand down (Gould-Davies 2021).

Putin and his surroundings had for a long time doubtless been aware of the problems that may arise in the transition from Putin to someone else after the 2024 elections. How indeed could legitimacy built on charisma be transferred? The provisional remedy was to transfer power from Putin to Putin. Health permitting, Putin may now continue as president for two more consecutive periods until 2036. This is in theory of course, as the succession issue at least for health and age reasons will perhaps need to be settled much sooner. However, through the constitutional maneuvers, Putin has bought himself and his regime time for deciding how to sustain the legitimacy painstakingly constructed during his first 20 years in power and increasingly challenged by the corona crisis and by Navalny in 2020 and after.

VIII

Conclusion

Charismatic leaders need a following, a devoted audience, since that is what defines them. It is as simple as that; if they do not have a committed audience, they clearly have no charisma. However, as has been discussed previously there are other actors besides the committed audience who are important for the charismatic leader to acquire a basis of support (Joosse 2018). One such supporting role consists of the "unworthy challengers", who cannot compete with the incumbent or are, like in the present Russian case, absent altogether. In what I have described as the Putin predicament there are similarities with traditional authority, as the situation of there being no-one around to contest the man at the top has persisted over a period of more than twenty years. The condition has been characterized as one of legitimacy by default (Gel'man 2010). There are simply no conceivable alternatives.

This situation became obvious at the time of the presidential elections in 2018, and it continues to be even more so after the constitutional amendments of 2020. As the incumbent grows older, physical age will increasingly put into question his position as the only credible alternative at the helm. This is where the crux of the Putin predicament lies. There is no alternative at hand, and the only available option, i.e., the president himself, appears to be progressively devoid of energy and unable to instill enthusiasm. The regime's major challenge is to transform the incumbent's charismatic authority—while it is still there—into a more sustainable ground for legitimacy.

What is more, other challenges have started to appear and multiply. Putin's most formidable political opponent of recent years is the person who-must-not-be-named, Aleksey Navalny. He has for several years challenged Putin on his home turf and is increasingly eclipsing him in terms of charisma. The attempted assassination in the summer of 2020 and the re-opened court case, where

Navalny's suspended sentence was converted into an unconditional one, served to add to the opposition leader's reputation. He
may not have been generally popular before, but more and more,
people came to resent the heavy-handed and merciless way that he
was treated by the authorities. As they realized that the system's
repression mechanisms were in some senses arbitrary and could
strike down on anyone, people started to wonder who might be
next. Having been an irritant for many years, from the summer of
2020 on Navalny grew to becoming a major threat to the legitimacy
of the regime. The question could rightly be asked: if an outsider,
an alleged maverick at that, eclipsed the president in terms of charisma, did this not spell the beginning of the end of the charismatic
authority of the incumbent president?

The ability to communicate convincingly with the public is a
crucial part of what defines a political leader's charismatic authority. Putin has increasingly excelled at his communication practices
and has manifested this in his widely televised media spectacles,
the Direct Line and the News Conference. At these marathon events
he has had few superiors. However, in other communication genres
he is vastly outsmarted by his unnamed opponent. The chief originator of catchy one-liners and powerful visual cues, Navalny is in
a league of his own. His use of the Youtube medium is masterful,
and the blows that he struck with his widely spread videos "Don't
Call Him Dimon" and "A Palace for Putin" really hit home. Dimitriy Medvedev never recovered politically from the Dimon blow,
and as of spring 2021 it is still unclear what effects his confrontational challenge to Putin himself will ultimately have. Slogans like
"the party of crooks and thieves", "Putin is a thief", and "Not our
Tsar" have caught on, but maybe the launch of the toilet brush as a
symbol of the "collective Putin" was the most dangerous of them
all for the ruling elite. As a meme the toilet brush had it all; everyone could relate to it, and everyone also knew what a toilet brush
was normally used for: to clear out dirt that otherwise threatened
to stick for too long to the surface. There was even a strike of irony
in the fact that it in a way took Putin full circle back to his early days
when he vowed to take Chechen separatist fighters out in the sh-
thouse.

Whereas there was no-one on the inside of the political elite who could even begin to rival the incumbent in terms of charisma, Putin seemed precisely in those terms to be no match for his disdained rival. This situation, should it persist, would be highly unlikely not to have long-time effects on Putin's general legitimacy. As he took up office in the earliest years of the 2000s, he had the great advantage of being young, strong, and energetic. In the early 2020s he was no longer young, it seemed as if his energy was starting to desert him, and he was widely overshadowed by Navalny in terms of charisma. The challenge through "A Palace for Putin" was tough enough, but the implications of the rhetorical jabs in Navalny's defense speech in the courtroom in 2021 were potentially even more devastating for Putin's legitimation strategies. Navalny argued that the incumbent president had been elevated to the presidential office by pure chance, and not due to his superior qualities. He had simply been available and acceptable for the contending political elites. Navalny chided the president as "the old man in the bunker" and as "Vladimir the poisoner of underpants", thus very deliberately eroding the political myths that had supported Putin's presidencies for so long. The hero, the dragon-slayer, the guarantor of greatness, the defender against disorder and chaos—all these grand epithets were suddenly seriously opposed. Could the good tsar take this? Would he respond or would it eventually transpire that the Emperor had no clothes on? Indeed, the latter was later to be suggested by Navalny in a desperate plea from inside his prison.

Respond Putin did, but in a manner not behooving a tsar posing as his subjects' benefactor. Navalny was deported to the penal colony, was long denied medical assistance, was threatened with force-feeding during his hunger strike, and had in the spring of 2021 unclear prospects of even staying alive. Meanwhile, measures were taken by legal instances to ban Navalny's Anti-Corruption Fund as an extremist organization, which would mean that its active members could be subjected to up to ten years of imprisonment. This could only be seen as an attempt to kill Navalny's movement, regardless of whether its initiator stayed alive or not. If the regime goes down this path, it will indeed seem as if the question of how the regime will sustain its legitimacy is a moot one. The

Putin regime would thus indicate that securing its legitimacy is not its priority since holding on to power by repression and brute force seems sufficient. Given the popular resentment that would be likely to follow, it is however uncertain whether such a solution would enable the regime to sustain power in the long run.

In recent years there have been ample signs that Putin's grip over the hearts and minds of the electorate is weakening. The widespread discontent about the pension reform in 2018 was one such indication, as were the demonstrations in the Far East protesting the discharge of the popular governor of Khabarovsk Krai, not to speak of course of the massive demonstrations in support of Navalny in early 2021. Whereas the unrest could still not match the 2011-2012 Bolotnaya manifestations in magnitude and intensity, the incidents seemed to occur with accelerating frequency. In addition to all this, there was the less than convincing handling of the corona pandemic, where Putin for once seemed disinclined to monopolize the center stage of politics. To more than one observer the overall impression was that the regime was starting to look as if it was past its prime. The massive hopes that it pinned on the Sputnik V vaccine as a panacea for more than the coronavirus itself did little to change the impression.

To be sure, however, the same overall impression of feebleness seemed to linger during the initial years of Putin's third term in office. The newly returned incumbent's charisma seemed to be waning, he seemed tired and somewhat disillusioned, but then came the year of 2014 and the annexation of Crimea. As if by magic, the regime's heavy-handed actions and enforcement of the great power ideal in Ukraine and Syria turned the tide of public opinion. Not only did the president manage to restore public trust in him to the same levels that he had achieved during his first two presidencies, but he even surpassed them and went on to keep his popularity ratings at a very high level for about four years. This was the period of the Crimean consensus.

At the ideational level, the tough response on the ground to the conflict in Ukraine was at that time accompanied by a revival of the political myths that the regime had used to legitimize its power. The rhetorical arsenal was invigorated, as the old formulae about the need to act and be respected as a great power and the urgency of avoiding a Time of Troubles were supplemented by a bout of heavily anti-Western and anti-American sentiments. What emerged was in essence a third and highly powerful political myth, the one about Russia as the lone defender of eternal values in a hostile world. Russia, and Putin personally, were slated as stalwarts against moral depravation and decay and as the principal guardians of tradition, the Orthodox religion, and family values. This turned out to be a popular move.

The question that arose in early 2021 is whether the regime will once again be able to muster and recover its strength in a similar manner as it did at the time of the initiation of the Crimean consensus. Can other forceful political myths be found to prompt and motivate collective action? The feebleness of the response to the corona crisis, and the abandonment of the vertical of power when it was needed the most, would suggest a negative answer. The president's frequent reverting to the use of the fall guy function, and his penchant for putting the blame on others when things go wrong can hardly be read as signs of vigor. However, there are also indications in a different direction. The paradigm shift in relations with the United States at the time of the Trump presidency, signaling great confidence that Russia was now in many respects the stronger party, seemed to hint at a way out of the present state of energy loss. Therefore, a repetition of the gathering-round-the-flag type of scenario, where adventures abroad are used to gain support at home, cannot be excluded. The annexation of Crimea worked like a miracle cure in boosting Putin's popularity and legitimacy, and in a situation where public support recedes at home there might be some temptation to use the old recipes once more, albeit perhaps in a new area of application.

In late April 2021 there were ominous signs that the Crimean consensus formula might be repeated against Ukraine, as there was for a while a massive buildup of Russian troops along the Russo-Ukrainian border. Whether this was a move to do some saber-rattling in relation to the new US presidential administration and test President Biden's resolve in the context of frosty relations and an intense verbal exchange, or whether it portended preparations for hard military action were still unclear at that time.

In view of all present challenges and in order to sustain itself, it will be necessary for the regime to transform Putin's still lingering personal popularity into authority with more durable grounds. This may take different forms. When charisma starts to recede, other means will be needed to sustain the political system. Legitimation is but one of the conceivable strategies to ascertain societal stability in hybrid and authoritarian settings, with the other main forms often indicated to be repression and co-optation (Gerschewski 2013). The overarching questions are whether the regime is willing and prepared to take on the costs of increased repression and whether it has the economic muscle to manage a massive buying-out operation to purchase loyalty. The dilemma can be put in simple terms: If the number of protests grows and the economy slows, the regime will find it difficult to survive (Hall 2017: 175)

Routinizing elusive charismatic authority is certainly cheaper than going for large-scale repression and co-optation but is easier said than done. When someone has had such a firm grip on political power as Putin has had for more than 20 years one would assume it to be natural for the regime to plan ahead carefully for how to carry on the political legacy. The renowned Russian sociologist Olga Kryshtanovskaya cautioned that throughout Russian political history, periods of instability and unrest, periods of *smuta*, have followed upon lengthy and stable periods of incumbency by the same ruler (Laurén 2018, Whitehouse 2018). Since Putin, as opposed to his predecessor Boris Yeltsin, has managed to construct his legitimacy on his reputation for restoring and keeping stability and order, it would be ironic indeed if his rule were to be succeeded by an unstable power vacuum. One can safely assume that these kinds of discussions have been going on inside the Putin team, and that the subject has been taken seriously. As Putin himself has repeatedly asserted, the question of a suitable successor has been on his mind ever since he first took office in 2000 (President of Russia, 10 March 2018, 27 June 2019; Financial Times 2019). Here, there are two striking things: firstly, he has had a long time to find a successor and, secondly, he has apparently had no great success in this endeavor.

On one occasion during his third tenure in presidential office, Putin himself referred to Russia's turbulent past and argued that many crises and internal conflicts had been prompted by unclear succession rules. This was a lesson that had to be heeded, lest history should repeat itself (Drozdova and Robinson 2019: 809). The acknowledgement seemed new coming from him, since he had on other occasions dodged the issue of succession whenever it was raised in public. In the spring of 2020, he seemed to have found his answer to the problem. He solved it by introducing amendments to the 1993 constitution and getting them accepted by both houses of the Federal Assembly, the regional parliaments, the Constitutional Court, and the public. The answer to who was to succeed Putin was — Putin. The more time passes and the older the president gets, the more untenable this answer will become. There is no doubt that Putin's singular position in Russian politics is a harbinger of problems to come should he, for some reason, need to exit from the political stage prematurely. He has no credible contender allowed to take part at the polls, which indicates a problem per se, even in a system of electoral authoritarianism such as that in Russia.

However, Putin's forced prolongation of his legal mandate is equally problematic. The norm to adhere to the constitution seemed for a long time to be a strong driving force on his part (President of Russia, 10 March 2018, 24 June 2018), and he often underlined that the president is its guarantor (President of Russia, 25 April 2013). Putin seemed to regard this as a central element of his legitimacy, and he managed to make several analysts believe in his sincerity. He gave the trustworthy impression that he would not be willing to go down in history as someone who had tampered with its letter. As events during the elections in 2011-2012 showed, Putin did not have any qualms about being flexible in his interpretation of the spirit of the constitution. This was an early warning sign, portending the U-turn that he completed during the spring and summer of 2020 when he managed to get through the amendments that permitted him, at least in theory, to go on serving as president until the distant year of 2036. At any rate, the amendments made it possible for him to avoid the lame-duck stamp that otherwise would have started to hem him in from around mid-term of his fourth period in office. The constitutional change was a fateful event where Russia seemed to go from being a hybrid regime to an all-out authoritarian one, and where Putin in his search for foreign models to emulate appeared to come closest to the Chinese model under Xi Jinping where the incumbent was made into president for life.

History shows that hybrid and authoritarian regimes are particularly exposed and unstable at the time of leadership transition. After the constitutional changes initiated in the spring of 2020, continuity up until the year of 2036 seems to be secured should Putin wish to seek it, but it is a continuity where human fragility and ill health may interfere. Great uncertainty would arise, should he have to make an untimely exit. If the situation persists and no potential contenders for the presidential office after Putin are allowed to step forward, this is indeed a sign of weakness of the political system (Pavroz 2020, Sakwa 2014). One way out of the conundrum would be for Putin to designate a successor, even if there is a glaring absence of visible contenders for the job who would also be acceptable to the establishment. An heir apparent may of course give rise to the crown prince problem and eclipse his mentor, but a younger successor might also be able to take up the challenge posed by the Navalny generation.

Just as nature abhors a vacuum, so does political life. In a situation where the incumbent vanished from center stage without having designated a successor, new actors would be likely to try to move into the field and claim it as theirs. They would need to gather a following by appealing to audiences that have earlier been attracted to or subsumed under the Putin platform. There is a risk that radical contenders would try to do so by speaking louder than everybody else and by going to great extremes in radical or populist fervor, with likely implications both externally and internally. The little we can know and predict about future political developments in post-Putin Russia makes at any rate the alternative of Russia turning towards Western-style democracy very remote (Gill 2015). The political myth about the turmoil and the *smuta* of the 1990s, when Yeltsin's Russia tried to introduce the Western liberal democracy ideal, is still too forceful for this to happen. Even if Putin according to an outside perspective might not be the most appealing of all possible leaders in Russia, his political agenda is despite his penchant for populism reasonably well known and preferable to the unfamiliar alternatives potentially waiting in the wings. Thus the Putin predicament is a problem not only for the Kremlin and the Putin regime itself, but for the domestic population and the world outside as well.

After the constitutional amendments adopted in 2020 it might seem that there is no great haste to find someone to replace Putin, that is if he remains in good physical and political health. That is a big "if", however. As was vividly demonstrated during 2020-21, the apparent stability in Russian society of the last couple of decades is deceptive. Developments during Putin's fourth presidential term have indicated intense simmering under the surface. The amendments to the constitution in 2020 postponed the succession problem, but the way things are at present, the Putin predicament nevertheless remains.

References

Al Jazeera (2020) 'Putin orders start of Russia's mass COVID vaccination programme', 2 December, https://www.aljazeera.com/news/2020/12/2/putin-orders-start-of-russias-mass-covid-vaccination-programme, accessed 4 December 2020.

Alagappa, Muthiah (1995) *Political legitimacy in Southeast Asia: The quest for moral authority*, Stanford, Ca: Stanford University Press.

Ambrosio, Thomas (2001) 'Russia's quest for multipolarity: A response to US foreign policy in the post-cold war era', *European Security*, 10: 1, 45-67.

Ambrosio, Thomas (2015) 'Leadership Succession in Kazakhstan and Uzbekistan: Regime Survival after Nazarbayev and Karimov', *Journal of Balkan and Near Eastern Studies*, 17: 1, 49-67.

Ambrosio, Thomas and Geoffrey Vandrovec (2013) 'Mapping the Geopolitics of the Russian Federation: The Federal Assembly Addresses of Putin and Medvedev', *Geopolitics*, 18: 2, 435-466.

Amnesty International (2021a) 'Amnesty International statement on Aleksei Navalny', 25 February, https://www.amnesty.org/en/latest/news/2021/02/aleksei-navalny-prisoner-of-conscience/, accessed 10 March 2021.

Amnesty International (2021b) 'Statement on Alexei Navalny's Status as Prisoner of Conscience', 7 May, https://www.amnesty.org/en/latest/news/2021/05/statement-on-alexei-navalnys-status-as-prisoner-of-conscience/, accessed 10 May 2021.

Andrews-Lee, Caitlin (2019) 'The Revival of Charisma: Experimental Evidence from Argentina and Venezuela', *Comparative Political Studies*, 52: 5, 687-719.

Andrews-Lee, Caitlin and Liu, Amy H. (2020) 'The Language of Legacies: The Politics of Evoking Dead Leaders', *Political Research Quarterly*, 1-16, https://doi.org/10.1177/1065912920930.

Apressyan, Ruben (2013) 'Power and society in Russia: A value approach to legitimacy'. In Per-Arne Bodin, Stefan Hedlund and Elena Namli (eds): *Power and Legitimacy: Challenges from Russia*, London: Routledge, 118-132.

Arnesen, Sveinung; Troy S. Broderstad, Mikael P. Johannesson, and Jonas Linde (2019) 'Conditional legitimacy: How turnout, majority size, and outcome affect perceptions of legitimacy in European Union membership referendums', *European Union Politics* 20: 2, 176-197.

Åslund, Anders (2020) 'Responses to the COVID-19 crisis in Russia, Ukraine, and Belarus', *Eurasian Geography and Economics*, 61: 4-5, 532-545.

Assmann Aleida (2010) 'From collective violence to a common future'. In Helena Gonçalves da Silva, Adriana Alves de Paula Martins, Filomena Viana Guarda, and José Miguel Sardica (eds): *Conflict, Memory Transfers and the Reshaping of Europe*, Newcastle upon Tyne: Cambridge Scholars Publishing, 8–23.

Bacon, Edwin (2015) 'Putin's Crimea Speech, 18th March 2014', *Journal of Soviet and Post-Soviet Politics and Society*, 1: 1, 13-36.

Baev, Pavel (2020) 'A Chain of Poor Choices Leads Putin Into a Serious Blunder', *Eurasia Daily Monitor* 17: 122, https://jamestown.org/program/a-chain-of-poor-choices-leads-putin-into-a-serious-blunder/?fbclid=IwAR0D_08NEahKVUltLIxdVIQujRp9TzLzGyp_fD1hhIFDRGINkco7lgteVTg, accessed 9 September 2020.

Bagger, Hans (2007) 'The Study of History in Russia during the Post-Soviet Identity Crisis', *Scando-Slavica*, 53: 1, 109-125.

Barany, Zoltan (2004) 'The Tragedy of the Kursk: Crisis Management in Putin's Russia', *Government and Opposition*, 39: 3, 476-503.

Barber, Lionel (2020) *The Powerful and the Damned: Private Diaries in Turbulent Times*. London: W.H. Allen.

Baturo, Alexander (2019) 'Continuismo in Comparison: Avoidance, Extension, and Removal of Presidential Term Limits'. In Alexander Baturo and Robert Elgie (eds): *The Politics of Presidential Term Limits*, Oxford: Oxford University Press, 75-100.

BBC News (2011) 'Russia PM Vladimir Putin 'booed' at martial arts fight', 21 November, https://www.bbc.com/news/world-europe-15818517, accessed 19 November 2020.

BBC News (2014) 'Ukraine crisis: Timeline', 13 November, https://www.bbc.com/news/world-middle-east-26248275, accessed 23 November 2020.

BBC News (2020a) 'Coronavirus: Putin postpones Russia's WW2 victory parade', 16 April, https://www.bbc.com/news/world-europe-52311934, accessed 7 May 2020.

BBC News (2020b) 'Russia holds World War Two victory parade in coronavirus shadow', 24 June, https://www.bbc.com/news/world-europe-53152725, accessed 28 October 2020.

Bell, Duncan (2003) 'Mythscapes: memory, mythology and national identity', *British Journal of Sociology*, 54: 1, 63-81.

Bellingcat (2020) '"If It Hadn't Been for the Prompt Work of the Medics": FSB Officer Inadvertently Confesses Murder Plot to Navalny', 21 December, https://www.bellingcat.com/news/uk-and-europe/2020/12/21/if-it-hadnt-been-for-the-prompt-work-of-the-medics-fsb-officer-inadvertently-confesses-murder-plot-to-navalny/, accessed 27 May 2021.

Beetham, David (1991) *The Legitimation of Power*, London: Palgrave.

Bennetts, Marc (2020) 'As corona casualties mount, Putin keeps a low profile', *Politico*, 16 April, https://www.politico.eu/article/coronavirus-russia-vladimir-putin-keeps-low-profile/, accessed 5 May 2020.

Blackburn, Matthew and Bo Petersson (2021, under review for *Post-Soviet Affairs*) 'The Year of Parade, Plebiscite and Pandemic: Performance, procedure and decreasing system legitimacy in Putin's 2020'.

Blackmon, Pamela (2020) 'After Karimov and Nazarbayev: change in Uzbekistan and Kazakhstan?, *Central Asian Survey*, 40: 2, 179-196.

Bloomberg and Henry Meyer (2021) 'Countries are lining up for Russia's once-scorned Sputnik vaccine after strong efficacy results', *Fortune*, 8 February, https://fortune.com/2021/02/08/international-sputnik-russia-demand/, accessed 1 March 2021.

BMJ (2021) 'Covid-19: Russia's statistics agency reports much higher death toll than country's health ministry', 12 February, https://www.bmj.com/content/372/bmj.n440, accessed 24 May 2021.

Boele, Otto (2011) 'Remembering Brezhnev in the New Millennium: Post-Soviet Nostalgia and Local Identity in the City of Novorossiisk', *The Soviet and Post-Soviet Review*, 38: 1, 3-29.

Boer, Roland (2009) *Political Myth: On the Use and Abuse of Biblical Themes*, Durham: NC Duke University Press.

Bottici, Chiara (2010) *A Philosophy of Political Myth*, Cambridge: Cambridge University Press.

Bottici, Chiara and Benoit Challand (2013) *Imagining Europe: Myth, Memory, and Identity*, New York: Cambridge University Press.

Brusis, Martin (2016) 'The Politics of Legitimation in Post-Soviet Eurasia'. In Martin Brusis, Joachim Ahrens and Martin Schulze Wesse (eds): *Politics and Legitimation in Post-Soviet Eurasia*, Houndmills, Basingstoke: Palgrave Macmillan, 1-17.

Buchanan, Allen (2002) 'Political Legitimacy and Democracy', *Ethics*, 112: 4, 689-719.

Bueno de Mesquita, Bruce and Alastair Smith (2017) 'Political Succession: A Model of Coups, Revolution, Purges, and Everyday Politics', *Journal of Conflict Resolution*, 61: 4, 707-743.

Burrett, Tina (2020) 'Charting Putin's Shifting Populism in the Russian Media from 2000 to 2020', *Politics and Governance*, 8: 1, 193-205.

Busygina, Irina (2019) 'Are post-Soviet leaders doomed to be populist? A comparative analysis of Putin and Nazarbayev', *European Politics and Society*, 20: 4, 502-518.

Butler, Judith. P., and Gayatri Chakravorty Spivak (2007) *Who Sings the Nation-State?* New York, NY: Seagull Books.

Calvert, Peter (1987, ed): *The Process of Political Succession*, Berlin: Springer.

Cassani, Andrea (2017) 'Social services to claim legitimacy: comparing autocracies' performance', *Contemporary Politics*, 23: 3, 348-368.

Casula, Philipp (2013) 'Sovereign Democracy, Populism, and Depoliticization in Russia', *Problems of Post-Communism*, 60: 3, 3-15.

Charteris-Black, Jonathan (2011) *Politicians and Rhetoric: The Persuasive Power of Metaphor*, Houndmills: Palgrave Macmillan.

Charteris-Black, Jonathan (2019) *Metaphors of Brexit: No Cherries on the Cake?* Cham: Springer Nature.

Chebankova, Elena (2015) 'Vladimir Putin: Making of the National Hero'. In Agnieszka Pikulicka-Wilczewska and Richard Sakwa (eds): *Ukraine and Russia: People, Politics, Propaganda and Perspectives*, Bristol: E-International Relations Publishing, 173-182.

Chen, Cheng (2016) *The Return of Ideology: The Search for Regime Identities in Postcommunist Russia and China*, Ann Arbor: University of Michigan Press.

Chernova, Anna, Zahra Ullah and Rob Picheta (2021) 'Russia reacts angrily after Biden calls Putin a 'killer', *CNN*, 18 March, https://edition.cnn.com/2021/03/18/europe/biden-putin-killer-comment-russia-reaction-intl/index.html, accessed 19 March 2021.

Chung Joong-Gun (1993) 'Charisma and regime legitimacy: political succession in North Korea', *The Journal of East Asian Affairs*, 7: 1, 79-115.

Clunan, Anne (2014) 'Historical aspirations and the domestic politics of Russia's pursuit of international status', *Communist and Post-Communist Studies*, 47: 3, 281-290.

CNN (2020) 'Putin, Xi and other strongmen haven't congratulated Biden yet. Their silence speaks volumes', 9 November, https://edition.cnn.com/2020/11/09/world/biden-win-russia-china-silence-intl/index.html, accessed 10 November 2020.

Cooley, Alexander (2016) 'Countering Democratic Norms'. In Larry Diamond, Marc F. Plattner and Christopher Walker (eds): *Authoritarianism Goes Global*, Baltimore: Johns Hopkins University Press, 117-134.

Davis, Vicky (2018) *Myth Making in the Soviet Union and Modern Russia: Remembering World War II in Brezhnev's Hero City*, New York: I. B. Tauris.

Dawisha, Karen (2015) *Putin's Kleptocracy: Who Owns Russia?* New York: Simon Schuster.

De Pury, Kate (2018) 'Putting Putin on the Spot', *British Journalism Review*, 29: 1, 21-27.

Deyermond, Ruth (2013) 'Assessing the reset: successes and failures in the Obama administration's Russia policy, 2009–2012', *European Security*, 22: 4, 500-523.

Diamond, Jeremy (2018) 'Trump: "Relationship has never been worse … that changed as of about 4 hours ago"', *CNN Politics*, 16 July, https://edition.cnn.com/politics/live-news/trump-putin-helsinki/h_569a5 2a7d2dc362ff45aefd8d24ce16c, accessed 15 February 2021.

Diamond, Larry (2002) 'Elections Without Democracy: Thinking About Hybrid Regimes', *Journal of Democracy*, 13: 2, 21-35.

Dik, Sergey (2020) 'Russia's city Khabarovsk rises against Vladimir Putin', *DW*, 4 August, https://www.dw.com/en/russias-city-khabarovsk-rises-against-vladimir-putin/a-54437316, accessed 2 October 2020.

Drozdova, Oksana and Paul Robinson (2019) 'A Study of Vladimir Putin's Rhetoric', *Europe-Asia Studies*, 71: 5, 805-823.

du Boulay, Sofya (2020) 'Sekrety dolgoletiya: strategii legitimatsii politicheskikh rezhimov v Rossii i Kazakhstane', *Obshaya Tetrad*, Vestnik Shkoly Grazhdanskogo Prosveshenia, 1: 78, 44-53.

du Boulay, Sofya (2021) 'Charismatic Legitimation: The Mucky Waters of Anointed Succession in Kazakhstan and Azerbaijan', draft paper, dated 30 March.

du Boulay, Sofya and Rico Isaacs (2019) 'Legitimacy and Legitimation in Kazakhstan and Turkmenistan'. In Rico Isaacs and Alessandro Frigerio (eds): *Theorizing Central Asian Politics: The State, Ideology and Power*, Palgrave Macmillan, 17-42.

Dukalskis, Alexander (2017) *The Authoritarian Public Sphere. Legitimation and Autocratic Power in North Korea, Burma, and China*, London and New York: Routledge.

Dukalskis, Alexander and Johannes Gerschewski (2017) 'What autocracies say (and what citizens hear): proposing four mechanisms of autocratic legitimation', *Contemporary Politics*, 23: 3, 251-268.

Dunning, Chester S. L (2001) *A Short History of Russia's First Civil War: From the Time of Troubles to the Founding of the Romanov Dynasty*, Pennsylvania: Pennsylvania State University Press.

Dutch Safety Board (2015) 'MH17 Crash', https://echo.msk.ru/files/2383070.pdf, accessed 5 May 2021.

Easton, David (1975) 'A Re-Assessment of the Concept of Political Support', *British Journal of Political Science*, 5: 4, 435-447.

Eatwell, Roger (2006) 'The Concept and Theory of Charismatic Leadership', *Totalitarian Movements and Political Religions*, 7: 2, 141-156.

Eckel, Mike (2019) 'Change the Russian Constitution? Might Be A Good Idea, Says Putin Confidant', *Radio Free Europe/Radio Liberty*, 16 September, https://www.rferl.org/a/change-the-russian-constitution-might-be-a-good-idea-says-putin-confidant/30167426.html, accessed 29 October 2020.

Edele, Mark (2017) 'Fighting Russia's History Wars: Vladimir Putin and the Codification of World War II', *History and Memory*, 29: 2, 90-124.

Edelman, Murray (1977) *Political Language: Words that Succeed and Politics that Fail*, New York: Academic Press.

Efimova, Anna and Denis Strebkov (2020) 'Linking Public Opinion and Foreign Policy in Russia', *The International Spectator*, 55: 1, 93-111.

Eisenstadt, S. N. (1968, ed): *Max Weber on Charisma and Institution Building. Selected Papers*, Chicago: University of Chicago Press.

Elder, Miriam (2011) 'Vladimir Putin mocks Moscow's "condom-wearing" protesters', *The Guardian*, 15 December, https://www.theguardian.com/world/2011/dec/15/vladimir-putin-mocks-moscow-protesters, accessed 19 November 2019.

Fedotenkov, Igor (2020) 'Terrorist attacks and public approval of the Russian president: evidence from time series analysis', *Post-Soviet Affairs*, 36: 2, 159-170.

Feldmann, Magnus and Honorata Mazepus (2017) 'State-society relations and the sources of support for the Putin regime: bridging political culture and social contract theory', *East European Politics*, 34: 1, 57-76.

Financial Times (2019) 'Vladimir Putin says liberalism has "become obsolete"', 27 June, https://www.ft.com/content/670039ec-98f3-11e9-9573-ee5cbb98ed36, accessed 6 November 2019.

Fish, Steven M. (2017) 'What is Putinism?', *Journal of Democracy*, 28: 4, 61-75.

Flikke, Geir (2020) *Russlands rebeller: Protest og reaksjon i Putins Russland (2011-2020)*, Oslo: Cappelen Damm.

Fredrikson, Stig (2019) *Ryssland utan Putin: friare, fredligare och rättvisare*, Stockholm: Carlssons.

Frye, Timothy; Scott Gehlbach, Kyle L. Marquardt, and Ora John Reuter (2017) 'Is Putin's popularity real?', *Post-Soviet Affairs*, 33: 1, 1-15.

FSU Brief (2020a) 'Russia's Most Influential Insiders, Part 2: The Second Echelon', 29 October, https://fsubrief.substack.com/p/russias-most-influential-insiders-30c, accessed 29 October 2020.

FSU Brief (2020b) 'Reforms in Uzbekistan—Illusion or Reality?', 17 November, https://fsubrief.substack.com/p/reforms-in-uzbekistan-illusion-or, accessed 17 November 2020.

FSU Brief (2020c) 'Putin's Dilemma', 1 December, https://fsubrief.substack.com/p/putins-dilemma, accessed 3 December 2020.

Gagné, Learry (2011) 'A Modern Interpretation of Machiavelli's Political Cycle', *Canadian Political Science Review*, 5: 2, 127-135.

Galeotti, Mark (2019a) *We Need to Talk about Putin: How the West Gets Him Wrong*, London: Penguin.

Galeotti, Mark (2019b) 'Is This Russia's Next Leader?', *Moscow Times*, 4 October, https://www.themoscowtimes.com/2019/10/04/is-this-russias-next-leader-a67599, accessed 18 November 2019.

Galeotti, Mark (2021), 'Navalny Also Needs to Reach Russia's "Men in Grey Suits"', *Moscow Times*, 3 February, https://www.themoscowtimes.com/2021/02/03/navalny-also-needs-to-reach-russias-men-in-grey-suits-a72816, accessed 7 February 2021.

Gandhi, Jennifer; Ben Noble, and Milan Svolik (2020) 'Legislatures and Legislative Politics Without Democracy', *Comparative Political Studies*, 53: 9, 1359-1379.

Gel'man, Vladimir (2010) 'Regime changes despite legitimacy crises: Exit, voice, and loyalty in post-communist Russia', *Journal of Eurasian Studies*, 1: 1, 54-63.

Gel'man, Vladimir (2013) 'Cracks in the Wall: Challenges to Electoral Authoritarianism in Russia', *Problems of Post-Communism*, 60: 2, 3-10.

Gel'man, Vladimir (2015) *Authoritarian Russia: Analyzing post-soviet regime changes*, Pittsburgh: University of Pittsburgh Press.

Gel'man, Vladimir (2017) 'Political foundations of bad governance in post-Soviet Eurasia: towards a research agenda', *East European Politics*, 33: 4, 496-516.

Gel'man, Vladimir (2021) 'Sputnik V: one more "success story"?', *Riddle*, 4 March, https://www.ridl.io/en/sputnik-v-one-more-success-story/, accessed 16 March 2021.

Gerschewski, Johannes (2013) 'The three pillars of stability: legitimation, repression, and co-optation in autocratic regimes', *Democratization*, 20: 1, 13-38.

Gill, Graeme (2015) *Building an Authoritarian Polity: Russia in Post-Soviet Times*, Cambridge: Cambridge University Press.

Gill, Graeme (2016) 'Russia and the Vulnerability of Electoral Authoritarianism?', *Slavic Review*, 75: 2, 354-373.

Gippert, Birte J. (2016) 'The sum of its parts? Sources of local legitimacy', *Cooperation and Conflict*, 51: 4, 522-538.

Glasser, Susan B. (2019) 'Putin the Great: Russia's Imperial Impostor', *Foreign Affairs*, 98: 5, 10 + 12-16.

Goode, J. Paul (2012) 'Nationalism in Quiet Times: Ideational Power and Post-Soviet Hybrid Regimes', *Problems of Post-Communism*, 59: 3, 6–16.

Goode, J. Paul (2020) 'Patriotism without Patriots? Perm'-36 and Patriotic Legitimation in Russia', *Slavic Review* 79: 2, 390-411.

Goode, J. Paul (2021) 'Patriotic Legitimation and Everyday Patriotism in Russia's Constitutional Reform', *Russian Politics*, 6: 1, 112-129.

Gould-Davies, Nigel (2021) 'Is Putin Doomed to Run in 2024?', *Survival*, 63: 2, 203-212.

Goscilo, Helena (2013, ed): *Putin as Celebrity and Cultural Icon*, London: Routledge.

Gulina, Olga V. (2021) 'Vaktsina protiv COVID-19: vopros zhizni ili geo-politicheskoy loyal'nosti?', *Riddle*, https://www.ridl.io/ru/vakcina-protiv-covid-19-vopros-zhizni-ili-geopoliticheskoj-lojalnosti/?fbclid =IwAR0cYeO0sMW1Od9RwYE9VmFYSiApRCAAO7AcAD6QzLO Vt4pH0Fw3HLMfpQY, accessed 1 March, 2021.

Guriev, Sergei and Daniel Treisman (2019) 'Informational Autocrats', *The Journal of Economic Perspectives*, 33: 4, 100-127.

Gutterman, Steve (2019) 'The Week in Russia: Do Kremlin Bosses Dream in Kazakh?', *Radio Free Europe/Radio Liberty*, 22 March, https://www. rferl.org/a/the-week-in-russia-do-kremlin-bosses-dream-in-kazakh -/29836266.html, accessed 25 September 2019.

Gutterman, Steve (2021) '"Alone" Among Allies? Why Putin Shunned the West in Victory Day Speech', *Radio Free Europe/Radio Liberty*, 10 May, https://www.rferl.org/a/russia-putin-victory-day-speech-shuns-west-allies/31248055.html?fbclid=IwAR2J5Wc-t-tE4JFHF2_dT_v_6f 0ahrtqJObALo7A-ZNDvHJdl_0gL97Y9Jk, accessed 12 May 2021.

Hale, Henry (2015) *Patronal Politics: Eurasian Regime Dynamics in Comparative Perspective*, New York: Cambridge University Press.

Hall, Stephen G. F (2017) 'Preventing a Colour Revolution: the Belarusian example as an illustration for the Kremlin?', *East European Politics*, 33: 2, 162-183.

Hanson, Stephen E (2011) 'Plebiscitarian Patrimonialism in Putin's Russia: Legitimating Authoritarianism in a Postideological Era', *The Annals of the American Academy of Political and Social Science,* 636: 1, 32-48.

Helms, Ludger (2020) 'Leadership succession in politics: The democracy/autocracy divide revisited', *The British Journal of Politics and International Relations*, 22: 2, 328–346.

Hemment, Julie (2012) 'Nashi, youth voluntarism, and Potemkin NGOs: Making sense of civil society in post-Soviet Russia', *Slavic Review*, 71: 2, 234-260.

Heritage, Timothy and Guy Faulconbridge (2012) 'Tearful Putin wins back Russian presidency', *Reuters*, 4 March, https://www.reuters.com/article/us-russia-election-idUSTRE8220SP20120304, accessed 19 November 2020.

Higgins, Andrew (2020) 'Russia's Highest Court Opens Way for Putin to Rule Until 2036', *New York Times*, 16 March, https://www.nytimes.com/2020/03/16/world/europe/russia-putin-president-for-life.html, accessed 23 April 2020.

Hill, Fiona and Clifford G Gaddy (2015) *Mr. Putin: Operative in the Kremlin*, Washington, DC: Brookings Institution Press.

Hinsey, Ellen (2013) 'Putin Cracks Down: The Russian Presidential Election and Its Aftermath', *New England Review*, 34: 2, 123-141.

Hodge, Nathan (2020) 'Best-laid plans were derailed by 2020 and pandemic—even for Vladimir Putin', *CNN* , 26 December, https://edition.cnn.com/2020/12/26/europe/vladimir-putin-2020-russia-covid-navalny-intl/index.html, accessed 28 December 2020.

Hoffmann, Bert (2015) 'The international dimension of authoritarian regime legitimation: insights from the Cuban case', *Journal of International Relations and Development*, 18: 4, 556–574.

Holmes, Leslie (1997) *Post-Communism: An Introduction*. Durham, NC: Duke University Press.

Holmes, Leslie (2016) 'Comparative Conclusions: Legitimacy and Legitimation in Eurasian Post-Communist States'. In Martin Brusis, Joachim Ahrens, and Martin Schulze Wesse (eds): *Politics and Legitimation in Post-Soviet Eurasia*, Houndmills, Basingstoke: Palgrave Macmillan, 223-245.

Horák, Slavomir (2018) 'Leadership Succession in Turkmenistan and Uzbekistan: Between Stability and Instability', *Central Asian Affairs*, 5: 1, 1-15.

Hosking, Geoffrey A. (2001) *Russia and the Russians: A History*, Cambridge, Ma: Harvard University Press.

Human Rights Watch (2018) 'Uzbekistan', https://www.hrw.org/europe/central-asia/uzbekistan, accessed 6 November 2019.

Huskey, Eugene (2013) 'Legitimizing the Russian executive: identity, technocracy, and performance'. In Per-Arne Bodin, Stefan Hedlund, and Elena Namli (eds): *Power and Legitimacy: Challenges from Russia*, London: Routledge, 46-58.

Hutcheson, Derek S. (2004) 'Disengaged or Disenchanted? The Vote "Against All" in Post-Communist Russia', *Journal of Communist Studies and Transition Politics*, 20: 1, 98–121.

Hutcheson, Derek S. (2011) 'Elections, International Observers and the Politicisation of Democratic Values', *Europe-Asia Studies*, 63: 4, 685-702.

Hutcheson, Derek S. (2018) *Parliamentary Elections in Russia: A Quarter-Century of Multiparty Politics*, Oxford: Oxford University Press.

Hutcheson, Derek S., and Bo Petersson (2016) 'Shortcut to legitimacy: Popularity in Putin's Russia', *Europe-Asia Studies*, 68: 7, 1107-1126.

Hutcheson, Derek S. and Bo Petersson (2021) 'Rising from the Ashes: The Role of Chechnya in Contemporary Russian Politics'. In Christofer Berglund, Katrine Gotfredsen, Jean Hudson, and Bo Petersson (eds): *Language and Society in the Caucasus: Understanding the past, navigating the present*, Malmö: Universus, 147-166.

Isaacs, Rico (2010) '"Papa": Nursultan Nazarbayev and the Discourse of Charismatic Leadership and Nation-Building in Post-Soviet Kazakhstan', *Studies in Ethnicity and Nationalism*, 10: 3, 435-452.

Isaacs, Rico (2015) 'Charismatic Routinization and Problems of Post-Charisma Succession in Kazakhstan, Turkmenistan and Uzbekistan', *Studies of Transition States and Societies*, 7: 1, 58-76.

Isaacs, Rico and Alessandro Frigerio (2019) 'Political theory and Central Asia: An introduction". In Rico Isaacs and Alessandro Frigerio (eds): *Theorizing Central Asia: The State, Ideology and Power*, Cham: Palgrave Macmillan, 1-13.

Isachenkov, Vladimir (2021) 'Russia to expel 10 US diplomats in response to Biden actions', *AP News*, 16 April, https://apnews.com/article/russia-us-sanctions-sergey-lavrov-biden-4a935cd62c5db333ed082df447feddb8, accessed 18 April 2021.

Jarbawi, Ali and Wendy Pearlman (2007) 'Struggle in a Post-Charisma Transition: Rethinking Palestinian Politics after Arafat', *Journal of Palestine Studies*, 36: 4, 6-21.

Joosse, Paul (2018) 'Countering Trump: Toward a Theory of Charismatic Counter-Roles', *Social Forces*, 97: 2, 921–944.

Judah, Ben (2013) *Fragile Empire: How Russia Fell In and Out of Love with Vladimir Putin*, New Haven and London: Yale University Press.

Kailitz, Steffen, and Daniel Stockemer (2017) 'Regime legitimation, elite cohesion and the durability of autocratic regime types', *International Political Science Review*, 38: 3, 332-348.

Kjellgren, Adam (2019) 'Mythmaking as a feminist strategy: Rosi Braidotti's political myth', *Feminist Theory*, 22: 1, 63-80.

Klapsis, Antonis (2015) *An Unholy Alliance: The European Far Right and Putin's Russia*, Brussels: Wilfried Martens Centre for European Studies.

Kniivilä, Kalle (2021) *Putins värsta fiende: Aleksej Navalnyj och hans anhängare*, Stockholm: Bokförlaget Atlas.

Koesel, Karrie J. and Valerie J. Bunce (2012) 'Putin, Popular Protests, and Political Trajectories in Russia: A Comparative Perspective', *Post-Soviet Affairs*, 28: 4, 403-423.

Koesel, Karrie J. and Valerie J. Bunce (2013) 'Diffusion-proofing: Russian and Chinese responses to waves of popular mobilizations against authoritarian rulers', *Perspectives on Politics*, 11: 3, 753–768.

Kolstö, Pål (2016) 'Crimea vs. Donbas: How Putin Won Russian Nationalist Support — and Lost it Again', *Slavic Review*, 75: 3, 702-725.

Kokkonen, Andrej, and Anders Sundell (2020) 'Leader Succession and Civil War', *Comparative Political Studies*, 53: 3-4, 434-468.

Kolesnikov, Andrei and Denis Volkov (2018) 'Do Russians Want Change?', *Carnegie Moscow Center*, 16 January, https://carnegie.ru/comment ary/75261, accessed 6 May 2021.

Kommersant (2020), 'Kak izmenitsya Konstitutsiya Rossii. "Ъ" sravnil deystvuyushchuyu i predlagayemuyu versii Osnovnogo zakona', 20 January, https://www.kommersant.ru/doc/4225908, accessed 19 February 2020.

Konrad, Kai A and Mui, Vai-Lam (2016) 'The Prince — or Better No Prince? The Strategic Value of Appointing a Successor', *Journal of Conflict Resolution*, 61: 10, 2158-2182.

Kukshinov, Eugene (2021) 'Discourse of non-participation in Russian political culture: Analyzing multiple sites of hegemony production', *Discourse & Communication*, 15: 2, 163-183.

Langdon, Kate C., and Vladimir Tismaneanu (2020) *Putin's Totalitarian Democracy: Ideology, Myth, and Violence in the Twenty-First Century*, Cham: Palgrave Macmillan.

Laruelle, Marlene (2016) 'The three colors of Novorossiya, or the Russian nationalist mythmaking of the Ukrainian crisis', *Post-Soviet Affairs*, 32: 1, 55-74.

Laruelle, Marlene (2021) *Is Russia Fascist? Unraveling Propaganda East and West*, Ithaca and London: Cornell University Press.

Laurén, Anna-Lena (2018) 'Experten: Kreml letar efter en kronprins', *Sydsvenskan*, 20 March, A 10-11.

Laurén, Anna-Lena (2021) *Sammetsdiktaturen: Motstånd och medlöpare i dagens Ryssland*, Helsingfors: Förlaget.

Levada Center (2017) 'Aleksey Navalny', https://www.levada.ru/en/ 2017/03/20/aleksey-navalny/, accessed 5 May 2021.

Levada Center (2020a) 'Kto i kak golosoval za popravki v konstitutsiyu zavershayushchiy opros', 7 August, https://www.levada.ru/2020/ 08/07/kto-i-kak-golosoval-za-popravki-v-konstitutsiyu-zavershayu shhij-opros/, accessed 9 September 2020.

Levada Center (2020b) 'Vdokhnovlyayushchiye lichnosti', 11 June, https://www.levada.ru/2020/06/11/vdohnovlyayushhie-lichnosti/print/, accessed 6 October 2020.

Levada Center (2020c) 'Political trust', https://www.levada.ru/en/2020/10/22/political-trust-3/, accessed 3 February 2021.

Levada Center (2021a) 'Fil'm "dvorets dlya Putina"', https://www.levada.ru/2021/02/08/film-dvorets-dlya-putina/, accessed 10 April 2021.

Levada Center (2021b) 'The coronavirus: vaccination and the origin of the virus', 1 March, https://www.levada.ru/en/2021/03/01/the-coronavirus-vaccination-and-the-origin-of-the-virus/, accessed 10 May 2021.

Levada Center (2021c) 'Indicators', https://www.levada.ru/en/ratings/, accessed 17 June 2021.

Lindholm, Charles (2018) 'Charisma', *The International Encyclopedia of Anthropology*, Wiley Online Library, https://onlinelibrary.wiley.com/doi/10.1002/9781118924396.wbiea1286, accessed 19 June 2021.

Logvinenko, Igor (2020) 'Authoritarian Welfare State, Regime Stability, and the 2018 Pension Reform in Russia', *Communist and Post-Communist Studies,* 53: 1, 100-116.

Lönnqvist, Barbara (2021) 'Navalnyj blir en symbol', *Nya Argus*, 114: 7–8, 239–240.

Lührmann, Anna and Lindberg, Staffan I. (2019) 'A third wave of autocratization is here: what is new about it?', *Democratization*, 26: 7, 1095-1113.

Macdonald, Terry and Kate Macdonald (2020) 'Towards a 'pluralist' world order: creative agency and legitimacy in global institutions', *European Journal of International Relations*, 26: 2, 518– 544.

Machiavelli, Niccolò (1996) *Discourses on Livy*, translated by Harvey C. Mansfield and Nathan Tarcov, Chicago and London: University of Chicago Press.

Mahase, Elisabeth (2020) 'Covid-19: Russia approves vaccine without large scale testing or published results', *BMJ*, http://dx.doi.org/10.1136/bmj.m3205, accessed 18 August 2020.

Makarychev, Andrey and George Spencer Terry (2020) 'An Estranged "marriage of convenience": Salvini, Putin, and the intricacies of Italian-Russian relations', *Contemporary Italian Politics*, 12: 1, 23-42.

Makarychev, Andrei, and Alexandra Yatsyk (2014) 'The Four Pillars of Russia's Power Narrative', *The International Spectator: Italian Journal of International Affairs*, 49: 4, 62–75.

Malinova, Olga (2017) 'Political Uses of the Great Patriotic War in Post-Soviet Russia from Yeltsin to Putin'. In Julie Fedor, Markku Kangaspuro, Jussi Lassila and Tatiana Zhurzhenko (eds): *War and Memory in Russia, Ukraine and Belarus*, London: Palgrave Macmillan, 43-70.

Malinova, Olga (2019) 'Russian Identity and the "Pivot to the East"', *Problems of Post-Communism*, 66: 4, 227-239.

Malinova, Olga (2020) 'Framing the Collective Memory of the 1990s as a Legitimation Tool for Putin's Regime', *Problems of Post-Communism*, DOI:10.1080/10758216.2020.1752732.

Mamonova, Natalia (2016) 'Naïve Monarchism and Rural Resistance in Contemporary Russia', *Rural Sociology*, 81: 3, 316–342.

Martus, Ellie (2021) 'Policymaking and Policy Framing: Russian Environmental Politics under Putin', *Europe-Asia Studies*, 73: 5, 869-889.

Mazepus, Honorata; Wouter Veenendaal, Anthea McCarthy-Jones and Juan Manuel Trak Vásquez (2016) 'A comparative study of legitimation strategies in hybrid regimes', *Policy Studies*, 37: 4, 350-369.

McAllister, Ian and Stephen White (2008) 'Voting "against all" in postcommunist Russia', *Europe-Asia Studies*, 60: 1, 67-87.

McKie, Kristin (2019) 'Presidential Term Limit Contravention: Abolish, Extend, Fail, or Respect?', *Comparative Political Studies*, 52: 10, 1500-1534.

Medical Xpress (2020) 'Russia says Sputnik V virus vaccine 95% effective', 24 November, https://medicalxpress.com/news/2020-11-russia-sputnik-virus-vaccine-effective-1.html, accessed 24 November 2020.

Meduza (2020) ''The patient': The Kremlin's spokesman is still fielding questions about Navalny's poisoning, while refusing to say his name', 26 August, https://meduza.io/en/feature/2020/08/26/the-patient, accessed 9 September 2020.

Meduza (2021) 'Rosstat: izbytochnaya smertnost' v 2020 godu sostavila 324 tysyachi chelovek. U poloviny iz nikh byl koronavirus', 8 February, https://meduza.io/news/2021/02/08/rosstat-izbytochnaya-smertnost-v-2020-godu-sostavila-324-tysyachi-chelovek-u-poloviny-iz-nih-byl-koronavirus, accessed 16 March 2021.

MEMR1 (2020) 'After Proposing Amendment to Reset Putin's Presidential Terms to Zero, First Female Astronaut Valentina Tereshkova, A Hero of the Soviet Union, Becomes An Object of Stormy Controversy', 20 March, https://www.memri.org/reports/after-proposing-amendment-reset-putins-presidential-terms-zero-first-female-astronaut, accessed 23 April 2020.

Meng, Anne (2021) 'Winning the Game of Thrones: Leadership Succession in Modern Autocracies', *Journal of Conflict Resolution*, 65: 5, 950-981.

Miller, Chris (2019a) 'Putin's Not Ready to Call It Quits', *FP*, 22 July, https://foreignpolicy.com/2019/07/22/putins-not-ready-to-call-it-quits/, accessed 28 October 2020.

Miller, Christopher (2019b) 'Death Toll up to 13,000 in Ukraine Conflict, Says UN Rights Office', *Radio Free Europe/Radio Liberty*, 26 February, https://www.rferl.org/a/death-toll-up-to-13-000-in-ukraine-confli ct-says-un-rights-office/29791647.html, accessed 23 November 2020.

Mio, Jeffery Scott T; Ronald E. Riggio, Shana Levin, and Renford Reese (2005) 'Presidential leadership and charisma: The effects of metaphor', *The Leadership Quarterly*, 16: 2, 287–294.

Mishra, Pankaj (2017) *Age of Anger: A History of the Present*, Toronto: Allen Lane.

Mjør, Kare Johan (2018) 'Smuta: cyclical visions of history in contemporary Russian thought and the question of hegemony', *Studies in East European Thought*, 70: 19–40.

Moscow Times (2014) '"No Putin, No Russia" Says Kremlin Deputy Chief of Staff´, 23 October, https://www.themoscowtimes.com/2014/10/ 23/no-putin-no-russia-says-kremlin-deputy-chief-of-staff-a40702, accessed 6 November 2019.

Moscow Times (2020) 'Russia's Mortality Hit 16-Year High in November, Official Data Says', 29 December, https://www.themoscowtimes. com/2020/12/28/russias-mortality-hit-16-year-high-in-november-official-data-says-a72505, accessed 20 January 2021.

Müller, Martin (2011) 'State dirigisme in megaprojects: governing the 2014 Winter Olympics in Sochi', *Environment and Planning A*, 43: 9, 2091-2108.

Nathan, Andrew J. (2020) 'The Puzzle of Authoritarian Legitimacy', *Journal of Democracy,* 31: 1, 158-168.

Navalny, Alexei (2021) 'Vladimir the Poisoner of Underpants: "It's the duty of every person to defy you."', *New York Times,* 4 February, https://www.nytimes.com/2021/02/03/opinion/navalny-putin-speech.html, accessed 5 February 2021.

Neumann, Iver B. (1998a) *Uses of the Other:" the East" in European Identity Formation*, Minneapolis, MN: University of Minnesota Press.

Neumann, Iver B. (1998b) 'Russia as Europe's other', *Journal of Area Studies*, 6: 12, 26-73.

Netelenbos, Benno (2016) *Political Legitimacy Beyond Weber: An Analytical Framework*, Cham: Springer.

Nikolskaya, Anastasiya and Mikhail Dmitriev (2020) 'The End of the Crimean Consensus: How Sustainable are the New Trends in Russian Public Opinion?', *Russian Politics*, 5: 3, 354-374.

Nokhrin, Ivan (2021) 'The populist political logic and Alexey Navalny's political discourse', *Academia Letters*, Article 344, https://doi.org/10.20935/AL344, accessed 19 May 2021.

Novitskaya, Alexandra (2017) 'Patriotism, sentiment, and male hysteria: Putin's masculinity politics and the persecution of non-heterosexual Russians', *NORMA*, 12: 3-4, 302-318.

O'Loughlin, John; Gerard Toal, and Vladimir Kolosov (2017) 'The rise and fall of "Novorossiya": examining support for a separatist geopolitical imaginary in southeast Ukraine', *Post-Soviet Affairs*, 33: 2, 124-144.

Oliker, Olga (2017) 'Putinism, Populism and the Defence of Liberal Democracy', *Survival*, 59: 1, 7-24.

Omelicheva, Mariya Y. (2016) 'Authoritarian legitimation: assessing discourses of legitimacy in Kazakhstan and Uzbekistan', *Central Asian Survey*, 35: 4, 481-500.

Orange, Mia (2019) *Sustaining Authoritarianism: Clientelism and Repression in Kazakhstan, Kenya, Kyrgyzstan and Tanzania*, doctoral dissertation, Lund: Lund University.

Orange, Mia, and Bo Petersson (2017) '"There Can Be No Other Sun in the Sky": Political Myth, Spirituality and Legitimacy in Contemporary Kazakhstan'. In Catharina Raudvere (ed): *Contested Memories and the Demands of the Past*, Cham: Springer International Publishing, 25-47.

Orenstein, Mitchell A. (2014) 'Putin's Western Allies: Why Europe's Far Right Is on the Kremlin's Side', *Foreign Affairs*, 26 March, https://www.saintjoehigh.com/ourpages/auto/2014/3/27/36730719/14-0326%20Putin_s%20Western%20Allies.pdf, accessed 28 October 2020.

Østbø, Jardar (2016) *The New Third Rome: Readings of a Russian Nationalist Myth*, Stuttgart: Ibidem.

Palasciano, Andrea (2021) '3 Things to Know About Navalny's 2014 Fraud Case', *Moscow Times*, 2 February, https://www.themoscowtimes.com/2021/02/02/3-things-to-know-about-navalnys-2014-fraud-case-a72804, accessed 3 February 2021.

Pannier, Bruce (2019) 'Kazakhstan Shows Managed Transition Not the Smoothest Path in Central Asia', *Qishloq Ovozi*, 14 May, https://www.rferl.org/a/kazakhstan-shows-managed-transition-not-the-smoothest-path-in-central-asia/29940129.html, accessed 6 September 2019.

Pavroz, Alexander (2020) 'Paradoxes of Public Support for the Political Regime of Vladimir Putin', *Russian Politics*, 5: 4, 454-476.

Pearce, Fred (2003) 'Global warming "will hurt Russia"', *New Scientist*, 3 October, https://www.newscientist.com/article/dn4232-global-wa rming-will-hurt-russia/, accessed 19 January 2020.

Persson, Emil and Bo Petersson (2014) 'Political mythmaking and the 2014 Winter Olympics in Sochi: Olympism and the Russian great power myth', *East European Politics*, 30: 2, 192-209.

Pertsev, Andrey; Farida Rusatmova, and Anastasia Yakoreva (2020) 'It's all Sobyanin's fault: How Moscow's mayor tried to tackle the coronavirus but ended up at odds with Putin', *Meduza,* 25 June, https://me duza.io/en/feature/2020/06/25/it-s-all-sobyanin-s-fault, accessed 20 January 2021.

Pertsev, Andrey and Maksim Solopov (2020) 'Chto chitayet Putin', *Meduza*, 16 July, https://meduza.io/feature/2020/07/16/chto-chitaet-putin, accessed 6 May 2021.

Petersson, Bo (2013) 'The eternal great power meets the recurring times of troubles: Twin political myths in contemporary Russian politics', *European Studies: A Journal of European Culture, History and Politics*, Brill Rodopi, 301-326.

Petersson, Bo (2017) 'Putin and the Russian Mythscape: Dilemmas of Charismatic Legitimacy', *Demokratizatsiya*, 25: 3, 235-254.

Petersson, Bo (2018a) *National Self-Images and Regional Identities in Russia*, London: Routledge Revivals.

Petersson, Bo (2018b) 'Mars 2018—och sedan? Om successionsfrågan i Putins Ryssland', *Nordisk Östforum*, 32, 123–134.

Petersson, Bo (2018c) 'Perspective on the Eastern Enlargement: Triumph of the EU or Seed of Its Destruction?'. In Antonina Bakardjieva Engelbrekt, Anna Michalski, and Lars Oxelheim (eds): *Trust in the European Union in Challenging Times*, Cham: Springer, 41-64.

Petersson, Bo (2020) 'Nationalism and greatness: Russia under the Putin presidencies. In Liah Greenfeld and Zeying Wu (eds): *Research Handbook on Nationalism*, Cheltenham: Edward Elgar, 371-381.

Petersson, Bo and Emil Persson (2011) 'Coveted, detested and unattainable? Images of the US superpower role and self-images of Russia in Russian print media discourse', *International Journal of Cultural Studies*, 14: 1, 71–89.

Petersson, Bo and Elena Sommers (2015) 'Cold War to the Rescue? Anti-American Sentiment in Russian Highest Level Political Discourse', Paper for the 20th Annual ASN World Convention, Columbia University, 23-25 April.

Petersson, Bo and Karina Vamling (2013, eds:) *The Sochi Predicament: contexts, characteristics and challenges of the Olympic Winter Games in 2014*, Newcastle upon Tyne: Cambridge Scholars Publishing.

Petrov, Kirill (2020) 'Elites and Color Revolutions: The Logic of Russia's Response', *Russian Politics*, 5: 4, 426-453.

Petrov, Nikolay; Maria Lipman, and Henry E. Hale (2014) 'Three dilemmas of hybrid regime governance: Russia from Putin to Putin', *Post-Soviet Affairs*, 30: 1, 1–26.

Peyrose, Sebastien (2012) *Turkmenistan: Strategies of Power, Dilemmas of Development*, Armonk, NY: M. E. Sharpe.

President of Russia (2000) 'Interview with the Chinese Newspaper Renmin Ribao, the Chinese News Agency Xinhua and the RTR TV Company', 16 July, archive.kremlin.ru/eng/speeches/2000/07/16/0000_type8 2916_127805.shtml, accessed 5 April 2013.

President of Russia (2005) 'Conversation with Students from Moscow Universities and Cadets after Laying Flowers on the Minin and Pozharskii Monument', 4 November, http://kremlin.ru/eng/speeches/2005/11/04/1556_type84779_96825.shtml, accessed 3 September 2010.

President of Russia (2007) 'Speech and the Following Discussion at the Munich Conference on Security Policy', 10 February, http://en.kremlin.ru/events/president/transcripts/24034, accessed 5 December 2019.

President of Russia (2013) 'Direct Line with Vladimir Putin', 25 April, http://en.kremlin.ru/events/president/news/17976, accessed 6 November 2019.

President of Russia (2013), 'Seliger 2013 Youth Forum', 2 August, http://en.kremlin.ru/events/president/news/18993, accessed 12 February 2018.

President of Russia (2013) 'Press-konferentsiya Vladimira Putina', 19 December, http://kremlin.ru/events/president/news/19859, accessed 6 November 2019.

President of Russia (2014) 'Obrashcheniye Prezidenta Rossiyskoy Federatsii', 18 March, http://kremlin.ru/events/president/news/20603, accessed 30 November 2020.

President of Russia (2014) 'Interview to TASS News Agency', 24 November, http://en.kremlin.ru/events/president/news/47054, accessed 28 April 2021.

President of Russia (2014) 'Poslaniye Prezidenta Federal'nomu Sobraniyu', 4 December, http://kremlin.ru/events/president/news/47173, accessed 2 December 2020.

President of Russia (2014) 'Bol'shaya press-konferentsiya Vladimira Putina', 18 December, http://kremlin.ru/events/president/news/47250, accessed 30 November 2020.

President of Russia (2015) 'Interview to American TV channel CBS and PBS', 29 September, http://en.kremlin.ru/events/president/news/50380, accessed 28 April 2021.

President of Russia (2016) 'Interview to Bloomberg', 5 September, http://en.kremlin.ru/events/president/news/52830, accessed 28 April 2021.

President of Russia (2016) Meeting of the Valdai International Discussion Club, 27 October, http://en.kremlin.ru/events/president/news/53151, accessed 17 November 2016.

President of Russia (2017) 'Answers to journalists' questions following Direct Line', 15 June, http://en.kremlin.ru/events/president/news/54794, accessed 6 February 2018.

President of Russia (2017) 'Press-konferentsiya po itogam sammita "Gruppy dvadtsati"', 8 July, http://en.kremlin.ru/events/president/news/55017, accessed 6 February 2018.

President of Russia (2017) 'Meeting with students from Sirius Educational Centre', 21 July, http://en.kremlin.ru/events/president/news/55114, accessed 30 April 2021.

President of Russia (2017) 'Zasedaniye Mezhdunarodnogo diskussionnogo kluba "Valday"', 19 October, http://www.kremlin.ru/events/president/news/55882, accessed 25 February 2021.

President of Russia (2017) 'Tseremoniya vrucheniya premii "Dobrovolets Rossii—2017"', 6 December, http://kremlin.ru/events/president/news/56318, accessed 6 November 2019.

President of Russia (2017) 'Bol'shaya press-konferentsiya Vladimira Putina', 14 December, http://kremlin.ru/events/president/news/56378, accessed 6 November 2017.

President of Russia (2018) 'Meeting with heads of Russian print media and news agencies', 11 January, http://en.kremlin.ru/events/president/news/56639, accessed 6 November 2019.

President of Russia (2018) 'Poslaniye Prezidenta Federal'nomu Sobraniyu', 1 March, http://kremlin.ru/events/president/news/56957, accessed 6 November 2019.

President of Russian (2018) 'Interv'yu amerikanskomu telekanalu NBC', 10 March, http://kremlin.ru/events/president/news/57027, accessed 6 November 2019.

President of Russia (2018) 'Vstrecha s predstavitelyami obshchestvennosti Sevastopolya', 14 March, http://kremlin.ru/events/president/transcripts/57065, accessed 6 November 2019.

President of Russia (2018) 'Answers to media questions', 18 March, http://en.kremlin.ru/events/president/news/57085, accessed 30 April 2021.

President of Russia (2018) 'Obrashcheniye k grazhdanam Rossii', 23 March, http://kremlin.ru/events/president/news/57121, accessed 23 March 2018.

President of Russia (2018) 'Vstrecha s initsiativnoy gruppoy grazhdan v Kemerove', 27 March, http://kremlin.ru/events/president/news/57139, accessed 6 November 2019.

President of Russia (2018) 'Plenarnoye zasedaniye Peterburgskogo mezhdunarodnogo ekonomicheskogo foruma', 25 May, http://kremlin.ru/events/president/news/57556, accessed 6 November 2019.

President of Russia (2018) 'Interv'yu avstriyskomu telekanalu ORF', 4 June, http://kremlin.ru/events/president/news/57675, accessed 7 November 2019.

President of Russia (2018) 'Pryamaya liniya s Vladimirom Putinym', 7 June, http://kremlin.ru/events/president/news/57692, accessed 6 November 2019.

President of Russia (2018) 'Press-konferentsiya po itogam peregovorov prezidentov Rossii i SShA', 16 July, http://kremlin.ru/events/president/news/58017, accessed 6 November 2019.

President of Russia (2018) 'Interv'yu amerikanskomu telekanalu Fox News', 17 July, http://en.kremlin.ru/events/president/news/58019, accessed 6 November 2019.

President of Russia (2018) 'Zasedaniye diskussionnogo kluba "Valday"', 18 October, http://kremlin.ru/events/president/news/58848, accessed 18 December 2018.

President of Russia (2019) 'Poslaniye Prezidenta Federal'nomu Sobraniyu', 20 February, http://kremlin.ru/events/president/news/59863, accessed 7 November 2019.

President of Russia (2019) 'Interv'yu gazete The Financial Times', 27 June, http://kremlin.ru/events/president/news/60836, accessed 26 August 2019.

President of Russia (2019) 'Presentation of officers appointed to senior command posts', 6 November, http://en.kremlin.ru/events/president/news/61991, accessed 7 November 2019.

President of Russia (2019) 'Vladimir Putin's annual news conference', 19 December 2019, http://en.kremlin.ru/events/president/news/62 366, accessed 15 January 2020.

President of Russia (2020) 'Poslaniye Prezidenta Federal'nomu Sobraniyu', 15 January 2020, http://kremlin.ru/events/president/news/62582, accessed 20 January 2019.

President of Russia (2020) 'Soveshchaniye po voprosam realizatsii mer podderzhki ekonomiki i sotsial'noy sfery', 6 May, http://kreml in.ru/events/president/news/63303#sel=16:11:Dwx,16:63:3ow, accessed 7 May 2020.

President of Russia (2020) 'Greetings to graduates of Russian higher military schools, 10 May, http://en.kremlin.ru/events/president/news /63332, accessed 11 May 2020.

President of Russia (2020) 'Parad v chest' 75-letiya Velikoy Pobedy', 24 June, http://kremlin.ru/events/president/news/63560, accessed 17 February 2021.

President of Russia (2020), 'Meeting with Government members', 11 August, http://en.kremlin.ru/events/president/news/63877, accessed 18 August 2020.

President of Russia (2020) 'Interview with Rossiya TV channel', 27 August, http://en.kremlin.ru/events/president/news/63951, accessed 14 September 2020.

President of Russia (2020) 'Vstrecha s m·erom Moskvy Sergeyem Sobyaninym', 4 September, http://kremlin.ru/events/president/news/ 64000, accessed 14 September 2020.

President of Russia (2020) 'Meeting with President of Belarus Alexander Lukashenko', 14 September, http://en.kremlin.ru/events/president /news/64031, accessed 17 September 2020.

President of Russia (2020) 'Beseda s Gerbertom Efremovym', 19 September, http://kremlin.ru/events/president/news/64058, accessed 21 September 2020.

President of Russia (2020) '75th session of the UN General Assembly', 22 September, http://en.kremlin.ru/events/president/news/64074, accessed 16 February 2021.

President of Russia (2020) 'Interv'yu telekanalu "Rossiya", 7 October, http://en.kremlin.ru/events/president/news/64171, accessed 9 October 2020.

President of Russia (2020) 'Zasedaniye diskussionnogo kluba "Valday", 22 October, http://kremlin.ru/events/president/news/64261, accessed 27 October 2020.

President of Russia (2020) 'Meeting with State Duma Speaker Vyacheslav Volodin', 26 October, http://en.kremlin.ru/events/president/news/64269, accessed 27 October 2020.

President of Russia (2020), 'Meeting with Government Ministers', 28 October, http://en.kremlin.ru/events/president/news/64293, accessed 29 October 2020.

President of Russia (2020) 'Soveshchaniye s chlenami Pravitel'stva', 18 November, http://kremlin.ru/events/president/news/64436, accessed 20 November 2020.

President of Russia (2020) 'G20 Summit', 21 November 2020, http://en. kremlin.ru/events/president/news/64460, accessed 23 November 2020.

President of Russia (2020) 'Zasedaniye Soveta po razvitiyu grazhdanskogo obshchestva i pravam cheloveka', 10 December, http://kremlin.ru/events/president/news/64638, accessed 5 February 2020.

President of Russia (2020) 'Congratulations to Joseph R. Biden on winning US presidential election', 15 December, http://en.kremlin.ru/events/president/news/64660, accessed 15 December 2020.

President of Russia (2020) 'Ezhegodnaya press-konferentsiya Vladimira Putina', 17 December, http://kremlin.ru/events/president/news/64671, accessed 18 December 2020.

President of Russia (2021) 'Meeting with university students to mark Russian Students Day', 25 January, http://en.kremlin.ru/events/president/news/64922, accessed 22 February 2021.

President of Russia (2021) 'Meeting with President of Belarus Alexander Lukashenko', 22 February, http://en.kremlin.ru/events/president/news/65046, accessed 24 February 2021.

President of Russia (2021) 'Meeting on increasing vaccine manufacturing and vaccination progress', 22 March, http://en.kremlin.ru/events/president/news/65181, accessed 8 April 2021.

President of Russia (2021) 'Poslaniye Prezidenta Federal'nomu Sobraniyu', 21 April, http://kremlin.ru/events/president/news/65418, accessed 27 April 2021.

Putz, Catherine (2020) 'Dariga Nazarbayeva Dismissed From Top Senate Seat', *The Diplomat*, 5 May, https://thediplomat.com/2020/05/dariga-nazarbayeva-dismissed-from-top-senate-seat/, accessed on 31 August 2020.

Radio Free Europe/Radio Liberty (2020) 'Russian Sputnik-V Producer Claims COVID-19 Vaccine Is 92 Percent Effective', 11 November, https://www.rferl.org/a/russian-sputnik-v-covid-19-vaccine-92-percent-effective/30942797.html, accessed 16 November 2020.

Rainsford, Sarah (2020a) 'Coronavirus: Russian PM Mishustin tests positive for virus', *BBC News*, 30 April, https://www.bbc.com/news/world-europe-52491205, accessed 7 May 2020.

Rainsford, Sarah (2020b) 'Putin strongly backed in controversial Russian reform vote, *BBC News*, 2 July, https://www.bbc.com/news/world-europe-53255964, accessed 18 August 2020.

Rak, Joanna and Roman Bäcker (2020) 'Theory behind Russian Quest for Totalitarianism. Analysis of Discursive Swing in Putin's Speeches', *Communist and Post-Communist Studies*, 53: 1, 13-26.

Reevell, Patrick (2018) 'The best of Vladimir Putin's responses from his annual marathon call-in show, including advice to his grandson', *ABC News*, 7 June, https://abcnews.go.com/International/best-vladimir-putins-responses-annual-marathon-call-show/story?id=55719406, accessed 28 October 2020.

Restad, Hilde Eliassen (2014) *American Exceptionalism: An idea that made a nation and remade the world*, London: Routledge.

RIA Novosti (2020) 'Putin poruchil pravitel'stvu reshit' vopros s rostom tsen za nedelyu', 13 December, https://ria.ru/20201213/tseny-1588988104.html, accessed 26 April 2021.

Robertson, Graeme (2013) 'Protesting Putinism: The Election Protests of 2011-2012 in Broader Perspective', *Problems of Post-Communism*, 60: 2, 11-23.

Rogov, Kirill (2017) 'Public opinion in Putin's Russia: The public sphere, opinion climate and "authoritarian bias"', *NUPI Working Paper* 878, Oslo: Norwegian Institute of International Affairs.

Roth, Andrew (2019) 'Kazakhstan president Nazarbayev steps down after 30 years in power', *The Guardian*, 19 March, https://www.theguardian.com/world/2019/mar/19/kazakhstan-president-nursultan-nazarbayev-steps-down-after-30-years-in-power, accessed 10 June 2019.

Roth, Andrew (2021a) 'Vladimir Putin receives first dose of Russian-made Covid vaccine in private', *The Guardian*, 23 March, https://www.theguardian.com/world/2021/mar/23/vladimir-putin-to-get-covid-19-vaccination-on-tuesday?CMP=Share_iOSApp_Other, accessed 6 April 2021.

Roth, Andrew (2021b) 'Russian prosecutors move to liquidate Navalny's "extremist" movement', *The Guardian*, 16 April, https://www.theguardian.com/world/2021/apr/16/russian-prosecutors-move-to-liquidate-navalnys-extremist-movement, accessed 30 April 2021.

Rutland, Peter (2017) 'Trump, Putin and the Future of US-Russian Relations', *Slavic Review*, 76: S1, S45-S56.

Rutland, Peter (2017b),'Imagining Russia post-Putin', *The Conversation*, 3 August, http://theconversation.com/imagining-russia-post-putin-8 1731, accessed 18 May 2018.

Ryazanova-Clarke, Lara (2013) 'The discourse of a spectacle at the end of the presidential term'. In Helena Goscilo (ed): *Putin as Celebrity and Cultural Icon*, London and New York: Routledge, 104-132.

Sakwa, Richard (2008) 'Putin's Leadership: Character and Consequences, *Europe-Asia Studies*, 60: 6, 879-897.

Sakwa, Richard (2014) *Putin Redux: Power and Contradiction in Contemporary Russia*, London: Routledge.

Samoilenko, Sergei (2017) 'The Benefits of Bureaucratic Leadership: When There is No Character to Assassinate', https://carplab.wordpress. com/2017/10/26/bureaucracy/, accessed 7 December 2018.

Schedler, Andreas (2013) *The Politics of Uncertainty: Sustaining and Subverting Electoral Authoritarianism*, Oxford: Oxford University Press.

Schlein, Lisa (2020) 'Civilian Casualties Drop in Eastern Ukraine as Ceasefire Holds', *VoA*, 19 September, https://www.voanews.com/europe /civilian-casualties-drop-eastern-ukraine-cease-fire-holds, accessed 5 May 2021.

Semenov, Andrei (2020) 'Team Navalny and the Dynamics of Coercion: The Kremlin's reaction to Alexei Navalny's 2018 presidential campaign', *PONARS Eurasia Policy Memo*, No. 655, http://www.ponars eurasia.org/memo/team-navalny-and-dynamics-coercion-kremlin-reaction-alexei-navalny-2018-presidential, accessed 23 June 2020.

Sharafutdinova, Gulnaz (2014) 'The Pussy Riot affair and Putin's démarche from sovereign democracy to sovereign morality', *Nationalities Papers*, 42: 4, 615-621.

Sharafutdinova, Gulnaz (2020) *The Red Mirror: Putin's Leadership and Russia's Insecure Identity*, Oxford: Oxford University Press.

Sharlet, Robert (2001) 'Putin and the Politics of Law in Russia', *Post-Soviet Affairs*, 17: 3, 195-234.

Sheiko, Konstantin and Stephen Brown (2014) *History as Therapy: Alternative History and Nationalist Imaginings in Russia, 1991-2014*, Stuttgart: Ibidem.

Shekhovtsov, Anton (2018) *Russia and the Western Far Right: Tango Noir*, London and New York: Routledge.

Sherr, James (2019) 'A President Losing His Voice? Putin's Address to the Federal Assembly', International Centre for Defence and Security, 25 February, https://icds.ee/a-president-losing-his-voice-putins-addre ss-to-the-federal-assembly/, accessed 7 November 2019.

Shevtsova, Lilia (1998) *Yeltsin's Russia: Myths and Reality*, Washington DC: Carnegie Endowment for International Peace.

Sil, Rudra and Cheng Chen (2004). State Legitimacy and the (In)significance of Democracy in Post-Communist Russia', *Europe-Asia Studies*, 56: 3, 347-368.

Siltitski, Vitali (2005) 'Preempting Democracy: The Case of Belarus', *Journal of Democracy*, 16: 4, 83-97.

Simes, Dimitri K. (1999) *After the Collapse: Russia Seeks Its Place as a Great Power*, New York: Simon & Schuster.

Snyder, Timothy (2018) *The Road to Unfreedom: Russia, Europe, America*, New York: Tim Duggan Books.

von Soest, Christian and Julia Grauvogel (2016) 'Comparing Legitimation Strategies in Post-Soviet Countries'. In Martin Brusis, Joachim Ahrens, and Martin Schulze Wesse (eds): *Politics and Legitimation in Post-Soviet Eurasia*, Houndmills, Basingstoke: Palgrave Macmillan, 18-46.

von Soest, Christian and Julia Grauvogel (2017) 'Identity, procedures and performance: how authoritarian regimes legitimize their rule', *Contemporary Politics*, 23: 3, 287–305.

Sokhey, Sarah Wilson (2020) 'What Does Putin Promise Russians? Russia's Authoritarian Social Policy', *Orbis*, 64: 3, 390-402.

Solovei, Valerii (2004) 'Rossiya nakanune smuty', *Svobodnaya mysl'*, 21: 12, 38–48.

Sperling, Valerie (2014). *Sex, Politics, and Putin: Political legitimacy in Russia*, New York, NY: Oxford University Press.

Spiegelberger, William R. (2020) 'Meet the New Boss, Same as the Old Boss: Putin "Changes" the Constitution', *Orbis*, 64: 3, 374-389.

Stacher, Joshua (2011) 'Reinterpreting authoritarian power: Syria's hereditary succession', *The Middle East Journal*, 65: 2, 197-212.

State Duma (2020) 'Viacheslav Volodin: Russia's strength is not oil and gas, but Vladimir Putin', 12 March, http://duma.gov.ru/en/news/48036/, accessed 5 May 2020.

Stent, Angela E. (2019) *Putin's World: Russia against the West and with the Rest*, New York and Boston: Twelve.

Stewart, Katie L. (2021) 'Building the Nation Through Celebrating the Nation: A Comparison of Holidays in Russia's Regions', *Europe-Asia Studies*, DOI: 10.1080/09668136.2021.1900074

Surkov, Vladislav I. (2009) 'Nationalization of the future: Paragraphs pro sovereign democracy', *Russian Studies in Philosophy*, 47: 4, 8-21.

SVT Nyheter (2018) 'Här vägrar Åkesson (SD) välja mellan Macron och Putin', 2 September, https://www.svt.se/nyheter/inrikes/har-vag rar-akesson-valja-mellan-macron-eller-putin, accessed 6 November 2019.

Swedish Center for Russian Studies (2020) 'State of the Russian Economy', *SCRS Briefs* 20-06, https://54502991-ebb0-4b9b-861a-72607686ef84.fi lesusr.com/ugd/455813_b92760d15c32418184ca7e3e2539681d.pdf, accessed 19 June 2021.

Tass (2020) 'Russian embassy urges Bloomberg to apologize for disinfor mation about Putin's ratings', 24 May, https://tass.com/politics/ 1159709, accessed 6 May 2021.

Teague, Elizabeth (2020) 'Russia's Constitutional Reforms of 2020', *Russian Politics*, 5: 4, 301-328.

Terzyan, Aram (2020) 'The Anatomy of the Authoritarian Rule in Russia: Mainstream and Critical Perspectives', *Eurasian Affairs Research Pa pers*, no. 1, Eurasia Institute, http://eurasiainstitutes.org/en/post/ aram-terzyan-the-anatomy-of-the-authoritarian-rule-in-russia-main stream-and-critical-perspectives/, accessed 19 June 2021.

The Guardian (2020) 'Russia admits to world's third-worst Covid-19 death toll', 28 December, https://www.theguardian.com/world/2020/ dec/28/russia-admits-to-world-third-worst-covid-19-death-toll-und erreported, accessed 29 December 2020.

Tolstrup, Jakob (2015) 'Black knights and elections in authoritarian re gimes: Why and how Russia supports authoritarian incumbents in post-Soviet states', *European Journal of Political Research*, 54: 4, 673–690.

Torbakov, Igor (2005) 'New National Holiday: Strengthening Putin's Stat ist Thesis', *Eurasia Daily Monitor*, 2: 206.

Toth, Mano (2021) 'On pluralist mythscapes', *Memory Studies*, https:// doi.org/10.1177/1750698020988746.

Troianovski, Anton (2020) 'Putin Endorses Brazen Remedy to Extend His Rule, Possibly for Life', *New York Times*, 10 March, https://www.nyt imes.com/2020/03/10/world/europe/putin-president-russia.html, accessed 23 April 2020.

Trump, Donald J. (2018) 'President Donald J. Trump's State of the Union Ad dress', https://www.whitehouse.gov/briefings-statements/presiden t-donald-j-trumps-state-union-address/, accessed 5 February 2018.

Tumarkin, Nina (2003) 'The Great Patriotic War as myth and memory', *Eu ropean Review*, 11: 4, 595-611.

Turchenko, Mikhail and Grigorii V. Golosov (2021) 'Smart enough to make a difference? An empirical test of the efficacy of strategic voting in Russia's authoritarian elections', *Post-Soviet Affairs*, 37: 1, 65-79.

Umland, Andreas and Pavlo Klimkin (2020) 'Putin's Devious Plans If Joe Biden Wins', *The Globalist*, https://www.theglobalist.com/united-states-2020-presidential-elections-joe-biden-russia-vladimir-putin-hybrid-warfare/, accessed 28 October 2020.

Valdai Discussion Club (2021) https://valdaiclub.com/about/valdai/, accessed 18 March 2021.

Versteeg, Mila; Timothy Horley, Anne Meng, Mauricio Guim, and Marilyn Guirguis (2020) 'The Law and Politics of Presidential Term Limit Evasion', *Columbia Law Review*, 120: 1, 173-248.

Watkins, Eli (2018) 'Mattis warns Syria on chemical weapons, doubts Russian missile claims', *CNN Politics*, 11 March, https://edition.cnn.com/2018/03/11/politics/james-mattis-syria-russia/index.html, accessed 6 November 2019.

White, David (2017) 'Modifying Electoral Authoritarianism. What the 2016 Parliamentary Elections Tell us about the Nature and Resilience of the Putin Regime', *Russian Politics*, 2: 4, 482-501.

White, Stephen and Ian McAllister (2008) 'The Putin Phenomenon', *Journal of Communist Studies and Transition Politics,* 24: 4, 604-628.

Whitehouse, Mark (2018) 'What Comes After Putin Could Be Trouble', *Bloomberg Opinion*, 25 August, https://www.bloomberg.com/opinion/articles/2018-08-25/putin-s-succession-plan-could-be-trouble-for-russia, accessed 6 November 2019.

Wijermars, Mariëlle (2019) *Memory Politics in Contemporary Russia: Television, cinema and the state*, London: Routledge.

Willerton, John. P. P. (2017) 'Searching for a Russian national idea: Putin team efforts and public assessments', *Demokratizatsiya*, 25: 3, 209-233.

Wilson, Jeanne L. (2010) 'The Legacy of the Color Revolutions for Russian Politics and Foreign Policy', *Problems of Post-Communism*, 57: 2, 21-36.

Wilson, Jeanne. L. (2019) 'Russia's relationship with China: the role of domestic and ideational factors', *International Politics*, 56: 6, 778-794.

Wilson, Kenneth (2021) 'Is Vladimir Putin a strong leader?', *Post-Soviet Affairs,* 37: 1, 80-97.

Wilson, Kenneth and Jaechul Lee (2020): 'Questioning Putin's Popularity', *Problems of Post-Communism*, 67: 1, 37-52.

Wood, Elizabeth (2011) 'Performing Memory: Vladimir Putin and the Celebration of World War II in Russia', *The Soviet and Post-Soviet Review*, 38: 2, 172–200.

Yaffa, Joshua (2018) 'The Trump-Putin Summit in Helsinki', *The New Yorker*, 16 July, https://www.newyorker.com/news/current/trump-putin-helsinki, accessed 6 November 2019.

Yatsyk, Alexandra (2021) '"From Russia With Love": The Kremlin's Covid-19 Charm Offensive', *PONARS Eurasia Policy Memo* No. 687, January, https://www.ponarseurasia.org/sites/default/files/policy-memos-pdf/Pepm687_Yatsyk_Jan2021.pdf, accessed 16 February 2021.

Youtube (2011a) 'President Dmitry Medvedev Promotes Badminton´, https://www.Youtube.com/watch?reload=9&v=eGE39YLRiyg, accessed 6 November 2019.

Youtube (2011b) 'Putin 'booed' at Moscow martial arts event', https://www.Youtube.com/watch?v=nS48UuVXbjQ, accessed 19 November 2020.

Youtube (2014) 'V.V.Zhirinovskiy — predlagaet naznachit" Putina imperatorom Vladimir -1. Zazhigaet krasivo', 14 August, https://www.Youtube.com/watch?v=gwNxAy_M7Hw, accessed 3 May 2021.

Youtube (2015) 'President Clinton and Boris Yeltsin laugh attack', https://www.Youtube.com/watch?v=mv7M0xmq6i0, accessed 26 October 2020.

Youtube (2017) 'On vam ne Dimon', 2 March, https://www.Youtube.com/watch?v=qrwlk7_GF9g, accessed 5 November 2019.

Youtube (2018) 'Putin's annual address to Federal Assembly', https://www.Youtube.com/watch?v=iDGvrdqQZVY, accessed 6 November 2019.

Youtube (2021a) 'Putin's palace. History of world's largest bribe', 19 January, https://www.Youtube.com/watch?v=ipAnwilMncI, accessed 24 January 2021.

Youtube (2021b) 'Russia: President Putin and DM Shoigu drive all-terrain vehicle in Siberian taiga', 21 March, https://www.Youtube.com/watch?v=EpP-B1EDXjY, accessed 12 April 2021.

Yudin, Greg (2020) 'Governing Through Polls: Politics of Representation and Presidential Support in Putin's Russia', *Javnost – The Public*, 27: 1, 2-16.

Zeleny, Jeff; Chandelis Duster, and Betsy Klein (2021) 'Biden and Putin summit to take place next month in Switzerland', *CNN Politics*, 25 May, https://edition.cnn.com/2021/05/25/politics/biden-putin-summit-geneva/index.html, accessed 27 May 2021.

Index

SOVIET AND POST-SOVIET POLITICS AND SOCIETY

Edited by Dr. Andreas Umland | ISSN 1614-3515

121 *Mykhaylo Banakh* | Die Relevanz der Zivilgesellschaft bei den postkommunistischen Transformationsprozessen in mittel- und osteuropäischen Ländern. Das Beispiel der spät- und postsowjetischen Ukraine 1986-2009 | Mit einem Vorwort von Gerhard Simon | ISBN 978-3-8382-0499-4

122 *Michael Moser* | Language Policy and the Discourse on Languages in Ukraine under President Viktor Yanukovych (25 February 2010–28 October 2012) | ISBN 978-3-8382-0497-0 (Paperback edition) | ISBN 978-3-8382-0507-6 (Hardcover edition)

123 *Nicole Krome* | Russischer Netzwerkkapitalismus Restrukturierungsprozesse in der Russischen Föderation am Beispiel des Luftfahrtunternehmens „Aviastar" | Mit einem Vorwort von Petra Stykow | ISBN 978-3-8382-0534-2

124 *David R. Marples* | 'Our Glorious Past'. Lukashenka's Belarus and the Great Patriotic War | ISBN 978-3-8382-0574-8 (Paperback edition) | ISBN 978-3-8382-0675-2 (Hardcover edition)

125 *Ulf Walther* | Russlands „neuer Adel". Die Macht des Geheimdienstes von Gorbatschow bis Putin | Mit einem Vorwort von Hans-Georg Wieck | ISBN 978-3-8382-0584-7

126 *Simon Geissbühler (Hrsg.)* | Kiew – Revolution 3.0. Der Euromaidan 2013/14 und die Zukunftsperspektiven der Ukraine | ISBN 978-3-8382-0581-6 (Paperback edition) | ISBN 978-3-8382-0681-3 (Hardcover edition)

127 *Andrey Makarychev* | Russia and the EU in a Multipolar World. Discourses, Identities, Norms | With a foreword by Klaus Segbers | ISBN 978-3-8382-0629-5

128 *Roland Scharff* | Kasachstan als postsowjetischer Wohlfahrtsstaat. Die Transformation des sozialen Schutzsystems | Mit einem Vorwort von Joachim Ahrens | ISBN 978-3-8382-0622-6

129 *Katja Grupp* | Bild Lücke Deutschland. Kaliningrader Studierende sprechen über Deutschland | Mit einem Vorwort von Martin Schulz | ISBN 978-3-8382-0552-6

130 *Konstantin Sheiko, Stephen Brown* | History as Therapy. Alternative History and Nationalist Imaginings in Russia, 1991-2014 | ISBN 978-3-8382-0665-3

131 *Elisa Kriza* | Alexander Solzhenitsyn: Cold War Icon, Gulag Author, Russian Nationalist? A Study of the Western Reception of his Literary Writings, Historical Interpretations, and Political Ideas | With a foreword by Andrei Rogatchevski | ISBN 978-3-8382-0589-2 (Paperback edition) | ISBN 978-3-8382-0690-5 (Hardcover edition)

132 *Serghei Golunov* | The Elephant in the Room. Corruption and Cheating in Russian Universities | ISBN 978-3-8382-0570-0

133 *Manja Hussner, Rainer Arnold (Hgg.)* | Verfassungsgerichtsbarkeit in Zentralasien I. Sammlung von Verfassungstexten | ISBN 978-3-8382-0595-3

134 *Nikolay Mitrokhin* | Die „Russische Partei". Die Bewegung der russischen Nationalisten in der UdSSR 1953-1985 | Aus dem Russischen übertragen von einem Übersetzerteam unter der Leitung von Larisa Schippel | ISBN 978-3-8382-0024-8

135 *Manja Hussner, Rainer Arnold (Hgg.)* | Verfassungsgerichtsbarkeit in Zentralasien II. Sammlung von Verfassungstexten | ISBN 978-3-8382-0597-7

136 *Manfred Zeller* | Das sowjetische Fieber. Fußballfans im poststalinistischen Vielvölkerreich | Mit einem Vorwort von Nikolaus Katzer | ISBN 978-3-8382-0757-5

137 *Kristin Schreiter* | Stellung und Entwicklungspotential zivilgesellschaftlicher Gruppen in Russland. Menschenrechtsorganisationen im Vergleich | ISBN 978-3-8382-0673-8

138 *David R. Marples, Frederick V. Mills (Eds.)* | Ukraine's Euromaidan. Analyses of a Civil Revolution | ISBN 978-3-8382-0660-8

139 *Bernd Kappenberg* | Setting Signs for Europe. Why Diacritics Matter for European Integration | With a foreword by Peter Schlobinski | ISBN 978-3-8382-0663-9

140 *René Lenz* | Internationalisierung, Kooperation und Transfer. Externe bildungspolitische Akteure in der Russischen Föderation | Mit einem Vorwort von Frank Ettrich | ISBN 978-3-8382-0751-3

141 *Juri Plusnin, Yana Zausaeva, Natalia Zhidkevich, Artemy Pozanenko* | Wandering Workers. Mores, Behavior, Way of Life, and Political Status of Domestic Russian Labor Migrants | Translated by Julia Kazantseva | ISBN 978-3-8382-0653-0

142 *David J. Smith (Eds.)* | Latvia – A Work in Progress? 100 Years of State- and Nation-Building | ISBN 978-3-8382-0648-6

143 *Инна Чувычкина (ред.)* | Экспортные нефте- и газопроводы на постсоветском пространстве. Анализ трубопроводной политики в свете теории международных отношений | ISBN 978-3-8382-0822-0